THE CINEMA OF

OLIVER STONE

NORMAN KAGAN

CONTINUUM | NEW YORK

1995

The Continuum Publishing Company
370 Lexington Avenue
New York, NY 10017

Printed in the United States of America

Library of Congress Cataloging-in-Publication Data

Kagan, Norman.
    The cinema of Oliver Stone / Norman Kagan.
      p.   cm.
    Includes bibliographical references and index.
    ISBN 0-8264-0817-6
    1. Stone, Oliver—Criticism and interpretation. I. Title.
PN1998.3.S76K35 1995
791.43'0233'092—dc20   94-41775
                              CIP

to Chris Stanowski
class, style, and elegance

I consider my films to be first and foremost dramas about individuals in personal struggles.

I consider myself to be a dramatist before a political filmmaker. In my films, an individual struggles for his identity and his soul—which has been stolen or lost—and gets it back in the end. I don't consider myself a pessimist but an optimist. I don't believe in the collective version of history, but in the higher dialogues of Socrates: know thyself.

—Oliver Stone

He took me to the little projection room . . . and showed me a montage he has made of McNamara's policy speeches and screaming women, clipped out of old horror movies. . . . Hilarity mounted to hysteria. Barry, very cool, kept apologizing for imperceptible nuances of error.

—Tom Disch
Camp Concentration

CONTENTS

I wish to acknowledge the help of
the following people in preparing this book:

. . . . .

BRIAN CAMP

OSCAR COLLIER

MARY CORLISS

JOAN FEINBERG

ANDY HAFTER

MIA KATOH

EVANDER LOMKE

CHRISTINA MARKUNIS

RON MAGLIOCZI

CHARLES SILVER

CHRIS STANOWSKI

ANDRÉA STASKOWSKI

1

BEGINNINGS

BORN IN New York City, September 15, 1946, Oliver Stone grew up in the upper middle class into the turbulent 1960s. In the Showtime Channel documentary *Oliver Stone, Inside Out* the writer-director describes himself as "born into conflict"—his father a native atheistic born-Jewish stockbroker having a dark pessimistic if not cynical view of life, his mother an upper-class Catholic Frenchwoman, never losing her immigrant's optimism. The couple had a full social life, the child raised largely by nannies.

His father, Lou Stone, wrote a monthly newsletter about economics and politics. "My father believed life was hard. The important thing was to earn a living."[8] Stone has clear childhood memories of visiting Wall Street, and that his father loved his life there. He was always telling his son to wear a suit, cut your hair, be a stockbroker. A man should not stand out for his behavior. Stone admits his relationship with his father was a stormy one, and he was "pretty much of a disappointment to his father for thirty years."[9]

Stone saw his father as very orthodox in his thinking, rigid, even a bit militaristic. As a youth he had huge fights with him, once putting LSD in his drink, "to blow his mind." Years later, when he'd loosened up, he said "Can't you give me some more of that stuff?"

Stone's mother was a vivacious French-Canadian woman, whom his father had met in Paris during the war. "Oliver doesn't like to talk so much about how he was raised rich," his mother, Jacqueline Goddet Stone, has said.

The Stones lived in Manhattan townhouses and Stamford, Connecticut, homes. Stone attended Tritiny School in New York City and Hill School in Pottstown, Pennsylvania (where Stone supported Goldwater in 1964). The five-year-old composed marionette show skits, casting his French cousins; at seven he wrote stories, and themes for which his father paid him a quarter each. The nine-year-old began a nine-hundred-page book about his family and life.

Stone's father was a man who supported the ranks of the rich until almost the end of his life. Stone has said: "My father used to take me to the movies and would often say, "Why do they make the businessman such a *characture?*"[4] In fact, Stone's father carried out multiple infidelities starting in the late forties—call girls and affairs with his wife's friends and wives of family friends. Meanwhile, he was having financial difficulties, headed toward bankruptcy—all this no doubt an influence on Oliver's worldview.

Stone's parents divorced in 1961, when he was fifteen. In *Oliver Stone, Inside Out*, he stated he was shocked, only then realizing they were already living separate lives: "When they were divorced, my father gave me the facts of life. He told me that he was heavily in debt. He said, 'I'll give you a college education, and then you're on your own. There's literally no money.'"[4] His father never recovered financially. Still in prep school, Stone made inquiries about going to the Congo to fight as a mercenary, and took up skydiving.

Stone finished private school, and spent a year at Yale University in liberal arts. In 1987 he stated that at that point he "saw himself as a product—an east coast solid economic product—and I wanted to break out of the mold."[4] He's also said that feeling that his parents had really lived apart for years made him feel betrayed.

Stone learned of a teaching position the free Pacific Institute needed to fill in Cholon, the Chinese district of Saigon. Inspired by Zorba the Greek, George Harrison's sitar music, and Lord Jim's redemption, Stone applied.

The young man arrived in Saigon in June 1965, an eighteen-year-old schoolteacher. Marines and First Infantry troops strolled around firing off their weapons. "We were the good guys," Stone has written. "We were going to win. It was the war of my generation. It was glorious."[13] Stone spent two terms teaching the Vietnamese–Chinese students English, math, geography, and history. Then he signed on as a wiper on a U.S. merchant ship, a lowly job that took him to several Southeast Asia ports, and eventually to Oregon.

In Guadalajara, Mexico, Stone finished a first novel, *A Child's Night Dream*, about his experiences in Asia. The book reached 1,400 pages. "It started out as a boy's suicide note—not that I was going to commit suicide, but I was very depressed. It was Jack

London–type experiences in a Joycean style. Totally insane, with great passages of lyricism here and there. I thought it was the best thing since Rimbaud. And when Simon and Schuster rejected it, I gave up. I threw half the manuscript in the East River and said, 'My father is right. I'm a bum.'"4

After another semester at Yale, Stone joined the army in 1967: "It was a way of announcing to my father that I was a man. Also, I had a serious dose of patriotism. I believed in the country, believed in the ideals, believed that the communists were undermining us everywhere."2 To speed things up, he turned down OCS, and insisted on infantry and Vietnam.

Stone's father, an intelligent right-winger, believed in the domino theory, but thought the war was a ridiculous waste for his son. The war was fine as long as other boys less economically sufficient would fight it.5

Returning as a combat soldier in 1967, Stone saw a different Vietnam. "The Vietnamese who had welcomed us in 1965 had now started the slow process of taking our dollars and hating us for it."13

Stone was very much aware of the growing corruption and prostitution across the war zone. "Many people came home in body bags from this war . . . while others made millions. . . . There were six or seven non-combatants for every combatant, many of them eating steak or lobster dinners each night. . . . We brought a corporate Miami Beach–Las Vegas mentality to Vietnam. . . . The ultimate corruption of course was President Johnson's sending only the poor and uneducated to the war—in fact, practicing class warfare while the middle and upper classes could avoid the war by going to college or paying a psychiatrist. I am sure to this day that if the middle and upper classes had gone to Vietnam, their mothers and fathers—the politicians and businessmen—would have ended that war a helluva-lot sooner."13

In September 1967 Stone was on the way to joining the Twenty-Fifth Infantry near the Cambodian border, as he celebrated his twenty-first birthday.

One day in the bush was enough to shatter his romantic illusions. "I was put on point my first day in the field. It was just so hard, so grimy, so tough. I thought I couldn't take it. I was about to pass out, with fifty pounds of equipment."

Stone's first action was very like the night ambush in *Platoon*. Three NVA soldiers walked up to him and he just stood there. "I remember my logical worldly brain of course trying to rationalize the whole thing. I said about the North Vietnamese: 'These must be lost GIs.'" Luckily, he was wounded, or he claims he couldn't have taken the other guys' derision.

There was never any ideological talk. But the blacks and poor whites, he realized, saw through "that 'upper class' bullshit. They don't buy into the rich guy's game. . . . They know the score. That score is: We've been fucked (Stone laughs) and we are over here in Vietnam."[11]

As the war dragged on, Stone became a better soldier, but his sense of right and wrong was eroded. Villages were burned and damage was done on a steady basis. In one village, he lost control and began firing at an old man's feet, a scene he used later in *Platoon*.

Stone found many soldiers were hostile to the antiwar protesters (Let *them* come over here and fight! Let *them* experience it!). Others, blacks especially, were more hippie-ish ("I'm here, man. I'm gonna smoke dope and I'm gonna make it and I'm gonna survive and I'm gonna make a lot of money!"). And the dope *was* great![8]

Combat grew fiercer, and Stone was wounded in the leg and behind. By then he simply wanted to survive. He began smoking pot heavily to blunt his awareness.

Eventually, Stone was transferred to Saigon for MP duty. Instead of receiving an Article 15 for insubordination, he made a deal to go back to long-range recon patrol and have the charges dropped. It was there he met a sergeant who was the basis for *Platoon*'s Elias character—a handsome black-haired Apache who looked like Jim Morrison and was later killed.

Stone went on to the First Cavalry, where he met a sergeant that the filmmaker transformed into *Platoon*'s Sergeant Barnes character.

Stone was hanging out with the blacks, using dope heavily, and began to wear beads and speak in black rap dialect: Hey, what you doin' man? What's happenin'? He states that the U.S. troops didn't think about the enemy. They considered them pretty tough, skilled, and mean, and wanted to kill them, because they wanted to kill the Americans.

Many soldiers had strong racist feelings about the civilian population, including women and children. ("All gooks are the same. The only good gook is a dead gook.") There were no ordered massacres, but there were random killings of civilians, as in *Platoon*, which were gotten away with. Stone actually saved a girl, as shown in the film.

Fragging of officers and noncoms also happened frequently. With no set objective, and no victory in sight, no one wanted to get killed. This survival tension led to both murders and fraggings. The officer corps, especially top sergeants, were pretty much hated, often because they were fat cats, getting rich in various ways but rarely risking their lives. Stone thinks such incidents were six to ten times as common as official estimates. Indeed a pamphlet was circulated at UCLA saying Stone participated in real counterparts of some of the *Platoon* scenes, and should be tried as a war criminal.

After fifteen months in Vietnam, Stone returned to the U.S. He has often stated that Vietnam was the formative crucible of his life, the source of his most powerful cinematic preoccupations: "What combat burned into our heads was the very real fact that we could be dead any moment. . . . The war formed me, it was the major shaping event of my life, but it never, never turns out the way you expect it to be. . . . It has nothing to do with heroism. Incoming fire is very random and can kill you as easily as the guy standing two feet away from you. And modern fire power is so devastating that the modern small battlefield is really a slaughter pit."[1]

Yet Stone sees such experiences of trapped helplessness, with terrible odds, as nevertheless having great significance: "It's wrong to always be in control. Most of the stuff I've learned in my life has been from humiliating defeat, or stretching myself and making a fool of myself. 'Excess leads to wisdom,' that's what Blake said. By really knowing the limits of life as much as you can, you find out about life. And the great moral choices are based on really being out there."

Out of the army ten days, Stone went to Mexico, and was caught at the border with two ounces of marijuana. He was jailed, facing a five- to twenty-year federal smuggling charge.

He found himself jailed with fifteen thousand young Americans, who told him: "Wake up! This is what America's really like man!" Reluctantly, Stone called his father who paid his court-appointed lawyer, and got his case dismissed in the "interests of justice." When his father heard all his black rapping, he exclaimed hatefully: "You turned into a black man!"

Stone says New York University Film School was his salvation: "I know it sounds corny, but I was saved by film school. . . .To be able to study movies in college, it was any movie lover's dream. It was cool, too, like studying to be an astronaut. Martin Scorsese was my first teacher. He was like a mad scientist, with hair down to here. He was someone on an equal wave of nuttiness. And he helped channel the rage in me."[4] Stone in fact has compared himself to Travis Bickle, the human time bomb in Scorsese's *Taxi Driver.*

The charismatic, electrifying Scorsese inspired Stone to make a series of short student films. Excerpts from them in *Oliver Stone, Inside Out*[8] show a disabled vet hobbling down a New York street, the dumping of a suitcase full of medals in the foaming wake of an ocean liner, and a young psychopathic student type slipping his Luger pistol into his waistband. Scorsese liked Stone's work, commenting: "I thought he was a real filmmaker. He'd been through a lot more than other students and had something to say. Some of it was a little excessive, but I think that excess is what's kept him going."[2]

In other interviews, however, Stone comments, "I was catatonic" and "The other students looked upon me as an assassin. It was never discussed, nobody would talk about it, but I think all the vets felt that silence."

Politically, Stone stated, Vietnam had turned him from a right-winger to an anarchist—alienated, hateful, suspicious. When Nixon invaded Cambodia, he thought about killing Nixon: "If you want to shake up the system, if you want a revolution, let's fuckin' have one! Let's kill cops." Ten years later, he still thought that was the only way a U.S. revolution could occur.[11]

Presumably at this time Stone began to develop his own ideas and work methods. Some of these appear in a later interview.

"Direction is really an extension of writing; you write it, and it's sort of natural to complete the process. It makes it more self-sufficient. You also help yourself as a writer if you direct the material. The differences are more. . . . Let me put it this way: writing is very internal and uncommunicative—antisocial. Directing is the complete opposite. It's like giving a party; as the host, you're very external and deal with the external. I like going from internal to external."[5]

In *Oliver Stone, Inside Out*, he adds that the director pushes, coaxes, uses guile, encourages, shakes up: "I don't like what you're doing" so the actor "will plug into his soul and find the resources to deliver."[8]

1. Director Oliver Stone on the set of *Natural Born Killers*. *(Copyright 1994 Warner Brothers Productions. Courtesy Museum of Modern Art Film Stills Archive.)*

"I generally work long hours," Stone says of his writing. "I work a morning shift, take a little break in the early part of the afternoon, and come back for a late afternoon/early evening shift. I can pretty well write anywhere—hotel rooms, foreign cities. I like to go to foreign cities. The only place I can't work is on the beach or near music and talk. I don't like that."[5]

"[Good filmmaking] depends on the persistent vision of two or three people, and they push it through a system that's geared to compromise and obstacles. . . . There are just so many collaborative elements, you have so many actors, you have to depend on locations; you have to depend on money; you depend on whether you wake up that day with a headache. It all comes down to thousands of little choices. And if you miss one of them, the movie is not going to be good.[11]

Out of school and without an agent, Stone turned out ten screenplays, while supporting himself as a cabdriver and xerox messenger.

In 1973, when Stone was twenty-seven, a Canadian company bought a feature screenplay, which according to the program notes was inspired by a nightmare he'd written down "in the early dark hours of the morning." The script was rewritten with Edward Mann, Stone commenting: "It was a low-budget film, even though it didn't look like one." Released in 1974, *Seizure* was made on a $150,000 budget.

Stone has stated that he and a friend named Jeff Kapelman actually raised the money for the film among Canadian investors. "We raised about 150 [thousand dollars] cash and 200 in deferments. I gave my blood to it, along with every last dime I could raise; I cut the film myself, while living in a forty-dollar-a-week hotel room. We eventually got chased out of Canada owing money, and I had to steal the answer print from the lab and run with it over the border in order to sell it."[7]

Like many moderately budgeted projects there are obvious economies in *Seizure*—a single location (perhaps the home of an investor), a lack of special effects, a small cast, a low shooting ratio, Stone's first wife Majwe Sarkis, as art director. (Stone's first marriage lasting from 1971 to 1977, was to an older, sophisticated woman, an Iranian who was an executive assistant at the Moroccan UN embassy, a relationship he referred to as "not so easy."[9]

Seizure opens with vistas of a lovely country lake at dawn, credits over. Into the bedroom where intelligent-faced, middle-aged author

Jonathan Frid is sleeping rushes a boy, whose playful "Daddy!" is met with a fearful shout. The weekend guests will arrive soon. The man goes in to shave, telling his youngish wife he's had the same apparently upsetting dream yet again.

Their first guest is a youthful lady's man. The next pair are a brash aging millionaire and his bored, modelish companion. The first insults a garageman before driving off in his BMW. An aging foreign aristocrat and his older mate arrive next, all sunning by the lake. A radio reports the escape from a mental hospital of a former Harvard prof, Jezebel Joyce, and two other inmates. Briefly we glimpse dark figures in the woods.

The writer's son pleads with him to find their dog, lost in the woods, while his wife rests in a bedroom, fantasizing a masked figure with a torch who enters and seizes her. . . . There's a knock, and her son in a plastic mask grabs her playfully.

Outside in the woods, to drumming music, the writer searches, the camera swinging elaborately around him, finally finding the dead dog hanging from a tree.

Indoors, the young stud is coming on to the aging rich man's woman: "What does it feel like?" "We do it by phone." They agree to rendezvous later.

Alone, rich man and lady's man confront: "Money is the root of all evil." "You're a failure, small-time, very small-time."

Over dinner, the conflicts intensify. The rich man grudgingly offers to put money into the aging count's projects—"Fun money"— offering a check across the table. "Last chance, Count!" The old man takes it.

For a moment, a frightening face appears at the window.

Outside, a teenage visitor heads for home in the darkness, then to owl hoots and drums panics and runs. A warrior figure in metal-studded leather chases, traps, approaches: "No, please, I'll do anything, please don't hurt me!"

The writer puts his son to bed. "I'm scared of something in me." But he loves his son, and his wife just as much.

The young seducer contemplates a book of Indian erotica.

The mother looks at the mist-covered lake. Her son tells her: "I'm scared . . . of daddy."

In his study, the writer tells his friend the count: "Something terrible is happening to me. . . . It's as if I'm dreaming—as if I've

2. *Seizure*. Martine Beswick as the Queen of Evil, about to destroy Mark (Troy Donahue): "We are without beginning and end, and our only purpose is death!" (*Cinerama Releasing Corporation. Courtesy Museum of Modern Art Film Stills Archive.*)

3. *Seizure*. The guests confront each other. Jonathan Frid as Edmund, Christina Pickles as his wife, Joe Sirola as Charlie, Mary Woronov as his mistress Mikkie, Roger de Koven as Sergei. (*Courtesy Museum of Modern Art Film Stills Archive.*)

seen it all before. A group of friends come to the house—strangers appear, I don't know who, but they're frightening."

Outside, backlit figures run toward the house.

The writer speaks of the dead dog, dead teen, face at the window—a face he'd sketched in the past.

We glimpse a dwarf, a black warrior, a tall imperious woman.

In the bedroom, the countess speaks to her dead husband, another voice promises youth. The aging distraught woman dances with herself. The dwarf offers magic ointments.

The seducer enters a bedroom, glimpses a female figure, is strangled gasping: "Who are you?"

The tall imperious woman, black warrior, and dwarf, all costumed, confront writer, wife, three guests. The woman chants: "Do not ask us who we are and where we come from. We are without beginning and end, and our only purpose is death. You will do as you are told!"

Others are gone, and "at dawn tomorrow, only one of you will be left!"

They're led outside, linked by a rope looped to each neck. They're to race around the home, the last to be executed: "God will not help, only lungs and legs!"

The count counsels: "We have no choice. With all our civilization, we must learn to accept that nature has no special respect for our disasters. Anyway, you have little to fear, I'm the oldest and weakest among you."

They run.

Upstairs, the older woman speaks to her lost husband. The dwarf mocks her, the ointments disfigure her. She leaps to her death.

Writer, wife, rich man, mistress, and count circle the house, gasping, chased by the warrior. Writer and wife try to use their car, but fail. The old count struggles, hopping on a bad leg, finds his dead wife. The rich man has a stroke, tries to buy the three off: "I'll give you a million!" But when they tear it up, tries subversion of the black: "You're quiet, but you're smart, I can tell, we'll be a team." Instead, obeying the woman, the warrior breaks his neck.

The wife faints, the men are locked up, the young mistress flees to the service station, appeals to the mechanic under a car—who emerges to be the dwarf!

Locked up, the count tells the writer: "The answer lies not in force, but knowing who they are. . . . She is Kali—true giver and destroyer of life! In her name, children were sacrificed by throwing them into the flames."

"*She* is the majestic embodiment of all our fears and desires— the mother and dark lady of the world."

The writer says that his last friend is mad.

"Edwin, you are the Faust . . . you have seen them before in dreams."

The writer is led to a room in which the Queen of Evil sits on a throne while the millionaire's athletic young mistress stands in a black bikini, the two companions on guard. The woman tells her it's her last chance: "Kill him and you go free!"

Writer and mistress circle, expressions fierce, long knives up-raised. She kicks at him, they circle, come together, struggle, and he stabs her.

"Kill her!" Instead the woman cuts the girl's throat. She lies crouched on the floor, legs drawn up.

"Please. What have you done to my wife?"

The woman caresses him, unbuttons his shirt, kisses him passionately.

"Very well, go to her—very few men or women have refused me in the course of centuries. I'll give you two hours to be with her— but then you'll be mine, forever!"

The parents take the boy to the attic hiding place in a trunk. They embrace.

"Edmund, it doesn't work anymore. Ever since the first day we were married, there was this mystery about you . . . your intellectual fantasies . . . whatever happens, I feel that you and only you are in control. You've invited your friends here to destroy them, me, Jason, and finally yourself."

"You're a coward, Edmund. I realized that tonight. There's no use lying to myself. I could have married worse things. At least you were gentle."

"Time's about to run out. Come here."

The writer wakes up on the bed, alone. The clock shows that two hours have passed. On the bathroom mirror, I LOVED YOU is printed in lipstick. On the tub's edge, a blood-splattered razor blade, and more bloodstains. His face is tormented.

From inside, he sees the old count led to a stump where the warrior waits with an ax.

"There's no need to be afraid. I'm a bit tired of myself. . . .I've come to believe that God is both good and evil . . . death is a companion, and not an enemy to life."

"Serge," the writer asks, "do you really believe in God?"

"I believe in myself and therefore I have faith in Him."

He puts his head on the block: "Make it quick, I have a pressing appointment to keep."

The Queen of Evil: "I've had the best of them all . . . and there can be only one survivor."

"There's the child!"

"You're a lump of mud, Edmund. You want so much to live, and you don't know how!"

"What would you do with him?" A flash fantasy image of murdering the son.

The artist speaks to himself: "I can start again! It was all an illusion. My love for them was an artist's love. I can create more!"

The attic hiding place is empty. The Queen of Evil sends her two agents to hunt the child down. But the writer ax-kills the warrior, then flees for the woods, the dwarf in pursuit.

The Queen of Evil finds the child, and lifts him.

"Leave my child alone! My husband? Yes. The child? Never!"

The mother's figure appears, her face silvered, unreal. Soothingly, she tells the boy: "Go to your room. I have to go away. You're growing up. Listen to your mother for the last time."

The Queen of Evil: "Then Edmund is mine."

"Take him!"

The camera spinning, the dwarf closes in on the fleeing writer.

The writer wakes up, shouting: "Nicole—I had the dream again!"

Sweaty, guilty faced, he walks through the bedroom: "It's over. It was a dream—it's all right." He starts to shave, then sees the same lipstick words on the mirror: I LOVED YOU.

He runs back to the bedroom. The figure in bed, smiling cruelly, is the Queen of Evil: "Yes, my darling!"

The house, in early morning. The milkman delivers. The writer's son runs happily to the woods, his wife smiles, carefree: "Jason! Wake your daddy up and tell him the guests will be here soon."

In the bedroom, the boy finds his face, his face dead white and motionless. A newscaster's voice tells us "The Edgar Allan Poe of American fiction, Jonathan Frid, forty-seven, died today of a heart attack. He leaves behind his widow Nicole and his ten-year-old child Jason."

Though it could be criticized as pretentious and overblown, *Seizure* is clearly an ambitious effort to use the horror genre to treat serious psychological and cultural ideas. The film clearly seeks to work on two levels (or perhaps have it both ways), being a melodrama of a group of social types menaced by society's outsiders, and as symbolic figures (avarice, intellectualism, mother love, carnality, romanticism, artistic aspiration) set upon by figures representing corruption and self-destruction. On both levels, each character betrays himself by his own single-minded view of the world (e.g., the intellectual mesmerized by various abstractions). *Seizure*'s view of the artist is particularly critical—an initially decent type who seems to confirm his wife's view that his ultimate love is of his own artistry, for which he'll give the Judas kiss to his wife and child for more intercourse with the Queen of Evil (symbolically speaking).

Seizure also creates a special cinematic "world" via its key motifs, motifs that prove central to each of the filmmaker's later film worlds, and so are keys to understanding Stone's career. Reality, here and elsewhere, is a veil of illusions and self-deceptions through which the protagonist must find his way, mostly alone. Parent figures (here Sergei the aristocrat and seemingly the writer's wife) provide wisdom that proves inadequate or irrelevant in the final crisis. Society also is nonsupportive. (One thinks of Alfred Hitchcock's "the police are never there when you need them.") Intellect is untrustworthy, emotion likewise a confusing guide, the women characters led into self-destruction, most easily. If the artist-protagonist survives the longest, it's rather through a combination of blind courage, ruthlessness, and guile, rather than any conventional beliefs or feelings. Stone has repeatedly quoted Blake's aphorism in defense of his work: "The road of excess leads to the palace of wisdom."

Seizure may in fact be looked at as Stone's most honest and bravest work about his deepest feelings and fears: of being manipulated and betrayed by powerful forces, of becoming trapped in a society of shallow, self-centered people; of the futility of art; of artistic impulses ruining human relationships. Perhaps he's never been so honest, or just never changed his point of view, so never needed to create anything like it again.

The film had several sympathetic reviews. Vincent Canby in the *New York Times* commented: "*Seizure*, an ambitious horror film made in Canada by a young New York director, Oliver Stone. Its cast includes a lot of good New York actors, including Jonathan Frid and Anne Meacham, and its plot (about three mysterious strangers who take over a house party, Manson style) has enough gore to keep a 42nd Street audience polite. The screenplay includes two or three too many twists but there is some genuinely funny, waspish dialogue. Mr. Stone, a graduate of the New York Film School, is now writing an original screenplay with Robert Bolt (*A Man for All Seasons*).[3]

The *New York Post*'s Francis Herridge commented, "As horror films go, *Seizure* deserves a high rating. Its fanciful story has imagination with a core of plausibility, its direction remains smartly realistic and the acting excellent. Although in most far out yarns, the ending is tricky, still this one is possible. . . . For sheer horror entertainment, it holds your attention throughout."[6]

The *New York Daily News*'s Jerry Ostler summed it up as "a sadomasochistic ditty that ought to have an aspirin break." *Variety*'s capsule comment on November 20, 1974, said *Seizure* was "stylishly filmed but a murkily plotted horror film."[10]

Seizure did not do well with audiences, but Stone kept struggling with the help of his first wife. He would not give up film and follow his father into the business world. A relative commented of this period: "It's a safe bet that his father thought that Oliver would never really be able to support himself."[2]

Stone's headaches with *Seizure* continued for years.[7] *Seizure* was acquired by Cinerama Releasing Corporation, ten years later. The writer-director still felt sharply disappointed by the handling of the film, and accused Cinerama, its parent American International, and the men who run them, of "almost criminal deceit of the artist."[7]

In 1981 Astral Bellevue Pathe owned *Seizure*, and kept it in distribution as a shock film. Stone commented: "The reason that sort of thing happens is that these companies are owned by an element in Canada who call themselves 'tax shelter specialists.' They buy films for some ridiculously low figure, never pay, and then own them outright. Because they make their profit by deferring taxes for the year that the film was bought, they have no incentive to make any further profit on it. . . . Now when I get contacts about getting the film to show in England, there's not a thing I can do about it. I can't even get the Canadian assholes on the phone, or to cooperate in any way. There's nothing I can do—except express my rage."[7]

In a final turn of fate, after the Oscar nominations for *Platoon* and

Salvador, the film was resurrected for foreign sale under the title *Queen of Evil.*

Immediately after making *Seizure,* Stone found himself totally disillusioned and spiritually depleted. He took a job with a "god-awful" sports film company, but meanwhile wrote fourteen more screenplays, five about Vietnam.

On July 4, 1976, the U.S. Bicentennial, Stone was almost thirty, his first marriage had broken up, and he was barely able to survive as a cabdriver. Then, within a few months, he'd written the *Platoon* screenplay. "I finally sat down and dealt with the war as I had known it realistically. It took me eight years to get that screenplay, because I couldn't deal with it before. I needed the distance."

The script impressed a number of producers and was optioned, but the producers didn't want to go up against *Apocalypse Now,* then in production. Instead, Columbia Pictures assigned Oliver Stone to write *Midnight Express,* with English producer David Puttman and director Alan Parker.

2

......

FALSE STARTS

FROM 1978 TO 1986, except for writing and directing *The Hand*, Stone worked for others as a screenwriter on various Hollywood big-budget films. *Midnight Express* (1978) was the first.

The nonfiction book of the ordeal of Billy Hayes in a Turkish prison for drug smuggling, on which the film was based, was cowritten with a professional writer. A carefully crafted job, the first chapter sets up a careless, unsympathetic college dropout. As the book proceeds, we see him learning to survive in a filthy, corrupt, nightmarish Turkish jail. In the foreigner's block, he establishes his strength, enduring a merciless beating. Later, he begins to acquire a new self-awareness: "I was becoming a con. It seemed that everyone was always waiting for something in prison. You waited for the cell to be unlocked, and for the bread to come in in the morning. You waited for the food at noon. . . . You waited for visits. You waited for courts. You waited to go free."[15]

Eventually, Billy Hayes is sentenced to four years. His father visits and discusses appeals. Billy speaks again and again of escape. But his father fears that he will be killed if he tries. Then Billy's case is reheard, his sentence increased to thirty years. The impact is overwhelming. Billy develops discipline, meditates, assembles escape preparations. The tension and austerity lead to a physical relationship with another prisoner.

After five years, the American decides to take matters into his own hands. In a special code, he writes to his parents that he won't wait for the "legal local"—he's going to take the "midnight express"—to try to break out. Transferred to a work colony, he assembles his escape gear. During a bad storm, he rows away in a stolen boat, and makes his way to Greece, where he is safe. His family sends money, and he flies home.

Despite critical carping, many reviewers give Stone credit for the film's success. Blauner notes: "Stone gave the screenplay the dramatic force of such classic prison movies as *Cool Hand Luke* and *The Great Escape*, tossing in a kind of ferocious, obsessive violence that would appear in most of his movies."[4]

Specific changes noted by Roberta Plutzik[27] and others include making the cocksure airport departure a sweating shaking headed-for-the-gallows sequence, creation of a horrifying disabling fight with a trustee, death of a malicious guard, a fierce court speech, and two escape attempts. The chronology is also rearranged; placement in the criminally insane wing really happened early, not at the end, and Hayes served in two prisons, not one.

Director Alan Parker commented: "The first problem [both writer and director] saw was one of construction. In the book, as in a lot of prison stories, the action wanders back and forth among a lot of characters. But in a movie we had to concentrate on the story."

Stone also transformed an escape attempt to a sequence showing how Hayes and other prisoners chipped away at cell walls to reach a maze of underground tunnels. Hayes: "That escape try really took place as we were cutting a bar on a window. But when Oliver Stone and I were talking about my experiences, I mentioned a story I'd written about the prison being built on catacombs. I guess he liked the idea."

When given his life sentence, Hayes prepared a speech "to touch those people somehow," but did not curse them. "I tried to make a statement that would affect them, so I said that from one society to another laws change, from one age to another laws change, but that's all. I was trying to maintain a balance, and I had a simple secret— to smile, to send out good energy no matter what. I'd gotten past screaming and yelling. I said to them, 'All I can do is forgive you.'"

Stone, however, asked him how he felt after returning to his cell with a merciless sentence. Hayes admitted underlying outrage, and Stone inserted that outrage into the screenplay's courtroom speech. The homosexual relationship in the book was more or less denied. The scene is treated in a romantic dreamlike manner, but ends with Billy backing off, supposedly to show Hayes was not homosexual. Hayes commented: "I like the dreamlike quality of the scene, but I wish they'd have the steam come up and fade out. But I'm very

4. *Midnight Express.* Brad Davis as Billy, Paolo Bonacelli as Rifki: "The more I see of him, the more I hate him." *(Courtesy the Museum of Modern Art Film Stills Archive.)*

5. *Midnight Express.* Brad Davis as Billy, Irene Miracle as his girlfriend. Susan: "They're calling you a pawn in the poppy game between Nixon and the Turks." *(Courtesy Museum of Modern Art Film Stills Archive.)*

happy that maybe somebody in the Midwest who is freaked out by the very idea of homosexuality can look at the scene and feel the delicacy of it. The line from my book expresses it best—"It's only love."[27]

Finally, Hayes's real escape, described in the book, involved an island prison far from the mainland. In a storm he swam to a fisherman's dingy, rowing to the mainland despite enormous waves. Later he swam a river to Greece. The boat sequence was dropped, though, for the escapee: "The experience was such an exhilarating one for me—holding those oars, I was literally holding my destiny. I realized I'd forgotten what it was like to be free, and though I might have drowned, it was worth it."

October 6, 1970. In earth-colored tones that dominate *Midnight Express* throughout, we see brief tourist vistas of Istanbul, Turkey: great domed temples and public buildings, busy canals, crowded markets. Turkish music, echoing horns, sets the mood.

In a plain bedroom, a handsome American youth tapes silvery rectangular drug packages to his chest. Eventually we see his face, anxious but determined. On the sound track, Billy Hayes's heartbeat pounds.

The airport is crowded with soldiers, black-dressed matriarchs. The youth kids and smiles with his blond young American girlfriend. Billy visits the men's room to wash and tape down the packages. More kidding on the airport bus, heart still pounding.

But the aircraft is surrounded by troops and customs men. "For God's sake, just get on that plane!" Billy tells her. He slips around the search line, has his feet on the ramp—then a soldier touches his shoulder. Face rigid, he's frisked, the soldier touching the packages and shouting. Dozens throw themselves flat, while the squad aims at the youth. To frantic music he's dragged off, girl watching, down a tunnel. In a dank room he's stripped, drugs removed, suitcase contents torn apart—clothing, camera, condoms—all tiny fragments. The beefy Turkish cops grin at each other, then slap faces angrily when he dumps packets they've missed from his boots.

A Texas-accented embassy man interprets an official's questions. There've been hijackings. If he cooperates he'll be on the next plane. Billy agrees to go back to the bazaar shop where he bought the drugs and finger the sellers. "Otherwise it'll be tough on your parents and girl."

To piping Turkish music Billy sits sweating in T-shirt and jeans in the crowded shabby restaurant, full of bored Turks and drugged-out-looking foreign youths. Seeing his chance, he ducks out, the awkward cops chasing. He slips through the crowds, into an alley holding stacks of caged roosters, dead ones hung up, a butcher at work. He hurries up a closed old courtyard's stairway, pauses, a gun muzzle appearing beside his head. Tex tells him: "You seem like a nice enough kid to me, but you try it and I'll blow your fuckin' brains out!"

A military truck delivers him to the big ancient prison, his head shaved as his voice says earnestly: "Dear Mom and Dad, this is the hardest letter. . . . I'm sorry for making it so difficult. . . . Will it ease the pain and shame? . . . Forgive me."

He's put in a shabby old cell, the bunk littered with debris. It's cold, there's no blanket. Another prisoner tells where to scrounge one. But in the middle of the night, with shouts and punches he's dragged into a basement in his undershorts. On his back, legs chained overhead, he is smashed in the feet with a club by the big cruel faced head guard. The chains lift his legs further, spread them.

Waking up days later, Billy meets the other prisoners; the always-excited Jimmy and a placid Swede. "The prison's like a cheap hotel, but room service is awful." In the prison yard, the inmates pace, play volleyball, brood. Billy's advised to take it easy. Sentences are long, it'll be a while before he eats a hamburger.

Max, a gentle older con, explains there are no straight lawyers in Turkey. They're all bent, they take courses in corruption at night school. If suspected of honesty, they're disbarred, " . . . catch the Midnight Express."

Billy has a visitor, a kindly faced middle-aged Irishman, his father. Embarrassed, they embrace. "I'll punch you in the nose later. Right now we've got to get you out." With him is a consulate man, and a grinning fat Turkish lawyer.

At the hearing in a third-world courtroom, the excited young prosecutor shouts and points at Billy. His fat lawyer is pleased: "The judge likes you!"

The sentence is four years, two months. His lawyer: "It is a great victory!"

Billy's dad says they're all working for him. "Don't get stupid. . . . They can play with your sentence." Upset, the old man threatens the head guard.

Billy sits in his shadowy, shabby ancient cell. Cell doors are un-locked, surrounding a sort of two-story commons, equally dilapi-dated, all earth-colored walls and dusty sunbeams. In underwear, on an iron cot, Billy contemplates his future: "Nineteen seventy has passed into 1971."

The inmates play volleyball in the yard, surrounded by tiers of cells like slums. Billy's voice explains that prisoners use a Turkish phrase that means "Like this, like that" for their harsh, arbitrary life. Homosexuality is forbidden, but common. Inmates stab each other's behinds—"Turkish revenge!" Of Rifke, a fat, sly-eyed middle-aged trustee, Billy says: "The more I see of him, the more I hate him!" He chisels the inmates on food, and hangs Max's pet cat. Max takes it down and holds it, weeping.

Billy's fat lawyer proposes an escape scam: "You could be released before the court discovers its stupid clerical mistake." Billy doesn't even reply.

Frantic Jimmy has a prison plan—involving blocked shafts that lead to the sewers. Max: "I swear I heard a couple of Christians singing down there." Impatient to escape, he's caught and beaten.

"Dear Susan," Billy's voice says, "poor Jim was caught and pun-ished so severely he got a hernia. In their own fashion, the Turks are draining my life away."

Billy exercises with the Swedish inmate, smiling in solace at each other. The Swede puts his hand on Billy's, slides it up his neck. Billy gently pushes away, kisses the fingers, shakes his head. . . .A little later, the Swede is released.

The consulate man visits with bad news. There's a new sentence. There are thirty-five judges, and twenty-eight voted for a life sentence.

Billy grabs the foreign service man's throat: "Life? For what? For what? I have fifty-three days!" He throws him backwards.

Billy faces his judges. "So now it's time for me to speak. What is crime, what is punishment? You can't put everybody in jail. I've served three-and-a-half years of my life in your prison, and I think I've paid for my crime. . . . I wish you were standing in my place . . . you'd know a society is based on a sense of fair play, a sense of justice. For a nation of pigs, it sure is funny you don't eat 'em. Jesus Christ forgave the bastards, but I can't. I hate you, I hate your nation, I hate your people, and fuck your sons and daughters because they're all pigs, you're a pig, they're all pigs!"

The judge: "My hands are tied by Ankara. I must sentence you for a term no less than thirty years. May it pass quickly." Half a dozen white-helmeted soldiers escort Billy out.

In his cell, dazed, he strums a guitar:

> Got the old Istanbul blues, they gave me thirty years
> Ain't got nothin' left to loose
> I was busted at the border, two keys in my shoes
> And they gave me thirty years, to learn the Istanbul blues.

Tapping the walls, the three pals find the old shafts, move stone blocks, slip down to the sewers with haversacks and flashlights. "The Turks must have blocked it off. . . . We'll come back every night til we get out."

But Rifke spots the disturbed mortar. Lined up, Jimmy blows up and is dragged off. Billy would kill him, but Max has a better idea—steal the money he's chiseled: "Steal his money and you steal his life's blood. It's in his radio."

Next morning Rifke fumbles with his radio, screams. The Keystone Kop guards rush in: smashing beds, tables, plates, slashing mattresses and pillows, shattering all. Finally, in the stove, ashes and a few fragments of burned dollars.

Rifke, ready to leave, appears in suit and suitcase. Max: "Soon he'll be back on the street. No friends. No money. Plenty enemies." He makes a throat-cutting gesture.

Rifke jumps him, sets him up with hashish so he's to be beaten.

Guards gone, Billy throws himself on Rifke, the two clawing as they roll, crawl, and tumble, struggling in the shabby commons. Rifke slashes at Billy, kicks, crawls under some sinks. Billy, hysterical, tears down the feeder pipes, as Rifke crawls out, up a filthy set of stairs. Screaming, Billy tackles him. Face-to-face, Billy jams his mouth to Rifke's and the stoolie's tongue is bitten out, flies off, Billy's face bloody, expression mad.

Seven months later, he's in the section for the criminally insane, a grim set of cavelike rooms crowded with white-dressed figures with unearthly faces: crazy smiles, numb blanks, frozen-postured shapes. Billy, daze-faced, wanders around the oddly timeless big room full of madmen.

In an echoing basement, other figures meaninglessly circle a massive pillar. As he joins them, an intelligent-faced man tells him: "I studied philosophy at Harvard. . . . We all come from the factory. You're one of the machines that doesn't work."

Time passes. Billy, slack featured, is taken to an outdoor building, its single room divided by a glass panel. His girlfriend Susan enters: "Oh my God, Billy! What have they done to you?" She weeps. "Your family's fine. . . . They're calling you a pawn in the poppy game between Nixon and the Turks."

Billy, slack jawed, only asks that she unbutton her blouse.

She does so, presses herself against the glass while he moans and strokes himself.

"I wish I could make it better for you. . . . please stop."

"I love you," she tells him. She's brought a family photo album with pictures of Ben Franklin. . . . Don't count on anyone but yourself. You're running out of time. If you stay here, you'll die. You've got to get out of here."

Billy goes back to the figures circling the pillar, circling the wrong way. Harvard tells him: "A bad machine doesn't know it's a bad machine. The factory knows."

Billy: "I know that you are a bad machine. I'm from the factory. I make the machines!" Harvard runs away.

Billy pushes through the bedlam, refuses the evening drugs, hides in a toilet, and tears hundred-dollar bills from the album, hiding them.

By the nodded-out Max he weeps: "I'm going away. . . . I've come to say good-bye. If I stay here I'll die. . . . I'm gonna come back for you, Max, I promise. You hang on for me."

At the gate, he offers a hundred dollars to the massive, hated head guard. He's let out, walks with him on a narrow footway circling the prison—not to freedom, but to the sanitarium! Billy pleads, but the guard takes him inside, screaming as the giant throws him against a wall, offering money as the guard takes down his pants. Desperate, he throws himself at the guard, so he slams the guard against the wall. A massive coathook, stabs the back of the guard's neck, so he falls, blood streaming.

Billy seizes his pistol, points it, can't shoot. Instead he slips on a guard's uniform and hat, down a stairwell. A guard throws him the keys.

He's outside. A light, hopeful Turkish tune commences. Billy moves along a street, arms reaching out from his sides in new free delight. The tune becomes triumphant. But a military vehicle with an armed soldier approaches. Billy's head goes down, shoulders slavishly high. The vehicle passes. He pauses, goes forward, runs! jumps!

That night he crosses the border, three days later lands at JFK. Black-and-white still photos show him embracing parents, girl, and a final zoom to his older, wiser eyes.

Stone's screenplay is interesting for its closeness to the themes and viewpoint of his first film, *Seizure*. Like its protagonist, Billy finds himself in an alien, manipulated environment, on his own resources.

Very quickly he must abandon his illusions about fair play and justice, let alone his privileged status as an American. Neither parents, nor society as represented by the U.S. State Department officials or the local legal system, nor the "prison society" he joins can help him—it all leads to the slow-motion suicide in the madhouse, a counterpart to the writer's occupied home in *Seizure*. Neither intellect (the Harvard madman) nor love (his girl: "Don't count on anyone") has the answer. Half-gone into madness, only by guileful excess does Stone's hero have a chance.

Though criticized, the screenplay is also skillful in calculated dramatization using a strong rising dramatic arc. Stone builds up to his protagonist's act of violence by showing the years of stress and abuse he's endured. Following Hollywood conventions, Billy only lashes out when pushed to the limit, and even then refuses to kill in cold blood. His ongoing good relations with family and friends confirm his basic decency and quiet strength. Not everybody can be an Indiana Jones, especially in real life.

Nevertheless, the major reviewers found the greatest fault with Oliver Stone's screenplay.

The *New York Times*'s Janet Maslin thought the film calculated and dishonest. "When Billy finally kills one of his captors and makes his escape, it's a triumph of the human spirit; his sanity reasserts itself just in time for the grand finale. . . . *Midnight Express* offers its audience the vicarious thrill of sharing Billy's depravity without making the viewer feel compromised."[23]

The *Village Voice*'s Andrew Sarris commented: "Characters are combined, episodes are transposed, the plot is simplified. All this is standard procedure for adaptation . . . but on this occasion there seems to be a pattern to the discrepancies. Brad Davis as Billy Hayes is directed as more of a crybaby than the person described in the book. His squeamishness and his hysteria are overemphasized. Positive experiences have been written out of the screenplay. For example, two prisoners successfully escape while Billy is incarcerated. Billy is impressed with the tactics they employ. These characters are not present in a movie dedicated solely to grotesque futility. Even Billy's escape, arduous to the point of being heroic in the book, is reduced to a gruesome accident in the movie, and is infinitely less believable in the process. . . .

"There is also remarkably little psychological or sociological curiosity in the movie. Everything has been hyped and hoked up to intensify feelings of helplessness and self-pity. And no opportunity has been lost to depict the Turks as fat, greasy, brutal, and perverted. *Midnight Express* is thus a thoroughly ignoble and exploitational film because of the curiously intoxicating feeling of hatred it arouses in the viewer."[29]

Stephen Farber likewise zeroed in on the screenplay. "The movie has uncomfortable jingoistic and racist overtones. . . . Every single Turk is portrayed as venal or sadistic. . . . The movie goes for the crudest, basest response—inciting the audience to hate another nationality. . . .

"The entire movie is offensively one-dimensional. Billy has no identity beyond that of a victim. He's been made as bland as possible, apparently on the theory that it's easier to identify with a character who has no strong traits or idiosyncrasies. . . . The relationship of Billy and his father is portrayed as purely loving and supportive. The tensions hinted at in the book have been left out of the movie. . . .

"The movie even manages to lose the point of Billy Hayes's story. Almost every page of the book underscores his fierce desire to escape. That determination to survive is missing from the vapid character on screen. Even his escape seems like an afterthought. In the movie, it's truncated and anticlimactic compared to the thrilling escape described in the book. . . . It's one of the year's most unpleasant and dishonest movies."[12]

Pauline Kael's critique, "Movie Yellow Journalism," is perhaps the harshest. "This innocent American is subjected to the most photogenic brutalization that the director, Alan Parker, and the screenwriter, Oliver Stone, can dream up. . . . This film is like a porno fantasy about the sacrifice of a virgin. . . . He's thrown in jail and, on his first night, he's hung up by the ankles and clubbed—and there's also the strong suggestion that he's sodomized by the head guard, Hamidou (Paul Smith), a huge sadistic bullock of a man with great clumps of hair growing from the rims of his ears like outcroppings of lust. . . .It's more like a brothel than a prison."

Kael goes on to speculate about the filmmaker's techniques and motives, focusing on the director. "*Midnight Express* is single-minded in its brutal manipulation of the audience: this is a clear-cut case of the use of film technique split off from any artistic impulse. . . . They're demonstrating that they can be vivid and ferocious enough for the international "action" market. . . . The film is a crude rabble-rouser: like a wartime atrocity movie, it keeps turning the screws to dehumanize Billy's jailers. . . . At the same time, it's sanctimonious about Billy's victimization. . . . There is no mention of the fact that it was the American government which put the pressure on the Turks to keep dope from being smuggled into the U.S.—we gave them an assistance program in criminology and trained their customs officials. The Turks have been trying to oblige us."[18]

All four reviewers make arguable errors to score their moral points. A few of the Turks are clearly sadistic, but most are simply indifferent, insensitive types that you'd expect as guards, criminal lawyers, or prisoners. Maslin's murder of a guard is Sarris's gruesome accident. Sarris's and Farber's crybaby is a stoical survivor who turns neither bitter nor hopeless in a difficult situation. Kael's note on U.S. drug policy ignores Billy's girl's shrewd comment about Billy being "a pawn in the poppy game between Nixon and the Turks." It's far easier to attack the filmmakers as racists than to question our fifty-year relationship to this cold-war, third-world ally, and how little being in "the free world" amounts to.

Despite all the carping Stone won an Academy Award for his screenplay of *Midnight Express*. His main memory of that night was the questions of the press about why he didn't follow the story line of the book more closely. He replied that a book is one thing, a motion picture another—the book would have made a poor film if the screenplay had followed it to the letter.

In an interview several years later Stone commented: "I think that there was a lack of proportion in the picture regarding the Turks. I was younger. I was more rabid. But I think we mustn't lose sight of what the movie was about. It was about the miscarriage of justice, and I think it still comes through."[26]

Nevertheless, it was a moment of triumph. "It was like a fairy tale. A great night. A lot of the old Hollywood was there. All of a sudden, I was thirty-two years old, the golden boy for a few minutes. But I really wasn't ready for it."[4]

Stone moved to California and began to get steady, lucrative work. He also exhibited much outrageous behavior—heavy drinking and long tirades against drugs at awards ceremonies. Stone's explanation is that he also spent the year trying to make his script about paralyzed vet Ron Kovic, *Born on the Fourth of July*, starring Al Pacino. He had crew, cast, rehearsals, sets, sites—when the money wasn't there, he became bitter.

Nevertheless, in 1981 Edward Pressman, a Hollywood producer, hired Stone as writer-director of a major horror film, a psychological suspense thriller with a 6.5-million-dollar budget starring Michael Caine—*The Hand.*

The novel on which it was based, *The Lizard's Tail* by Marc Brandel,[5] centers on a talented professional cartoonist, who loses his drawing hand in a freak auto accident, so he then loses his livelihood as well as the affections of his wife. His wife, unhappy with their marriage, leaves him, taking their daughter. Brandel's prose has been described by Gerald Peary as "gentle, quietly emotional and strangely sane. . . . He knows how to write about loneliness." The reader never "sees" the severed hand, never knows if it has taken on a life of its own, or the cartoonist is murdering while suffering blackouts. Brandel subtly develops his characters as well: the cartoonist starts off sympathetic, intelligent, and decent; gradually it becomes apparent he's a "control freak, never happier with his wife than when she's paralyzed in a wheelchair."[25]

Describing what he set out to do in the screenplay, Stone said, "There's nothing worse than to mislead a horror fan, and I truly believe that any horror fan will be disappointed . . . expecting a *Jaws*-like monster hand and its progressive subjugation of society. It's not about that—its about the character played by Michael Caine; the hand of the title is only a manifestation of his will."[22]

The original novel only suggested the hand, never showed it. After some consideration, Stone added a visible hand, and changed the title. Stone notes: "But the hand itself is only a manifestation of the character's anger. The true emphasis of the movie is Caine's, as you watch him change from an ordinary man to a very angry man, to a disturbed man, and finally a ruined man."[22]

First shooting was done on sound stages, then at locations in Los Angeles and the nearby countryside, concluding in the San Bernardino Mountains. A key element of the production was a radio-controlled mechanical hand designed by the special-effects expert Carlo Ramoloi. Over thirty different hands were designed for the film, each used in a different situation—a crawling hand, a walking hand, a strangling hand.

Stone later commented: "There was a lot of studio pressure. I wanted the picture to succeed, so I bowed. The trouble was that the studio wanted more hand. We spent close to a million dollars on this series of hands—forty or fifty of them. It was as if you had to be a mechanic to make this movie. It's better to work with a shark or a gorilla, because you have more space. But a hand?"[26] Out of a seventy-to-eighty-day shooting schedule, they spent twenty on the hand.

Stone was happy with the mechanical hand, but joyous about his actors. Michael Caine proved sweet and easy to work with, punctual, willing to rehearse and do retakes, and a stabilizing factor in the production. Stone saw his as a very dark role, that of a man who eventually becomes psychotic. "[But] we wanted to go with an out-wardly healthy, normal, family man."

Andrea Marcovicci played Anna Lonsdale, the cartoonist's discontented wife. Stone: "She has a quality that is something like young Elizabeth Taylor, and a steely, sort of waspish bitchiness that the part requires."

Commenting on postproduction, Stone has said: "When I did *The Hand* in 1981 . . . we cut too quickly. Before I knew it, we would be at an assembly of two and a half hours, but I would not really remember the alternatives I had. Having to go back and reconstitute took longer than to shrink down at a slower rate initially."[3]

A traveling air view of a lakeside community: pines, expensive lakeside homes, docks. In a greenhouselike studio, cool thoughtful-faced cartoonist John Lansdale finishes his Conan the Barbarian–type comic strip, *Mandro*. "Now that I control you, how can you best serve me?" a captor's speech balloon reads. Lansdale signs the strip, light flashing off his signet ring.

In his home his sultry but cool wife Anne does yoga. They have

6. *The Hand.* Michael Caine as Jon Lansdale, rehearsing with writer-director Oliver Stone: "The trouble was the studio wanted more hand." *(Copyright 1981 by Orion Pictures Company. Courtesy Museum of Modern Art Film Stills Archive.)*

7. *The Hand.* Michael Caine as Jon Lansdale, Andrea Marcovicci as his wife Anne: "You'll get a good income out of it, we won't have to worry about Lizzy or the rent or what we'll do after Christmas." *(Copyright 1981 Orion Pictures Company. Courtesy Museum of Modern Art Film Stills Archive.)*

a dinner date with another couple: "You'll talk about work, we'll listen." His wife wants to get a small apartment in Manhattan, take courses at the Origin Institute: "I want to do something on my own."

Sweating, Lansdale chops wood, cuts off a lizard's tail. His daughter sees the tail move, but "it's only a reflex." The cat runs off with it.

Anne drives their car, arguing with John about the apartment. "Where am I supposed to work?"

"I thought you wanted to stay here."

"You mean that's what *you* want."

A slow car ahead boxes them in as the argument grows. "Get back, you sick cow!" Lansdale yells to the driver. There's no way he's going to let them separate to think about the marriage.

Another car speeds toward them in the opposite lane, a hay truck closes in behind. The artist sticks his arm out to furiously signal. Suddenly, in a freak accident, the blocker car sheers off Lansdale's hand, blood splashing over him and the car interior!

Agonized, clutching the stump, more blood splashing, his wife brakes.

On a gurney the unconscious artist is put into an ambulance, while wife and patrolmen search the grass.

His wife, a physician, and the calm-faced artist look at the healed arm stump. "How does it feel?"

"Like it's still there. Like my fingers are still moving." He'll have such a feeling for years.

His daughter tries to console him: "On TV someone lost a finger, and they sewed it back."

"To sew it they've got to find the hand right away. Mommy went to look for it, but it ran away."

His wife is glad he told her, caresses him.

In bed with her, he loses control. Sad faced, he begins to cry: "It's so ugly!" She soothes him.

At night, he goes out to his studio, sits, and tries to draw with his other hand. The face he produces is crude. Expressionless, he studies his professional *Mandro* strip.

Abruptly the family cat, excited, leaps, mewing, onto his work table, then plunges out the window, smashing a glass panel. The artist peers after it.

At the accident site, Lansdale stares around. Out in the grass, the hand, in a black-and-white image, rests on the ground. Lansdale walks through the grass, seen from the hand's point of view, "looking" up at him. He finds his signet ring. He continues searching, while the hand tracks him at a distance. At last he walks away.

In New York, Lansdale talks with his agent, a middle-aged businesswoman. He's had an offer to teach. The agent says the strip might go on: "There's this young man who loves it."

In dark-blue black shadows, the hand clenches into a fist, twists.

Still dining, his agent says: "It's time to get used to things." For an instant, the lobster dinner's claws wave merrily. But he's reluctant—"because the moment you're back on your feet, your wife will leave you!"

At the Origin Institute, sleek women in leotards exercise to a young man's New Age patter. His hands move on Mrs. Lansdale. From a balcony, her husband watches.

In a loft building, Lansdale and wife bicker. He won't see an analyst: "After ten thousand hours, he'll tell me I'm sane again. No doubt we're all crazy."

In black and white, the hand crawls into a drawer, puts on the signet ring, scurries away.

A doctor helps the artist put on a prosthetic hand, steel fingers, and a palm. "With practice you can button your shirt." "Drawing?" The doctor doesn't answer. He puts a black glove on over it.

At home, angry, the artist looks at his replacement's work: "He's mine. I've created him. Why should I give him up?"

His wife: "You'll get a good income out of it. We won't have to worry about Lizzy or the rent or what we'll do after Christmas."

In the shower, the handles morph into hands, morph back.

In a midtown office, Lansdale confronts his editor and a scruffy young artist. "I brought it up to date!"

Lansdale: "You weakened the character . . . you made him look deeply into himself. You made him think. . . . You've cut the balls off Superman!"

Lansdale, furious, says they want him to leave Mandro to them. The editor and young artist take out the new strips—now all crossed out. "How could you!"

In the street, he bumps a bum similarly disabled, shoves him aside. In black and white, in an alley, the hand attacks the drunken homeless man, choking him.

Entering the loft, Lansdale sees the young trainer and wife on knees, the wife weeping. He turns away.

His daughter didn't like the new drawings, but didn't touch them.

His wife was "counseling," she can't talk about it. He can't give them Mandro. For money, he's taking the California teaching job.

In black and white, the hand hides under the furniture.

In California, another college teacher, Brian, explains the new milieu. "I teach psych . . . anything I can get the jerkoffs to enroll for. . . . You should do okay, the kids have heard of you, big culture hero!"

His class is less than bright looking, unattractive youths, and a few adults. One sensitive pretty girl, Stella, catches his eye.

His new home is a depressing cabin. Lansdale cooks burgers and eats alone, calls his family. "I miss you, Daddy." His wife wants to wait until Christmas to join him. Lizzy has made friends and is at a good school. "I miss her very much."

Rain beats at the window, a branch smashes through the pane, Lansdale cries out! He finds his signet ring on the pillow.

A class ends: he chats with the sensitive-faced girl.

Lansdale tries to draw, the girl visits. Summing up college: "The only thing I was good at was bookkeeping. And who wants to be a bookkeeper? That's why I picked this place. You never have to graduate. None of that shit about making it. I like the way you look at me." She pulls off her sweater.

In bed, she's face-to-face with him, touching the prosthetic device.

She'll come back tomorrow. Her sketches are childish. But with them is a shocking image of a naked girl controlled by a giant powerful hand!

In a noisy bar, the artist talks with the psych teacher about his apparent blackouts: "I found this drawing and I don't remember doing it."

"You never know what you can do. The unconscious mind is capable of anything . . . you can do anything you dreamed of and never had the guts to do. You'll never know who the fuck you are."

Outside, Lansdale stops before a shop window. A hand seems to leap toward him, shattering the glass in the grayish dark.

Lansdale interrupts Stella at her cashier's job, speaks intently.

In the cabin, the couple make love, moaning. His wife's coming for Christmas, Stella: "Fuck Christmas." She's going to L.A. Lansdale has a present for her, a teddy. Holding the romantic garment, she twists her face with painful feelings and they embrace. "I'll be here at 11:00."

In the noisy bar, the psych teacher shouts: "Hey, Mandro!"

He's getting out for two weeks. "L.A. Two weeks shacked up with 115 pounds of pussy. I get to screw her night and day any time I want."

Lansdale's face is agonized.

Alone in the cabin, Stella opens a gift. A hand grabs her, she cries out. Her ecstatic face moves around and around in multiple focus, openmouthed.

Night, rain, windshield wipers, RENO on a sign, Lansdale driving.

Wife and daughter arrive at the cabin. Ducking in ahead, he sees the place is empty. Lizzy admires the Christmas tree, his wife finds the teddy in the bedroom. "Is this for me?"

The family has dinner. Lizzy: "Uncle Bill says steak is bad for you. Makes you get angry at people." Lansdale's steel hand crushes his wine glass.

In the bedroom, his wife has something to say.

"Has he been fucking you?" Lansdale speaks out.

"I don't think that's any of your business. . . . I don't think you ever loved me. You loved your work. Loved Mandro."

"You hate me. You've always hated me." He seizes her neck.

"I think you should get me out of here. Get me out of this house. Get me out of this life."

Lizzy comes in, and they cheerfully exchange gifts.

In the garage, his wife can't start the car. "And what's that smell?" The hand, bluish and unreal, seems to creep up the back of the driver's seat. But she drives off.

Lizzy wants her mommy. "She may have car trouble."

A flash image: a fire-covered car hulk tumbling along. But Mom arrives safe and okay.

In the bar, the psych teacher grumbles the L.A. girl copped out.

He drives his jeep drunk, stops, yells at Lansdale: "You had to talk her out of going to L.A.!"

Lansdale, frightened, confused, says he only saw her at the bar, and drove to Reno alone.

In bluish light, the hand leaps to seize the psych teacher's throat. Bones crackle.

In bed alone in the cabin, Mrs. Lansdale reads Carlos Castaneda.

Lansdale stands silhouetted, frighteningly rigid, at the bedroom door. His wife's leaving with Lizzy.

"You're not taking her away from me. You're not."

The hand's enormous shadow jumps on the wall. His wife reacts, Lansdale's face is furious.

The hand jumps, seizes her by the throat. She struggles.

Lansdale runs into the bedroom, as the hand seems to dodge out the window. The woman sprawls on the bed, seemingly dead.

Lansdale tells his daughter to call the police, rushes out with a flashlight. In the garage he moves slowly ahead. Suddenly the hand drops from the ceiling to his neck, seizing him! Struggling, shouting, he drops to the floor. It lets go, then rushes forward to grab his remaining hand. Bones crackle.

He bites it, so it slides away. He seizes a knife, stabs through it! It hurries away to hit a tire to puncture it, air hissing out. Then it jumps up to grab his throat! He beats it with his arm, blacking out, the world going black and white.

Flashlight beams touch the artist's face. The sheriffs and his scared daughter stand over him: "I must have blacked out. My wife."

"She's okay."

They're looking at him oddly. There's a powerful smell coming from the car trunk. They found the psych teacher's Jeep.

The car trunk holds the dead-faced bodies of Stella and the psych teacher. His daughter screams.

Lansdale, in hospital pajamas, is strapped to a special chair in a lab. Electrodes on his head are wired to an EEG machine. A white-haired intense woman therapist speaks authoritatively to the oddly smiling man. "It's an old rage . . . an ancient rage. . . . You chose to eliminate someone else's life, just to fulfill your own."

The therapist tells him Lizzy saved him, stopping his attack before he killed his wife: "The struggle is not over yet. Go into the pain. Go into it. Sense it, feel it, touch it. I'm here to help you."

The EEG pens wiggle on the graph paper.

"I think that you're seeing the illusions. I think that someday you'll be able to say, 'I love'!"

The pens are wiggling wildly.

"What are you feeling now? Do you want to tell me something, John?"

"The hand . . . near your neck. It wants to kill you."

"Why? Why does the hand want to kill me?"

"Because it hates you!"

"Take responsibility for it. There is no hand!"

Suddenly the cold blue hand leaps to seize the therapist by the neck, throwing her over. Her skull hits the geometric logical pattern of black-and-white floor tiles and blood pours across it. Her blind eyes stare up at us.

The artist smiles. He begins to pull off the Velcro restraints and laugh. The camera rises away from him, and continues to rise.

The Hand was a critical but not a popular success. Interestingly, no one commented on Stone's subtle visual approach to the ambivalent nature of the hand—those sequences showing it are always in black and white or bluish, suggesting the events depicted might be a dream or a fantasy of the protagonist, not a real event.

More important, *The Hand* is notable for continued use of Stone's characteristic themes from *Seizure*, as might be expected in a film over which he has full artistic control. Again the protagonist, again an artist, is menaced by metaphysical forces that are counterparts of his psychological nature. Once more these show up the weaknesses of his prosaic links with the world career, marriage, and love relationships dissolving into veils of illusions. The closest things to parental figures, his agent and editor, move quickly to replace him with a new, more stylish, amiable, and subservient technician, his rewarding calling exchanged for empty insecure teaching of dull, insensitive, or broken-spirited youths. In this heartless, time-serving society, wife, daughter, and lover cannot accept or understand him, and the intelligent therapist offers a form of love that can only inspire his raging hatred. As in *Seizure*, it remains unclear to the end what is ultimately dream and truly real.

The critical response to *The Hand* was mainly positive, at least by the major writers. The *New York Times*'s Vincent Canby called it "a clever horror tale"—a suspense horror film of unusual psychological intelligence and wit . . . about his growing realization that the hand has taken on a life of its own. . . . The hand seems to share Lansdale's jealousies, his depressions and his fury over their separation, yet it also resents Anne, as if blaming Anne for what was, after all, an accident. . . . One of the things that Mr. Stone has done is to construct a screenplay that can be taken two ways with equal grace. At its most obvious, *The Hand* is a horror film, one in which some not easily describable "thing" terrorizes the countryside. It's also about anger so profound that it goes unrecognized, being accepted as an aspect of what might be called "normal" behavior until it goes out of control."[6] Canby thus links the film with

Seizure. He goes on to praise Stone's screenplay as precise, consistent, and self-assured. ("When Mr. Stone crosscuts between a scene of Anne in her yoga class . . . and . . . the severed hand crawling, crablike, across a field far away, there is mad method at work as well as extremely dark humor.")

Andrew Sarris saw *The Hand* as "one of the more intelligent efforts to combine psychological analysis with scary spectacle. . . . Stone never makes it clear whether the severed hand on the movie is a supernatural force, or the delusion of a deranged mind. In the end he plays it both ways, and gets away with it because of a satisfyingly dark humor in the treatment of the situation."[30]

Sarris notes perceptively that *The Hand* works ". . . to show us both the growing madness of the character, and the struggle of his cool intellect to control his raging emotions. The struggle is reflected in the film itself by the persistent tension between the realistic treatment of the milieu and the fantastic premise of the plot. . . . By the time Caine is face to face with the hatefully knowing psychoanalyst of Viveca Lindfors, we are being pulled one way by the vestigial morality of the Caine character, and another by the vicious imperatives of the genre. . . . The ending is perversely satisfying though hardly edifying or enobling."

Those critics that disliked the film tended to compare it unfavorably to the novel. Gerald Perry's review stated that "*The Hand* is insistently heavy handed. It's the real thing, a hairy slab of fingered meat. It goes after a surly derelict and murders him in an alley. It crawls around in the back seat of a car. It just acts bad, even choking its one time owner in one particularly stupid scene towards the end."[25]

Other reviewers found all the characters hateful throughout. As a watcher apparently quipped: "When you're Oliver Stone, the whole world is Turkish!"

The Hand was not a success, and people who wanted Stone a year ago didn't want to talk now. Once again, he felt like a pariah. Years later, he commented: "Part of the reason I did *The Hand* was that it was obvious the studios weren't going to do the more dramatic material. So I thought, at least they'll do a horror movie for money. That's why I compromised, and I made a serious mistake—I wanted to work as a director."[26]

On June 7, 1981, two months after its release, Stone married

Elizabeth Cox, his assistant on the movie. The next film he would be involved in would be a very different affair.

Conan the Barbarian began as a 1930s pulp-magazine hero created by writer Robert E. Howard. A heroic fantasy of masculine power, the character battles evil warlords, black magicians, and other enemies in Howard's imaginary ancient pagan Hyborian Age. The first Conan tale, "The Phoenix and the Sword," was published in the December 1932 issue of *Weird Tales*. Conan was "afire with the urge to kill, to drive his knife deep into the flesh and bone, and twist the blade in blood and entrails. . . . He moved with the supple ease of a great tiger, his steely muscles rippling under his brown skin."

Eighteen Conan tales were written during Howard's lifetime (he died at thirty in 1936, a suicide). In the early 1950s, hardbound collections of the stories were published by the Gnome Press, New York, and in the 1960s, mass-market Conan paperbacks were issued, utilizing muscular yet sensuous heroic artwork by Franz Franzetta. In the 1970s, Marvel comics released pictorial versions of the character.

The Conan movie project had its start in 1976, when producer Edward Pressman first formed his own production company. Scion of a toy-manufacturing company family, Pressman was impressed by "the whole world based on it. It was exciting—beyond any expectations that I had ever had. I saw the comic books, the paperbacks, and hardback books, the various fan publications, the fabulous Franzetta paintings—just everything that had been done about Conan. Immediately the significance of this hit me, and I knew I had to be the one to do the Conan movie."[21] Pressman wrote the first version of the script in 1976.

Getting the movie rights took four years, since Conan was controlled through posthumous collaborations, managers of his estate, and rights ownership through story publication. The character's potential, as well as tentatively signed up, but then unknown Arnold Schwarzenegger, drew Pressman on. Eventually a syndicate, Conan Productions, was formed to handle all aspects of the Conan property. An important contract stipulation was that the filmmakers would remain true to the spirit of Conan (i.e., not "camp it up"). The syndicate also picked up options on other Howard characters.

While still negotiating for the rights, Pressman had met Oliver Stone, who at the time also wished to prepare a Conan film. Press-

8. *Conan*. Arnold Schwarzenegger as Conan: "Arnold Schwarzenegger's Conan looks petulant, as if someone has left chewing gum on his favorite barbell" (Canby). *(Copyright 1982 Universal City Studios, Inc. Courtesy Museum of Modern Art Film Stills Archive.)*

9. *Conan*. Arnold Schwarzenegger as Conan, Sandahl Bergman as Valeria. "[Arnold] is so in love with his abilities and with himself that there's no room for anyone else" (Aufderheide). *(Copyright 1982 Universal City. Courtesy Museum of Modern Art Film Stills Archive.)*

man found Stone's vision of Conan was similar to his own, and felt Stone's track record with *Midnight Express* would be helpful in getting studio and financial backing for the Conan project. Pressman was also producer of *The Hand*.

Stone prepared a second Conan script, which began with the beginning of Conan's life. It also used another Conan character, Thulsa Doom, as the antagonist. In a 1981 interview Stone stated: "When I was asked to write the movie I was given a pretty free hand. Because the budget had not yet been finally determined."[22] Stone's version had the planet being taken over by mutant armies, and Conan the lonely pagan mythic hero—Tarzan, or Roland at the pass. Stone loved the fact Conan had been enslaved and suffered, then *rose* from peasant to king. In Stone's ending, King Conan tells his princess: "I can't be a king this way, as your husband. I can't inherit the throne. I will earn my throne." Then he rides off to a second adventure, and more sequels a la James Bond.

Director John Milius joined later, commenting: "It's an unbelievable script. He had armies of mutants in it, things it would have taken years to make up, but I read it and said: 'Jesus, they're gonna make a Conan movie and I've got to do it.'"

A complex deal was eventually cut that made John Milius director, Dino De Laurentis producer, and Pressman executive producer. Milius prepared a third screenplay, which reportedly filled in Conan's youth. It was praised for setting up Conan's history, motivation, and character development—from a child slave to a proud warrior.

Though one cannot be sure, the final Milius script clearly contains significant themes, characters, and relationships that are present in Stone's other projects.

In a Cimmerian village, Conan's father tends a forge, creating a steel sword, his mother nearby, the nine-year-old clinging to her skirts. The father lets him hold the weapon, and speaks of the steel's secret.

Barbarian raiders sweep into the peaceful village, led by an evil warrior, who kills Conan's parents and enslaves the child—Thulsa Doom. Growing into a powerful youth, Conan is purchased and trained as a gladiator, and finally mysteriously freed. He outwits an evil witch and her fiery orgasm, teams up with her feisty captive, and the two visit the local capital, dominated by an evil religion:

"Two, three years ago it was just another snake cult, but now. . . ." Allied with a blond beauty, the three thieves raid the cult's temple, whose decor recalls his parents' murders, seizing its treasures, fleeing, celebrating, and being arrested.

The local king wants the three to recapture his daughter from the evil master priest of the cult. Conan goes alone, meeting a wizard before reaching a stronghold filled with Mansonish fanatics, only to be captured. Conan confronts his parents' murderer, who demonstrates his evil powers—youths suicide at his command. Yes, he tormented Conan, "But look what it made you!" Finally, Conan is crucified by Thulsa Doom.

His three comrades in arms, and the wizard, that night rescue him yet again from evil spirits, then plot to rescue the princess. Creeping into the evil citadel past scenes of total human degradation, the band rescue the girl and escape—though the blond beauty, Conan's woman, is mortally wounded. The remaining comrades fight off Doom's warriors, breaking Conan's father's sword.

High up on the front of the temple, Thulsa Doom exhorts his followers—then Conan appears. Doom claims to be his "true" father. Conan seems to hesitate—but then beheads Doom. Conan then sets the temple afire, and departs for new adventures.

As in all Stone's previous projects, normal life is a veil of illusions—family, community, strengths, and other familiar ways easily annihilated by the forces of chaos and darkness. Conan's parents disappear in an instant and leave him utterly helpless; even a king cannot hold on to his daughter or her loyalty. Society is barbarism at best, slavery at worst. Intellect and emotion are absent or impossible—the blond beauty who loves Conan does not make contact with his feelings, let alone have her love returned, and can only die for him. Conan's victories are victories of excess—strength, tenacity, distrust, aggressiveness. *Conan the Barbarian* can be seen as the ultimate Oliver Stone movie of mistrust and isolation.

In fact, the reviews of *Conan the Barbarian* focus on the extreme view of human existence that the screenplay and film portray. "At the center of it all," Vincent Canby notes, "is the Milius–Oliver Stone screenplay that has no discernible point of view, unlike the screenplays for *Star Wars* and *Raiders of the Lost Ark*. . . .The images are as empty as the narrative, which, among other wrong things, begins on a fairly exciting note, and then becomes progressively less suspenseful until it just sort of stops. In moments of stress, as when he beheads Thulsa Doom, [Arnold Schwarzenegger's Conan] looks petulant, as if someone has left chewing gum on his favorite barbell."[7]

David Denby perhaps clarifies Canby's complaints about the script. "Yes, *Star Wars* also had its medieval overtones, its grandiloquent passages and mumbo jumbo, but George Lucas gave the story a parodic edge—he lets you know you were watching pop, and so, depending on age and inclination, you could enjoy *Star Wars* either as romantic adventure or as mass culture parody. . . . Working with a pop pastiche, Milius hasn't got much of a story, and he provides little narrative energy or rhythm of his own. The movie comes in blocks, each in a different style (*Seven Samurai*, then *Spartacus*, then *Thief of Baghdad*, [then *Seven Samurai* again]). The dreary, uninvolving narrative lurches from brutal "realism" to crudely oracular pomp to zippy fantasy to Christian and phallic symbolism"[10]

Variety's Berg summed up the project as monumentally boring and uncentered. "Conan has no real soul and thus leaves the film without much of a core. [The script] is no more than a series of meaningless adventures and ambiguous references until the final expected confrontation. . . . By that time, it's a case of much too little, much too late." The writers, Berg fears, also alternate between period conversation and contemporary vernacular, using the former where they need realism and the latter for comic relief. "The result is almost as if someone is telling audiences that despite the effort spent on creating the mood of mythic times, this is all one big inside joke. If only it were."[2]

Paula Aufderheide sees the movie on different terms: "This is not a movie about good or evil, or men and women, or barbarism and civilization. Instead it's about technique . . . the mere execution of tricky maneuvers. Arnold Schwarzenegger . . . works against the movie as a movie. He's so in love with his abilities and with himself as a technician that there's no room for anyone else."[1]

Stone went to Russia in 1982 and spent a year on a screenplay called *Defiance*, a love story about a dissident and his wife. In a 1987 interview he calls it the best work he'd ever done about a man-woman relationship. "Unfortunately," he stated in the early 1980s, "the executives were very much into high concept kid gloss movies—*War Games* rip-offs, *Star Wars* rip-offs, it was a depressing time. . . . I really should have been directing *Platoon* or *Born on the Fourth of July,* but there was no way they were even going to make those movies, let alone let me direct them. So I went into a phase of cynicism from around 1980 to 1985, which was a period in which no one was making any serious movies."[26]

Stone's next writing project, *Scarface,* was conceived in 1980 by its producer, Martin Bregman, who saw the 1932 Howard Hawks classic *Scarface* on late night TV and decided to make an updated version with Al Pacino, shaped around today's cocaine traffic. Stone has stated he worked on *Scarface* only because Pacino wanted him.

From the late seventies into the eighties cocaine was an everyday thing for Stone. "Cocaine took me to the edge. I finally realized that coke had beaten me. I hadn't beaten it."[26]

Stone, who had dealt with aspects of the drug world in *Midnight Express,* carried out two months of research, much of it in South Florida's Latino underworld. He interviewed federal agents (including FBI agents), narcotics investigators, Miami Police Department homicide detectives, and members of Florida's Dade and Broward County sheriff's departments.

He also met with some of the young criminal "bandidos" hired to unload contraband from offshore freighters, street hustlers who cut and peddled coke, and businessmen who funded drug deals and siphoned off the profits. In addition he did research in Colombia, Equador, Peru, and Bimini—an island link in the drug delivery chain. Stone described the experience as "overwhelming—I felt my life was on the line. Most of my work, for obvious reasons, was done between midnight and dawn. That's not the safest time to be out alone when you're dealing with people who might decide—on second thought—that they had told you too much."

Elsewhere Stone stated: "I conceived the picture in terms of a comic opera. Some of my friends call it *Scarfucci.* I modeled it on *Richard III.* Brian De Palma, who directed it, has a slower camera than I do, so some of the script had to be cut. But I was very pleased with the movie. It's got me a lot of free champagne all over the world from gangsters who asked me how I know all these things." Stone told another reporter he researched the film stoned, but wrote it totally straight.[26]

To dramatic news footage of the May 1980 Mariel Harbor, Cuba, to Miami "boatlift," and Castro's oratory, titles mention the 125,000 fleeing refugees included 25,000 criminals.

Distrustful U.S. lawmen interrogate a slim, sly-faced Marielito, Tony Montana. He smiles roguishly: "My father take me to the movies. I watch the guys like Humphrey Bogart, James Cagney. I learn how to spe' from those guys. I li'e those guys." In ragged clothes and cardboard shoes, he says he always knew he would come to the U.S.

One cop spots a crime gang tattoo. "I'm Tony Montana, a political prisoner."

"Send him to Freedomtown, let them look at him!"

Freedomtown is a refugee camp—tents under a freeway cloverleaf, fenced in, jammed with refs. His tall, dark, and handsome friend Manny tells him there's a job and green card for him if he'll kill a ref who tortured the brother of the guy with the job: "For a green card, I'll carve him up real nice."

In a camp riot, Montana does it and gets his walking papers.

As dishwashers, the two can see a glamorous club. Tony wants money, Manny wants women. Two toughs from their job connection assign them to pick up two kilograms of coke from some newly arrived Colombians.

A team of Marielitos pulls up at a sordid beachfront motel. Tony and a pal go inside, where the Colombians are waiting. They have the keys close by, they say. Tony says he has the money close by.

Abruptly the Colombians pull guns, gag and tape his pal in the shower. "You want to give me the cash, or I kill your brother before I kill you." They hold guns to their throats. The Colombian pulls out a chainsaw and carves the pal. Blood splashes everywhere. "Last chance!"

The others burst in, guns blasting, the wounded sawman leaps to the street. Tony shoots him in the forehead and heart, and they race away.

Tony and the survivors enter a luxurious condo, are greeted by the overweight syndicate head, Frank: "I need a guy with steel in his balls. A guy like you."

Tony gives him the keys. "You'll find your biggest problem is what to do with all the Colombia cash."

Tony catches sight of Elvira, Frank's sultry, stunning, strung-out ex-debutante mistress. They'll go to the Babylon Club. Elvira, intelligently: "We always go there. If someone wants to assassinate you, you won't be hard to find."

The Babylon Club is a sumptuous, multilevel nightclub complex

10. *Scarface*. Al Pacino as Tony Montana, Robert Loggia as Frank Lopez, Michelle Pfieffer as Elvira: "Lesson two—don't get high on your own supply." *(Copyright 1983 Universal City Studios. Courtesy Museum of Modern Art Film Stills Archive.)*

11. *Scarface*. Al Pacino as Tony Montana: "You need a fucking army to take me!" *(Copyright 1983 Universal City Studios, Inc. Courtesy Museum of Modern Art Film Stills Archive.)*

with black lacquered tables, Greek statuary, dancing fountains, bright neon, dazzling mirrors. Frank points out a bloated old drug lord: "A real *hazza*— a Yiddish word for pig. Lesson number one. Don't underestimate the other guy's greed."

"Lesson two," Elvira tells them, "don't get high on your own supply."

While Tony and Elvira dance, Frank's henchman confides: "He's a fucking peasant. But he'll break his back for Frank."

Tony tries to be friendly to Elvira and replies: "I've got enough friends. I don't need another, especially one that just got off a banana boat."

"You got a look in your eyes, like you haven't been fucked for a year." Dancing with her, he says the boss looks soft. But he's going to get "the world and everything in it."

Months later, Tony and Manny are looking over the young bikinied beach beauties. "This town is like a great big pussy waiting to get fucked!" Yet a pickup effort—wiggle your tongue and they go crazy!—fails.

Tony: "In this country you got to make the money first, then get the power, then you get the women."

Tony goes after Elvira. She won't go driving, so he shops with her for a $43,000 Porsche, cash. "The machine-gun turret is extra," a savvy salesman murmurs.

At sunset, Tony visits his aging mother and affectionate sister Gina living in a modest bungalow. His mother refuses money: "It's people like you who are giving a bad name to our people! Son? I wish I had a son! We haven't heard from you in five years. Get out!" But sexy young Gina embraces him passionately: "It doesn't matter how long you've been away. You're my blood—always!" Seeing Manny's excited expression, Tony tells him: "Hey, you stay away from her!"

At his palatial Bolivian estate, Frank's connection, Alexandro Sosa tells Frank's top aide Omar and Tony, surrounded by rolling green lawns, rose gardens, and ornamental fountains, that he can guarantee two hundred kilograms a month. But Frank must cover the risk of moving it. Tony proposes taking on the risk in Panama. Angrily, Omar says he's doing the talking, Sosa studying them. Outraged, Omar copters out.

Tony says simply: "You've got everything a man could want." The aristocratic drug lord responds: "I like you Tony. There is no lying in you."

Overhead, Omar is lynched from the copter. Sosa had recognized him as a squealer. Tony tells him: "All I have is my word and my balls, and I don't break 'em for anyone!"

"I think you and I can work things out. Just remember: Don't ever try to fuck me."

Night at Frank's condo. Frank and Tony, furiously: "You made a deal for 18 million!" "We got to think big." "Like your friend Sosa. . . . The guys that want it all . . . they don't last."

Tony visits Elvira's sundeck. "I hear you and Frank aren't working together anymore."

"I hear this is the land of opportunity. . . . You like kids? . . . I come from the gutter. I know that. I got no education. But I know the street, and I'm making the right connections. . . . I want you to marry me. I want you to be the mother of my children. . . . Just think about it."

At the Babylon Club, Tony sees his sister dating, Elvira, Frank, and a cynical cop who sketches his monthly payoffs: "We tell ya who's movin' against ya. I got eight killers workin' for me—when they hit it hurts."

Tony tells a pal Frank set the crooked cop on him, chases his sister so her date flees, but she shouts: "You got some nerve. If I want to fuck them I'll fuck them!" Tony, expressionless, watches the club entertainment. Two Latinos with concealed Uzis get ready.

Driving her home, Manny is teased by Gina: "Why don't *you* take me out?"

The assassins pull their weapons, mirrors exploding, guests screaming and fleeing, Tony dashing ahead of the bullets, firing back, finally driving off, tires shrieking. He then arranges a pre-timed phone call.

At Frank's, Tony, arm in a sling, arrives with his gunmen. Frank answers the phone, revealing he set the hit up: "I brought you in. I made you!"

"I stayed loyal to you. I made what I could on the side but I always stayed loyal to you."

Frank pleads for his life, promising ten million, crawls, bows, kisses Tony's shoe. "Shoot that piece of shit!" They kill Frank. Tony shoots the crooked cop, but offers Frank's gunman a new job.

Tony pulls back satin curtains on Elvira's enormous, satin-covered bed. "Where's Frank?" "Just come with me."

In the night sky, a blimp flashes: THE WORLD IS YOURS! From his new elaborate offices, Tony smiles at it.

A pounding driving rock then plays: "Push it to the limit . . . walk along the razor's edge . . ." A montage: Dollars pouring through counting machines; Sosa and Tony laugh, money sacks delivered to a bank while a Kennedyesque banker smiles; the new Montana Management offices; Gina's new club (she hugs Tony); Tony and Elvira's elaborate marriage at a fortresslike estate; security system TV screens in the citadel's war room.

Tony's money-laundering aristocratic banker tells him he is cleaning so much cash, he has to raise his rates. Anyway, there's no place else to go. Alone in the fortress villa, Tony curses him savagely.

In his war room, he tells Manny they must sweep for bugs, check out a lingering cable TV truck. But countersurveillance is 12 percent of their profits. "It helps me sleep."

Watching a glib TV business reporter from a pool-sized circular bubble bath, Tony swears: "You know what capitalism is—getting fucked!"

"A true capitalist if ever I saw one," Elvira mocks. Tony reminds her she uses too much coke. Elvira: "Nothing exceeds like excess. You should know, Tony!"

A politician on TV proposes drug legalization: "Bankers, politicians, *they* make it illegal. To help get votes!"

Elvira: "You're an immigrant spic millionaire who can't stop talking about money!"

Tony: "You know what your problem is? You've got nothing to do."

In a shabby warehouse office Tony works with a fat dishonest-looking man and his money-laundering team, putting bills through money counters. Two million, eight hundred thousand is heaped everywhere. The man pulls a gun and arrests Tony; a video camera has recorded everything.

Tony meets with his tough bright lawyer: "I guarantee you walk on conspiracy. But they'll come back on tax evasion. . . . When you got a million in undeclared dollars staring into a video camera, its hard to convince a jury you found it in a taxicab—"

Tony meets with Sosa in Bolivia, together with an industrialist, minister and a high U.S. government type. They can solve his tax problem if he'll help their disposal expert get rid of a certain anti-drug crusader.

At a nightclub a stoned Tony tells Manny and Elvira: "This is what it's all about—eating, drinking, fucking, sucking, snorting. When you're fifty you got a beer belly and you're looking like these rich fucking mummies. This is what it's all about!"

He glares at Elvira: "I look a' her. I got a fucking junkie for a wife. Her womb is so polluted I can't even have a baby with her."

"You sonofabitch. What makes you so wonderful? You kill people. You don't even know how to be a husband. I'm leaving you. I don't need this shit anymore." She goes, never to return.

Tony, face furious, addresses the Wasp club patrons: "You're all a bunch of assholes. Because you don't have the guts to be what you want to be, so you need people like me so you can point your fingers and say—that's the Bad Guy! That makes you good? You just know how to hide from life. I don't have that problem, I always tell the truth, so say good night to the bad guy!"

Tony, his gunmen, and the disposal expert put a bomb under the public figure's car—to be triggered in front of the UN. But when his wife and kids go along (making faces out the back window), Tony, tormented, kills the demo man instead.

At his Florida citadel, his mother calls to report Gina's disappearance. Tony snorts a colossal line of cocaine. Moments later Sosa calls, furious. The UN speech was given, security is now up to here. "So you want to go to war—we go to war!"

Tony finds out about Gina's new place. At the door, seeing Manny, he has a paranoid vision of the lovers, and belly shoots his friend. Gina, in a dressing gown, weeps: "We got married yesterday, we were gonna surprise you." Tony's men drag her out, leaving a dead Manny.

At home Tony slumps at his desk, while on the security TVs, slim figures advance over the walls. Tony: "We're gonna eat that Sosa for breakfast!" While Tony sprawls dazed, the raiders advance, strangling and knifing his own security teams.

Gina appears, lovely in a dressing gown, smiling wildly, pulling a gun. "Here I am, I'm all yours now. . . ." She starts firing, but first a raider leaps in, kills her, and is killed by Tony. He caresses his dead sister: "Gina, listen, I love you, I love you."

The raiders enter the immense red velvet–walled living room, past its THE WORLD IS YOURS silver pylon, like an old RKO titles icon. They close in on his door.

Tony pulls a grenade-launching machine gun from his desk and wipes out the raiders beyond the door. He sweeps the muzzle around the room, killing, killing, killing, unkillable! "You need a fucking army to take me!"

The Bolivian raiders are all firing up at him on the interior balcony. But behind him a tall aristocratic figure in sunglasses, face hidden, appears. Sosa fires his shotgun into Tony's back, so he flies forward, spread-eagled, descending into the room's interior pool. He floats, blood pours out. Above him the pylon glitters, THE WORLD IS YOURS.

Somber organ music sounds as the tall aristocrat, eyes covered, collects his troops.

Scarface is remarkable for its use of Oliver Stone's characteristic thematics from previous films. At the start, its young protagonist even declares he learned what the United States was like from watching Jimmy Cagney and Humphrey Bogart films—veil of illusions indeed! He ignores his family and they in turn provide little comfort—his mother denounces him and his sister's behavior only inflames his obvious pathological concern. Society teaches the wrong lessons—figures representing business, government, finance, and foreign cultures all enthusiastically further his drive toward crime, corruption, and self-destruction. The most intelligent and cultured individuals—his lawyer and ex-debutante lover—are no less cynical, except for his wife's futile last bitter critique of their life together.

In fact, Tony's "You hide from life—I always tell the truth" speech is interesting as one that could have been spoken to their opponents by the obsessed, isolated protagonists of *Seizure, Midnight Express,* or *The Hand.* (It's also interesting as a defense of the filmmaker or artists in general.) In the end, in Tony's endless massacre of swarming, anonymous enemies, the protagonist of *Scarface* demonstrates the Stone hero's obsession with survival at any price.

An early version of the script (draft three, May 1982) suggests its structural evolution, featuring more sequences of the young Tony advancing in the drug trade: robbing drugstores to bankroll future drug deals; coordinating a dramatic night drug freighter pickup run;

masterminding a multiple bypass of U.S. customers by drug-running nun, retiree, mother and baby, and teenager.

Wife Elvira kisses him as she sadly departs: "Too bad the two of us never grew up." These scenes were apparently less important than executive suite dealings which, as Pauline Kael suggests, try to make drugs unattractive by portraying the drug trade as tedious and treacherous when not murderous. This seems the film's real weakness—arguing that U.S. drug lords at heart are just business-men gone wrong and denying that drugs can be exciting and may be the only way out of poverty.

The moviemakers are of course straightjacketed by "public opin-ion"—they can't show users having a good time (except for big-time pushers) and to show the users suffering would destroy sympathy for their protagonist (let alone letting them show *why* users use). All that's left *is* a sort of comic dope opera of drug-trade big shots. The TV news sequence is a cynically accurate view of the drug trade's frequent role in politics, but since it isn't dramatized it seems only background for a marital spat. (Perhaps a bit should have been added about Hollywood's deliberate distortion of the drug problems for its own profit.)

Critical responses to *Scarface* dwelled on the film's violence and coldheartedness, while noting its parallels and comments on U.S. business and Hollywood itself.

In the *New York Times*, Vincent Canby's detached review com-mented, "This *Scarface* . . . contains not an ounce of sentimental-ity. . . . [It] has the impact of a single breathless anecdote. . . .*Scarface* is a relentlessly bitter, satirical tale of greed, in which all supposedly decent emotions are swept up for the possible ways in which they can be perverted. . . . Mr. Stone follows the general outline of the (1932) Hecht screenplay with at least one notable difference. Tony's fall comes not only because he ignores the under-world maxim to the effect that one should never underestimate the other man's greed. To his misfortune, he also ignores a second rule, 'Don't get high on your own supply.' This is a major switch on the work of Hecht. . . . I'm not at all sure what the film means to say about American business methods, though I suspect Mr. De Palma and Mr. Stone would not be unhappy if it were seen as an ironic parable. For all his evil ways, Tony Montana, unlike some legitimate businessmen, always deals in first class goods, though this may have less to do with his commitment to fair trade than with a desire to save his neck."[8]

Kael feels the story is so badly realized it's not effective as social criticism. "The joke is how shallow [Tony] is, how degraded. He's a pig rooting around in money and cocaine, and, as things go wrong, he snorts more and more. . . . But the scenes are so shapeless that we don't know at what point we're meant to laugh. The ludicrousness that the moviemakers are showing us can't be sorted out from the ludicrousness of the movie itself. . . . The film's message (or rationalization) that Tony is an honestly brutal businessman—he isn't a hypocrite like the WASPS. . . . When Tony, the drunken, corrupted peasant, tells off the old rich, he appears to be speaking for the writer and director. And from the film's point of view, he knows the truth about power and how it works (It may be that Stone and De Palma got into these cheap distortions by using the movie business as their model for the world)."[16]

Andrew Sarris likewise saw the film's problem in the script as a misinterpretation of a subgenre. "The trouble with the movie is that there are about twenty minutes of action and 2½ hours of attitudinizing. . . . Al Pacino's Scarface is cast in the mold neither of tragic hero nor of comic rascal, but of a glumly alienated antihero. In his later scenes . . . he resembles nothing so much as a road company Richard III attempting to articulate his disgust. . . . All I know is that the movie runs out of coherent plot very quickly, and that it never achieves any convincing characterizations."[28]

A number of other writers more or less wrote off the film, providing a variety of reasons for its failure.

David Denby summarized simply: "Every scene is designed to make the same point about Tony's crazy, beautiful courage and recklessness. Tony has the heaviest *cojones* of all time. . . . After a while [DePalma] loses everything that's special about Tony—he's become a myth, and his death is mere spectacle. . . . Tony, it seems, isn't very smart or interesting. Yet the movie treats him as a classic tragic hero—we get a pattern, not the working out of an individual destiny. There are no depths to Tony to reveal, and Pacino wears himself out finding new ways to explode into rage. . . . The movie turns into a mechanical remake of *Scarface* and other famous movies. [He marries Elvira] and we get obvious all too predictable empty scenes of their marital discord—*Citizen Kane* without the wit. Even worse, Tony's boringly moralistic mother and twitchy hot-to-trot sister are such clichés from old movies that they unintentionally approach camp parody."[11]

Enrique Fernandez saw *Scarface*'s sins as starting with producer Martin Bregman. "Bregman wanted to *Zap, Bang, Pow*—if not, why had he got Oliver Stone to write the screenplay? Stone can hardly be accused of delicacy, but he's good at delivering punch. . . .His *Scarface* is less chauvinistic than [*Midnight Express*] only because after all the central character is not an American innocent abroad but a Latin malevolent stateside. But *Scarface* is shallow precisely because Stone is unable to project himself into any kind of otherness. *Midnight Express* works because it's told from the protagonist's point of view, *Scarface* fails for the same reason. . . . I don't see Tony Montana, I see Al Pacino, acting."[13]

James Wolcott in Texas Monthly sees the film as "attempting an epic as rich and criminal as *The Godfather* but madder, kinkier. . . .If *Scarface* had been conceived of as a taut, subversive thriller, it might have had the makings of a classic, but it has been mounted as if it were a Brechtian epic of power mania run amok— a punk faced *Arturo Ui*. . . . Where *Scarface* goes mortally wrong is in spelling out all of its messages in pink neon. Once Tony becomes the Prince of Paranoia, staggering like Elvis through his red velvet hell as his subordinates tremble, the movie becomes ever more bloated, disconnected, didactic, and druggily adrift. Plot elements that should be handled suggestively, like Tony's semi incestuous love for his sister, become porno blatant with sis (mad with grief) fondling her breast and using the *F* word. Other sequences, as when Tony is dispatched to New York City to knock off an anti-coke-cartel crusader should never have gotten off the drawing board. A strict regime of diet and exercise would have done wonders for this waddling script. William Blake to the contrary, the road of excess doesn't always lead to the palace of wisdom. In *Scarface* it leads to the palace of excess, where dead bodies litter the screen in layers like lasagna."[33]

Interviewed about the politics of *Scarface*, Stone said: "In *Scarface* I don't back down for one second. I think it's clear that not all Cubans are drug dealers. This guy is, and his mother even says he is no good. It's classic gangster stuff, but people get oversensitive. . . . I mean, every nationality wants to believe there are no gangsters, and the Cuban right wing is a very scary group. Honestly, even to talk about them is dangerous; they may be the single most dangerous group of guys I've ever met. . . .

"The politics of it are buried by a lot of superficial trivia. To some, it's a movie about cars, palaces, money, and coke. It's not just about that. It's about what these things do to you and how they corrupt you. The theme gets lost. I think Tony Montana—Al Pacino—has a Frank Sinatra dream of the United States, okay? So he becomes a right winger in this sense: 'I hate communists, and this is the good life with the big steaks in fancy restaurants and the blond and the limo and the whole bit.'"[26]

After *Scarface*, Stone's next Hollywood writing project was also drug related—*Year of the Dragon*. Robert Daley's 1981 novel, *The Year of the Dragon*, from which it was adopted, was a best-seller with the feel of truth—Daley himself has an extensive background in police work. In the book a conventional intelligent careerist policeman is by political bad luck assigned as head of New York's Chinatown precinct, where his career is on the line. To save his job, he's forced to begin to probe the only conjectured Chinese drug Mafia, throwing himself and those around him into increasing jeopardy.

Stone and Michael Cimino did an enormous amount of research, but it was impossible to get the Chinese to talk about the gangsters. They went to dozens of fifteen-course Chinatown banquets, gorging themselves, trying to make friends. No luck. Finally they contacted a dissident on-the-outs gangster group, who took them to Atlantic City to give them the inside story on the gambling world: youth gangs as little surface fishes to knock off, exploit, run numbers; deep-down whales running the enormous Southeast Asia drug shipping—more heroin traffic than the Mafia.

Great scarlet and white paper dragons dance, Chinese costumed lion dancers march, Chinese bands play, strings of firecrackers explode, smoke and steam, and dust billows. It's Chinese New Year.

A few old men meeting quietly in a restaurant are surprised by a gang youth who stabs one, then flees.

In severe black and white, figures move in a solemn parade down the same streets, some supporting some with large images of the slain elder, a bit like a Peking party pageant. A beautiful young Asian-American TV reporter, Tracy Tzu, identifies the survivors' relatives: "This means a war of tongs!" Among the mourners is a tall handsome businessman, Joey Tai.

Meanwhile, the youth gang bursts into a candy store, demanding a weekly payoff. The owner: "You chinks will wind up with a garroting wire around your necks!" Bullets explode into his forehead.

Striding up to the parade is a fierce-looking Stanley White (Mickey Rourke) most decorated N.Y.C. cop, just given Chinatown. Meanwhile the mourners won't speak with the TV team. The girl concludes: "And so with the passing of Harry Yung, a chapter of Chinatown history closes."

White grabs an Asian youth, the two entering a basement gambling parlor. "Tell Uncle Harry I'm looking for him."

In an Asian bank executive suite, several Chinatown businessmen, led by old-guard leaders, angrily confront White. "We'll have the same arrangements. No police ever in our gambling clubs!"

White responds: "There's a new marshal in town . . . new rules . . . no more street violence. I don't want to see Asian faces unless they're serving spareribs. Get 'em jobs!"

"For thousands of years, no Chinese went to the police. Nobody will come to see you. If our citizens regard extortion and robbery as part of the cost of doing business, why should you be concerned?"

"Fuck you! I'm tired of China this and China that. This is America and it's two hundred years old. You're not special and you're not above the law. Start doing something about it fast."

White argues with his boss at city hall: "I told you to stick all this on the youth gangs, not the old guys."

"The Mafia was invented in China a thousand years ago."

"You want to attack Chinatown with the Eighty-second Airborne?"

At night, White arrives at his modest Queens two-story home. He and his wife are two terminal Catholic workaholics: "You missed target practice Wednesday—the day of my ovulation. You want a kid, you'd lay me once in a while."

Another evening. The top cop meets the Asian-American reporter-beauty at a glittering Chinatown restaurant. They talk Chinese-American history. Thousands of Chinese immigrants died, their bones scattered all over the west. He shows her the famous intercontinental railroad golden spike photo: "Look, not one Chinese worker, they died anonymous."

Outside the restaurant, two Asian youths pull down ski masks.

"Harry Young's head of Chinatown, got to be involved in the Chinese Mafia," White tells her. Chinatown stinks—crime, drugs, sweatshops, prostitution, extortion, gambling, slave rings. "The highest rate of TB and mental illness in the city." He wants her to splash it all over the tube. Each day they'll peel another layer.

The two youths with machine gun and shotgun run in, open up. The diners scream and riot as the killers blast people, chandeliers, bar. White fires back so they turn, flee in a getaway car. Around the couple victims are carried out on gurneys while the beautiful reporter weeps, and White kisses her.

In their executive suite, Chinatown's leaders quarrel. Joey Tai says the killers are from Toronto, to make them look weak: "There's a tourist falloff, the Italians are angry, they call us yellow niggers!" His answer: "It's time to consider more vigorous leadership. Sell direct to the blacks and Puerto Ricans."

At city hall, the cops quarrel. The commissioner's mad about the Shanghai Palace. White wants one undercover cop: "Get some results! That's it!"

Joey Tai and his black bodyguard hurry through a sweatshop, a Chinese kitchen, to a crummy apartment where the assassins are being sheltered by his special youth gang. He tells the others: "You know what's expected."

Captain White tells his young cop Herbert to go where the Chinese Mafia go, to see what they see. The radio reports two male Asians shot dead. "You're undercover now!" White and his team hurry into a kitchen where the bodies of the assassins lie in a great vat of bean curd. "Young people, no respect," an old cook rants, "rob, shoot, kill."

In one restaurant, White's trying to sell his exposé series to the reporter-beauty: "You're acting like there's something between us." Outside, his wife glances in.

In a restaurant, Joey Tai, apparently a drug lord, tells the families of the youths he'll pay college expenses.

White confronts Joey Tai, and is told "Chinatown can be very easy or very hard. . . . Say a contract for security work after you retire at one hundred thousand a year."

"I'll take the same amount you're gonna make off your next fifty keys of heroin."

At home, White finds his clothes dumped on the front lawn. "Hey, I was only twenty minutes late. What's the matter with you?"

Driving slow, he talks out the window to the striding reporter-beauty: "I thought it's over. . . . There's something between us."

The reporter's gloriously hi-tech apartment has a spectacular

12. *Year of the Dragon.* Mickey Rourke as Stanley White, Ariane as Tracey Tzu: "The first time I saw you I knew you were crazy and racist too." *(Copyright 1985 Dino De Laurentis Corporation. Courtesy Museum of Modern Art Film Stills Archive.)*

13. *Year of the Dragon.* John Lone as Joey Tai, Mickey Rourke as Stanley White: "I'll take the same amount you're gonna make off your next fifty keys of heroin!" *(Copyright 1985 Dino De Laurentis Corporation. Courtesy Museum of Modern Art Film Stills Archive.)*

night view of the East River bridges. Tracy: "The first time I saw you I knew you were crazy and racist too."

White: "I think I hated you before I even met you. . . . On television you destroy people's feelings. . . . That's why I want to fuck you so bad."

They go into a clinch.

At headquarters, White addresses ranks of policemen: "I want you to destroy the entire commerce of Chinatown. I want chaos!"

In a crowded gambling club, TV reporters and police bust in together, and the Asians are loaded into paddy wagons: Reporter Tracy confronts the smooth Joey Tai: "A major drug conspiracy case is rumored to be pending. Is there a Chinese Mafia?"

The old Asian businessmen meet with a voiceless Mafia don using an electronic larynx pickup. Vibrator: "I have nothing left but my brain! You people are flying too high."

In a small room, ancient white missionary nuns working with the police listen to wiretaps on the drug lords' obscure Asian languages: "They're talking around things, not about things. . . . They're flying into Bangkok."

White confronts his pal/superior, who cries: "We wanted to shake them up, not turn the city upside down! They go to the Manhattan Borough president, who goes to the mayor, who goes to the commissioner, who comes to me."

"You're gonna call off the investigation of the Chinese Mafia?"

"What Chinese Mafia? It's all in your mind."

"This is like the fuckin' war. This is like Vietnam all over again. Nobody wants to win."

Naked under a robe, Tracy opens her door for White, carrying a suitcase and a pile of books about China: "Maybe everyone's right— same as Nam, we lost because you were smarter than us."

"You can't stay here."

"You're the only friend I have left. . . . I don't know anybody else. . . . I feel like such an asshole. . . ." They're silhouetted against the blazing bridge.

"I love you. Did you hear what I said?"

"There is no Chinese word for love."

On an exclusive floating restaurant in Bangkok, Joey Tai greets his Asian connection. He'll have to consult directly with the warlord drug king about the new arrangements.

Captain White goes home to his wife: "I don't know what got into me. . . . It just happened."

"I'm out of time. I'm thirty-five, slidin' into forty. . . . It's okay, Stanley. Now will you get out of here."

As White pauses on the stoop two teen Asian assassins attack. One quickly slashes her throat, White guns him down, then shoots the escape car so it explodes against a wall. Madly he tries to drag out the killer's flaming corpse.

In Thailand's Gold Triangle, Joey Tai and bodyguard meet drug lord/warlord Ban Sung and his horse soldiers in the jungle. His mountaintop village holds hundreds of tribesmen and troops. They embrace, the old former leader a crouching sweating zombie ("The general likes heroin in his soup").

They bargain: 4,500 a key? 6,500 a key? A prisoner traitor is dragged up, and Joey Tai "buys " him. Deal concluded, Tai suddenly holds up the sawed-off traitor's head: "Let no motherfucker ever raise his head against us!"

The funeral for Captain White's wife is a tragic if dignified affair, the church ceremony in Polish, banked flowers by the open coffin, police cadres in full uniform.

His only friend visits White at his house: "You think you're on a crusade. . . . We got an arrangement, a treaty, we get along."

"The arrangement is what killed Connie."

Tracy confronts Joey Tai: "The death of Captain White's wife implicates you. . . . Did you meet with the drug lords?"

"There are ethical boundaries for the press!"

Photos and White's team are spread across Tracy's extraordinary apartment. White: "I'm going for Joey's throat! We got to get a tap into Joey Tai's office. You can do it, Herbert!"

The young undercover cop works in the Tai kitchen.

The Asian businessmen meet with Tai. A new shipment is coming in: "We are very upset, very unhappy. . . . White has a wire in your office."

Joey looks over his staff. When Herbert tries to report, he's gunned down. He gasps out the arrival pier number to White.

At a rock club, to pounding music and flashing strobes, White seizes Tai, drags him to a men's room full of dopers, and punches his nose. When a pretty girl guard shoots at him, he chases her outside, exchanging shots, so she lies, legs spread, in the street. "You look like you're gonna die, beautiful."

At Tracy's apartment, teen assassins trap the journalist.

The businessmen meet with Tai: "We look back at older, more stable leadership." Joey tells them: "We've survived by not turning on each other. I will be there at Pier 11."

At the TV station, a shaken Tracy tells White: "I can't go there. . . . I was almost killed for you. I was raped. . . . You're selfish, callous, indifferent to suffering. Your wife was right! Now go away and leave me alone!"

At home, he's told he's been reassigned. "You care too much."

Tai and bodyguard reach the pier—to be rammed by White, who pulls a gun: "Just tell me—" A third car sideswipes him, so the two flee.

A train races past White, pushing the hulk of the escape car. On the track, Tai and White run toward each other through the night, firing.

White stands over the dying Tai: "Tell me where it is."

Tai does. White hands him his gun, and he kills himself. Cops rush in.

Funeral music, another Chinatown parade for the late Joey Tai. Tracy covers it. Abruptly Captain White appears, in splints and bandages, leaping forward to attack the older drug businessmen: "I'm arresting these people—"

Tracy, overwhelmed, supports the hopeless crusader.

"I'd like to be a nice guy, but I don't know how to be nice."

"You're really cracked, you know that?"

While he was only half of the writing team and was working with the director who had control of the film's final vision, Stone exerted strong thematic influence on *Year of the Dragon.* Unlike previous projects, the protagonist's behavior is shaped less by personal obsessions than a social purpose achieved in a social context. Nevertheless Stanley White ignores social appearances, public and personal, as contemptible "arrangements"; disregards the paternal figures of the city government and Chinatown alike; betrays his wife's love and his friend's support to follow his single mania to the point where it virtually destroys career, marriage, relationships, and lives including nearly his own. Stanley White must be acknowledged as yet another Oliver Stone protagonist.

In terms of conventional plausibility and dramatic organization there clearly are great flaws in *Year of the Dragon.* Most of them could have been avoided had the film used the novelist's motivation—that his hero had no other way to save his career and job but to attack the conjectured Chinese Mafia. Making him a mad crusader looking for a sort of domestic Vietnam makes sympathizing increasingly difficult.

The creative team use a number of devices to deal with the problem. White operates within the laws of decency, as far as we can tell. Though he shows prejudice, he's clearly in a love relationship with at least one Asian-American, and father figure to another. Toward the film's close, *Year of the Dragon* carefully contrasts White's hotheaded decency (his wife's death and funeral) with the psychopathic drug lords (their contempt for their ancestor-patron and the head severing). By then, however, the audience is burned out. Critics have compared the White character to the contemporaneous Rambo and Dirty Harry movie heroes, but those two carry a mood of lonely cynical individualistic virtue in a corrupt world, while White chooses to represent the distrusted establishment, a sort of cop Lyndon B. Johnson (or as several critics argue, a cop Cimino figure).

The critical response to *Year of the Dragon* was almost uniformly negative, the screenplay by Stone and Cimino often particularly condemned.

In the *New York Times*, Janet Maslin commented: "*Year of the Dragon* gives the impression that some other crowded, ornate film about New York's Chinatown has been tossed into the air and shattered, only to have its pieces rearranged in a completely illogical way. . . . [Mr. Rourke] is entirely lost in the underwritten role of a middle-aged policeman. He must also grapple with the flat-footed, heavily scatological dialogue. . . . *Year of the Dragon* is . . . lacking in feeling, reason, and narrative continuity."[24]

Andrew Sarris also finds fault. "*Dragon* is a thoroughly rotten movie, but much more so to the ear than to the eye. The screenplay . . . is dedicated to the proposition that the Chinese underworld is engaged in a worldwide conspiracy to take over the drug traffic. . . . Still, Cimino's attitude towards this explosive situation is never made clear. The narrative point of view keeps shifting back and forth between the criminals inside the organization and the very divided police on the outside. . . . Cimino is all climaxes, all orgasms, with no build up, no foreplay. . . . Detective White destroys everything and everyone in his path, much as director Cimino destroyed United Artists."[31]

Pauline Kael goes to some length analyzing the script. "Stone and Cimino don't bother their heads with distinctions among Asian peoples. To hear Stan White tell it, New York's Chinatown is the hub of international evil. . . . It's hysterical, rabble-rousing pulp, the kind that generally goes over with subliterate audiences—people who can be sucked into believing that the movie is giving them the low-down dirty truth about power. It doesn't have the crude populism of good pulp storytelling. . . . It's directed too listlessly to be enjoyable pap. . . . The movie is an extension of what goes wrong in *Scarface*. It's sunk in torpor. . . . Viewers are distracted from what they're looking at by one of the tawdriest and stupidest scripts that could ever have been put into production as a major film. . . . It's mixture of maladroitness, sleaze, and ignorance might have been devised by some little white schoolboys on a very hot day. The characters share a flat stunted vocabulary—about twenty-five words, most of them the basic four-letter expletives. And the plot devices have some of the canned, echo chamber effects that the later scenes in *Scarface* had. . . . In terms of any kind of controlled moral intelligence, Oliver Stone and Michael Cimino are still living in a cave. . . . (Two brazen vulgarians) and both xenophobic bring out the worst in each other. . . . Neither one knows when he has become a public embarrassment."[17]

Several years later, Stone commented on *Year of the Dragon*: "The Chinese want to believe that there are no gangsters among them. That's all horseshit! The Chinese are the greatest importers of heroin in this country. We knew this five years ago! As for the lead character, played by Mickey Rourke, he is a racist and we wrote him as a racist. . . . But I think people cheered him for other reasons, not for his racism. At least I hope not. But there might be an element of it. The guy, no matter how prejudiced, is still trying to get something done—as an underdog. That's why I'm rooting for him. But I should say that I think it was the least successful of my scripts."[26]

Stone's next project, *Eight Million Ways to Die*, began as another crime novel, one by Lawrence Block about an alcoholic ex-cop. Little of the original remains. It was moved to L.A., the mystery excised and updated to center on cocaine rather than prostitution. Reviewer Jay Carr argued that "what makes Scudder [the novel's detective] interesting is his vulnerability—you feel he can backslide any time. In switching locales, the film ceases to be a character study." Reportedly a number of writers besides the two credited worked on this project.

Overviews of Los Angeles from a cruising helicopter and exchanges between two cops set the mood, and in passing explain the film's title:

"There's eight million stories in this city."

"In this town we got eight million ways to die."

A posse of sheriff's deputies in canvas jackets armed with shotguns move through a cemetery, past big expensive tombstones. One cop, Matthew Scudder, pauses to drink from a liquor bottle in his cap. They surround a shack where a Latino family is at dinner. The husband-father, excited, pulls out a baseball bat and Scudder shoots him in the chest.

Scudder is questioned, and gets falling-down drunk with a pal from the bust. At his suburban home, he turns away from wife and daughter.

To a cloud of colored headlights, he rumbles: "I Detective Sergeant Matthew S. Scudder request a leave of absence for medical reasons."

At an Alcoholics Anonymous meeting, six months later, the ex-cop tells them drinking cost him his job, his home, and his wife. But "he'll always be Connie's daddy." Outside, he's given a note from a "Sunny," and cash.

Scudder takes a streetcar uphill to a glamorous cliffside Beverly Hills after-hours club. Inside, well-dressed "players" and their beautiful women are socializing, drinking, watching wall-sized TV images of a prizefight.

Scudder is embraced by beautiful stranger Sunny, a neurotic high-class hooker, and meets Sarah, equally lovely but cool, tawdry mad-dog cocaine dealer Angel in an iridescent yellow suit, and black pimp and entrepreneur Chance. Scudder once busted Chance, which set him on the road to owning "all this." Scudder identifies Angel to Chance as a drug criminal.

"He's never been busted."

"I didn't say unsuccessful."

"He's my customer. I'm not his."

Sunny and Scudder go to his apartment to discuss possible business.

"You're a cop, right. Now you go around fixing things."
"I'm real good at major felonies."
She'll pay him five thousand dollars. She takes some lines of coke, strips, and comes on to him.
"You're not just a whore, you're a dumb whore—you're showing I'm predictable, not reliable—getting fucked is getting fucked."
Hysterical, she explains she wants him to tell Chance she's quitting. "You can tell him we're gonna get married."
At Chance's estate he delivers the message. Chance explains he's not her pimp. He sets the girls up, pays for their apartments, takes his payoff.
"I hate money," Scudder responds. "If it's new it cuts your fingers. If it's old it stinks."
Sarah looks him over distrustfully. She doesn't like cops. The outcome: Sunny is free to go.
At his humble place, Scudder finds Sunny stoned and toying with his gun. "It's an act, he's gonna hurt me!" the coked-up beauty cries. "Please stay with me until I go to the airport."
With Sunny in his car, Scudder shops for a birthday gift for his kid. He finds the car empty, a tire slashed, a van rushing off. Inside it, Sunny screams and struggles. Scudder gives chase, torn tire flapping. The van stops at a bridge, rushes on. Scudder stops, sees Sunny's blood-soaked body on the rocks.
Hospital walls, a derelict's face, rows of beds. An unshaven Scudder staggers to the nurse's station. He's been there two days.
At headquarters, his bust pal has been put on Sunny's murder; thanks to Scudder the division looks very bad.
At home, his wife won't let him speak to his kid. In her suitcase he finds Sunny's address book, with a list of names with two-digit numbers beside them, a contact phone number, a diamond necklace matching one worn by Angel. There's also a plastic bag of hundred-dollar bills.
Scudder visits a supermarket, going backstage where piles of Colombian bath sponges are being stored. The black businessman Chance finds him there, the two confront each other in his car. Sunny told Scudder she was scared of Chance. The two angrily shove each other, back to back. "Are we gonna continue with this adversarial relationship?" Who was close to Sunny? Sarah can tell him about her.

14. *Eight Million Ways to Die*. Rosanna Arquette as Sarah, Jeff Bridges as Scudder: "For a half-assed hooker, you're an extremely arrogant woman." (*Copyright 1986 Tri-Star Pictures, Inc. Courtesy Museum of Modern Art Film Stills Archive.*)

15. *Eight Million Ways to Die*. Jeff Bridges as Matt Scudder, Alexandra Paul as Sunny: "The street lamp makes my pussy hair glow in the dark." (*Copyright Tri-Star Pictures, Inc. The Museum of Modern Art Film Stills Archive.*)

At the club, Sarah's just finished with a blubbery client. "Thanks, Sarah!" "'Bye, teach!"

Sunny, Sarah tells him, was a natural born victim. It won't happen to her, because she doesn't have the ex-cop protecting her. She won't talk to him. Angel appears, Scudder grabs Sarah, carries her off struggling in the tramcar. He tells her Angel wears the same jewelry Sunny had in her address book. Anyway, Sarah tells him, Scudder enjoyed manhandling her.

"For a half-assed hooker, you're an extremely arrogant woman."

Angel Maldenado's been trying to get Chance into his business. Somehow it revolves around Chance's legit work.

They're drinking heavily. Sarah senses Scudder's grief. "I'm gonna fuck you so good!" But she's sick, then passes out.

Next morning Scudder makes a date with Angel. Scudder talks about his daughter. Sarah's father is dead, she came to L.A. and got into The Life.

"It's hard to reach out for help."

Sarah cries, then: "Fuck! I'm not a crybaby!"

The pair meet Angel and his hoods at the L.A. Coliseum. The ex-cop and dealer swirl around each other in a vicious, macho line exchange:

"Sara's my fuck for today. . . . I know you killed Sunny. . . . I've got $250,000. I want equal weight in the white stuff."

"Is that a movie about astronauts? . . . We're putting together this snow cone franchise. Go to Chance to borrow 250,000. I need 500,000, so call me."

Sarah goes with Angel.

Scudder sees a jogging Chance. "Angel killed Sunny. I've got to get $250,000." Chance's bodyguard runs off, Scudder pulls his gun: "You're big, but you can still bleed."

The black businessman lets Scudder off at the drug dealer's home, a priceless whipped-cream confection of a Gaudi house.

"What're you gonna do, Scooter? How do you like my pad? Gaudi said, 'Without beauty there could be no truth.' Gaudi had no predecessors and no successors. It's the best."

Sarah: "He wants to fuck me and kill you."

They can't deal, and as for Sunny, Angel tells Scudder, "Sometimes it pays to advertise. Make it messy. . . . I love Sarah as much as you. And I loved Sunny as much. So she's in your hands, don't make a fucking mistake."

Scudder meets Chance. Sunny, they realize, worked for Angel. That was why she lied. "It was easier to hire someone to protect her from a pimp than from dealers."

"Chance wasn't in business with Angel—but Angel was in business with Chance!" The unsold bath sponges, "made in Colombia," of course. Breaking them open, the two find keys of cocaine. Chance's employees are held, while the ex-cop and businessman load the dope into his BMW.

In his home, Angel puts the moves on a coked-up Sara, telling the hooker beauty: "Everything you need, everything you ever wanted. . . ."

Scudder calls. If you want your dope back, meet him on the San Pedro docks. "I'll forget my coke, if you go away with me." But she won't.

Scudder's drug-bust squad is poised nearby. A big empty warehouse has narcs hidden in the roof supports, the sponges piled high on the floor. Angel comes in at one end, a woozy blindfolded Sara has her throat taped to a shotgun muzzle carried by a gunman.

"You're blowing it, Angel!" Scudder cries from beside the coke. "Cut her loose or we're gonna burn your shit!" He has lighter fluid, smoke grenades.

The two swap snarled obscenities, then Scudder starts burning the coke. "Put the fire out!" "Cut her loose!" Flames climb, Chance appears and starts shooting. In the smoky room Chance is shot, so are cops and crooks, but Angel escapes.

Scudder and Sara return to Sara's expensive address, take the streetcar, and Scudder shoots it out with a waiting gunman and then Angel, the dead drug dealer sprawled on the tramway tracks.

There's an AA meeting on the beach. "I failed the first time. This time I may do it," Scudder's voice-over tells us. We see him and Sara walking along the surf line in long shot: "I'm in love. What can I say? It's a great feeling."

Like other Stone protagonists, but this time through guilt and alcohol, the Scudder character dissolves conventional links to career, family, and relationships, as well as society—AA in the film is a brotherhood of isolates who make speeches to each other. For most of the film Scudder associates only with prostitutes and others who all distrust him as a former cop. In fact he lacks the conventional movie detective's professionalism as compensation. He is unable to forge emotional relationships or think his way out of his problems without killing off his friends; except for the added-on happy ending he's actually gone downhill, for all that he's solved the crime through risking his life.

Looked at as a drama or a realistic depiction of its milieu the film has great weaknesses. For example, everything the drug dealer does from running his dealing out of another business's unguarded supermarket to offering to throw it all away for a woman seems highly unlikely. The final shoot-out feels like something cobbled together after other scenes failed to come off. The actors survive on what star power they can muster, rather than their improbable characterizations.

Reviewers' responses to *Eight Million Ways to Die* were very mixed. Though Stone was only a cowriter, his contribution was often pointed out, usually for the worst.

New York Times reviewer Walter Goodman states: "There is no detection in this detective story, and no story. Between Scudder's unconvincing meeting with the prostitute and the unbelievable final shootout, the movie . . . marks time. The time is taken up with filler material, credited to Oliver Stone and David Lee Henry. It is full of unmeaningful pauses, undeleted expletives, and unbearable exchanges: 'From your daughter?' 'Yes.' 'She's cute.' 'She's my best friend.' 'She looks like you.' Several of the scenes seem to be improvisations by actors with no knack for the work. 'You really liked Sunny, didn't you?' 'Yes I did.' 'So did I. What did you like about her most?' 'What do you like about anybody?'"[14]

Steve Vineberg likewise gives up. "The whole movie has the same glassy eyed, halting rhythm; it reels and stumbles and zones out as the nonsensical scenes collide with one another like so many billiard balls. . . . It's fun to pick up on the different voices in the screenplay since no attempt was made to integrate them. One of the writers must be an alcoholic, because Scudder gives not one but two solemn speeches at AA meetings. . . . One writer has a taste for florid action: the howler that broke up the audience at my preview was 'The street lamp makes my pussy hair glow in the dark,' which Alexandra Paul speaks in a tone of almost religious wonder. One of them must have had a puritan streak: Scudder becomes involved with two hookers, both of whom crawl all over him, but he never gets laid—the closest he comes to erotic contact is a scene where Rosanna Arquette vomits on his crotch. The litany of 'fucks' I take to be Oliver Stone's special contribution. He manages to beat his *Scarface* record in less than two thirds the running time."[32]

Pauline Kael takes the film and Stone's contribution on their own terms. "It's permeated with druggy dissociation and you can't always distinguish between what's intentional and what's unintentional. Plot points don't connect, as though they don't matter. . . . As far as the narrative is concerned, [the] macho shouting matches might be intermissions. . . . The script, credited to Oliver Stone and David Lee Henry . . . is crude stuff, but it suggests more narrative drive than Ashby delivers. . . . The story isn't filled in, and the spaces in the narrative contribute to the coked out feeling. . . . *Eight Million Ways to Die* is like a continuation of other drug traffic movies that Oliver Stone has written. . . . It's pulpier, and tawdrier than you might expect from Ashby, but it's also woozy, and it luxuriates in the glamour of being physically and emotionally spent, as if droopiness were sexy."[19]

Only David Denby argued that it was a good movie. "*Eight Million Ways to Die* has the seriousness of the old thrillers which no matter how farfetched were always obsessed with the honor of the lonely incorruptible man. . . . The whole movie explodes in a prolonged final confrontation."[11]

Dino De Laurentis had promised that if Stone could write *The Year of the Dragon*, he would produce Stone's *Platoon* script. But when he couldn't find a U.S. distributor, he backed out.

Stone had spent four or five years writing other people's movies, and had learned from it. But now nothing was coming to Stone from the studios. Richard Boyle, a friend, gave him some notes on the way to the airport. "Here, you may like this." The notes were sketches of his trips to El Salvador.

Stone's mind clicked. "This is it. I am going to make *Salvador*."

3

Salvador

STONE HAS CITED the influence of Latin American literature and film, especially the movies of Glauder Rocha of the sixties, and the novels of Gabriel García Márquez: "In *Salvador* I tried to give a flavor of Marquez where you combine comedy, tragedy, sexual excess and madness—what I love about Spanish cultural tradition."[19]

The specific origins of *Salvador* are in the late 1970s, when Stone became friends with the real Richard Boyle. Stone said of him: "[Boyle] was always broke, always needing to be bailed out of jail, always on drunken driving charges. He was a womanizer and a drinker, yet he would always be popping off to these small places, like Ireland or Lebanon, and doing these stories." In fact Boyle had covered Vietnam and Cambodia, and written a book, *Flowers of the Dragon*.[11]

After 1978, Boyle made several trips to El Salvador, becoming involved with a local woman, reporting on the civil war involving the U.S.-backed government, right-wing death squads, and left-wing guerrillas. It led to thousands of Salvadoran deaths, the assassination of Archbishop Romero, and the rape murder of two nuns and a U.S. Catholic lay worker. In December 1984, Boyle gave Stone the unpublished material that became the core of the film.

But it was Stone's interest in Boyle that led to the basic story for *Salvador*. "I was interested in the character of Boyle as this sort of renegade journalist, a selfish rascal, who through his exposure to the country becomes more unselfish, and who, through his love for the woman, starts to become something he wasn't in the beginning. It's a transformation, a liberation, call it what you want. . . . [In following that intention] I got very involved in the background story of El Salvador. . . . I was really quite shocked to see how black and white it was. . . . We tried to blend the two together. Obviously, you know where the film came down—it opposes the U.S. policy of taking sides with the military in El Salvador.[7]

Stone pretty much adhered to Boyle's point of view in the screenplay but also did his own extensive research. He found Boyle's ideas confirmed and documented in Raymond Bonner's book *Weakness and Deceit*.[2] Stone also read eyewitness accounts of such events as the "bullet passing" scene. His scenes of the FMLN rebels executing prisoners was based on Boyle's memory, an aberration left in by the producers, perhaps to balance the film's politics. The attack on horseback by the rebels, however, was made up, symbolic of the government's superior weaponry.

Stone tried to talk with U.S. Ambassador Robert White about the first treatment, which the two wrote over a few weeks. But White would not talk with him, claimed not to remember Boyle, and didn't respond to the version of the script Stone sent him. The director commented: "His attitude seemed to be that it just didn't have the gravity of a State Department document. . . . Our script had that ambiguity in White's character because it raised the question at what point he reinstated military aid. . . . The character of the ambassador is played by a sort of liberal muddlehead like Michael Murphy."

Nevertheless the film script largely uses real people and real historical events. Major Max is a renamed Robert D'Aubisson, and the photojournalist John Cassady is based on real photographer John Hoagland. The events that happened over a two-year period, however, seem to occur in only a few months.

At first, Stone and Boyle tried to shoot the film in El Salvador. They actually met with advisors of D'Avisson, the right-wing leader who reportedly led the death squads. "They liked Oliver because they loved *Scarface*," Boyle said.[1]

"They wanted us to do the movie," said Stone. "I think we sold them a bill of goods. We didn't give them the full script. We gave them a version of the script which we sort of doctored, making it very neutral, almost pro government; the guerrillas were the bad guys. We planned to shoot about three quarters of it there and the rest outside the country."[16] The approach would even reportedly allow them to use Salvadoran armed forces and equipment, as if Steven Spielberg had used a dummy script to get Hitler and the Nazis to bankroll *Schindler's List!*

Stone paid for his visits, as well as for scouting trips to other areas. The projected film was a very low-budget, almost cinema-verité drama with Boyle and Doc Rock portraying themselves. The plan went askew in March 1985 when Ricardo Cienfuegos, Stone's military liaison, was executed by the rebels. Government support died.

Stone feels *Salvador*'s script was just too anti-American for the U.S. money people. Mostly, studios would "pass," meaning they didn't say why. Admittedly, the track record for similar films was poor—*Missing* did no business in the U.S., and *Under Fire* was a near disaster. Stone felt he sold his project to the English (Hemdale) because they saw it as ironic, and his two main characters almost in funny Monty Pythonesque terms—"Laurel and Hardy Go to Salvador." Now he had a larger budget and real actors. To help financing, Stone agreed to invest his own money and direct without salary, not expecting any money; "But it was worth every single moment of it!"

According to an expert, *Salvador*'s logistics—the numbers of locations, schedule, number of actors—made it a very hard film to do. There are ninety-three speaking roles, one thousand extras, horses, tanks, helicopters, aircraft—all in a film with a seven-week shooting schedule.

The crucial battle of Santa Ana sequence was originally to be shot in Acapulco at a collapsed bridge, which was being rebuilt when the filmmakers arrived. Eventually, it was done in Tlayacapan, a tiny hamlet, with a five-hundred-year-old church and cobblestoned streets, to which second stories, new house fronts, and other set dressing were added. Shooting took over a week, utilizing its Mexican army soldiers with their tanks, trucks, and other hardware. One hundred and fifty villagers played the rebels and civilians. Filming had a reportedly surreal quality: battle scenes of tanks, bombing planes, soldiers, and burning cars were ringed by an audience of the local population.

Stone described the scene. "We took over this entire town for a week to shoot the battle of Santa Ana, and we blew it to pieces! The mayor was great. He loved movies and he said 'Go ahead, blow up the whole fucking city hall!' We even redesigned his office and used it as a whorehouse set (with real prostitutes). He liked the decor so much he kept it that way, red walls and all."[1]

The film was brought in at under five million dollars, and as shot was two hours, forty minutes—impossible to distribute. Stone commented: "The original concept was that it would go from light

16. *Salvador.* James Woods as Richard Boyle, John Savage as John Cassady: "You gotta get close to get the truth. You get too close, you die." *(Courtesy Museum of Modern Art Film Stills Archive.)*

17. *Salvador.* James Woods as Richard Boyle, Jim Belushi as Dr. Rock, Elepedia Carrillo as Maria. Major Max: "There are no death squads in Salvador!" *(Courtesy Museum of Modern Art Film Stills Archive.)*

to dark a lot . . . that Latin sort of blending that you find in a García Marquez novel—jumping from high seriousness to absurdity." Specific cuts included Doc Rock getting sex under a table, and Boyle's trying to speak with a drunken colonel as he has sex and tosses human ears at a champagne glass: "Left-wing ears, right-wing ears, who gives a fuck? Here's to Salvador!" Test audiences had no clear response to this, although Stone felt Latino audiences would have. Also in the script but missing from the film are scenes showing U.S. ad execs shaping the Major Max campaign ("That Hitler stuff won't fly in the states. . . . We sold Nixon. We had the Shah and Somoza.") and the U.S. nuns raped to right-wing political campaign songs.(!)[17]

James Woods said of the Boyle role, "I found it interesting that this man, with all his shortcomings and vices, would be interested in finding the truth. He goes back to El Salvador, even though he's on Major Max's death list, and this is just to make some money. But then he gets swept up in it on a personal level and becomes truly interested in finding the truth. . . . He is by his own admission a sort of charming guy with a whole lot of self-centered indulgences. But at the same time he has taken the risks to avail his presence at these very dangerous places."[16]

Woods also commented that working with Stone was like "being caught in a Cuisinart with a madman. And he felt the same with me. It was two Tasmanian devils wrestling under a blanket. But he's a sharp director. He starts with a great idea, delegates authority well, scraps like a street fighter, then takes the best that comes out of the fracas."[6]

James Belushi saw Doc Rock as "ignorant of Central American issues, of which I think most of the American general public is likewise, so I feel like a touchstone for the audience."

John Savage viewed his Cassady photojournalist as more of an "ethereal spirit who loved people from the artist's point of view of an outsider."

Stone's father died in 1985, just as he was about to make *Salvador*.

In a seedy San Francisco tenement, weary yet defiantly feisty fortyish photojournalist Richard Boyle wakes to a TV newscast reporting "chaos has descended on tiny El Salvador. . . . In two months more than a thousand people have disappeared. . ." Presidential election polls show Ronald Reagan leading. Boyle's landlord tells him: "No bucks, no Buck Rogers, Boyle. You and this Italian bitch are out. Today!"

Boyle scrounges for work, but his rep is poor. Driving, a cop stops him: he has no license and forty-three unpaid parking tickets. He's bailed out by unemployed DJ Doc Rock. The two commiserate: "I can't deal with yuppie women. Fuckin' Walkmans, running shoes, they'd rather go to aerobic jazz class than fuck." "They got these pussy exercises." "Latin women are better. They don't speak English."

Boyle's wife has gone back home, so the two pals head south. Boyle: "You'll love it here, Doc, you can drive drunk, you can get anybody killed for fifty bucks. Best pussy in the world. Where else can you get a virgin to sit on your face for seven bucks? Two virgins for twelve bucks."

But entering El Salvador, they're held at a roadblock by vigilantes, spread against Boyle's MG, guns pointed at them. They're "saved" by Smiling Death, a slender, oddly grinning National Guard officer, who will take them to Boyle's pal Colonel Figueroa.

At a square, a dozen locals lie in the dirt, unable to show their *cédulas*—ID papers. A young student type is questioned, knocked to his knees, prays. The pals are shoved into an armored car, see Smiling Death pull his pistol and casually kill the student. Doc Rock becomes hysterical.

They're taken to Figueroa, a handsome if drunk officer with three seminaked whores running around his office: "My amigo here . . . wrote me up in the U.S. newspapers—The Patton of El Salvador." They party, speaking of Major Max's forces, the rebels, the weak government junta.

Next Boyle meets his lover, the beautiful young Maria, at an idyllic beach shack, where he moves in with her, her two children, grandma, and fifteen-year-old brother.

In San Salvador, full of orphans, beggars, drunks, the two men meet John Cassady, a youthful working photojournalist. Doc, frightened, wants to go home, but there's no money.

Boyle and Cassady visit El Playon, the city dump, dozens of fresh tortured naked bodies strewn on the rubbish heaps. The two begin photographing the corpses. Cassady speaks of his idol, Capa: "You gotta get close to get the truth. You get too close, you die."

In front of the church, various groups meet—refugees, students, news teams, aid workers, people seeking their "disappeared," leafing through photo albums of the tortured dead. Boyle gives them his pictures, greets Cathy Moor, a pretty young woman helping nuns working with crippled orphans.

In the U.S. Embassy, Americans feed off a massive buffet as the election returns come in. There are many military present, and Ambassador Kelley who says it's his duty to support the president's policy. Boyle: "Can you believe some guy who was a straight man to a chimpanzee is gonna be president. Doesn't it depress you?" Boyle meets Jack Morgan, a youthful blond Yalie strategist, and tough Colonel Hyde, who tells him: "You know, I never understood why you guys like commies so much. If you were a Vietnamese, you'd be working in a reeducational camp pulling up turnips." Moran says the rebels are Cuban-backed, in five years Cuban tanks will be on the Rio Grande.

Boyle tries to hustle work from the journalists, including a "glamour reporter," arrogant Pauline Alexander, who'll do a net stand-up, an ordered rah-rah democracy speech, not mentioning all the killings. Doc Rock drugs her drink, as Boyle declaims: "You don't have one of these *cédulas* stamped Election Day, you're dead—'course they get their stories published, cause they kiss the right asses in New York." On the rooftop, the woman, mike in hand, collapses into an LSD giggling fit.

In ARENA party headquarters, a dozen men, some military, speak with Major Max, a tough undersized Latino: "Who will rid me of Roméro?" he asks, referring to the archbishop who has been "poisoning the minds of Salvadoran youth." All twelve jump up.

That night, Doc Rock, Carlos, and Boyle anger some local toughs, mocking Major Max's TV appearance. In the street, the toughs occupy Boyle's MG, looking lethal. Boyle provides beers, apologizes, manages to get them all away.

But later, the thugs put Rock and Carlos in the local jail. Hurrying in with Cathy Moore, Boyle bribes Doc out with liquor and a TV set, but can't free young Carlos.

Boyle and Moore meet with Ambassador Kelley, who says there's no record of the arrest. He sums it up: "I know, pathological killers on the right and who knows what on the left and a gutless middle." Boyle pleads for a *cédula* for Maria—Carlos's arrest means she's likely to be taken too. He tells Maria he'll marry her, it's the only protection.

Boyle confesses in church, wheedling, boyish but on the level: "If God gave me this woman, then there must be a God."

In the cathedral, ringed by threatening soldiers, Archbishop Romero pleads for an end to repression: "We are poor. You in Washington are so rich. Why are you so blind?"

Boyle and Maria take communion, but moments later the assassin shoots Romero, blood on his white raiments.

The next day, Major Max announces his campaign for president. Boyle at the press conference asks about the candidate's involvement with the death squads: "There are no death squads in Salvador," says Major Max.

At Maria's shack, Boyle is told that Carlos has been found. At the city hall, his body is laid out. Maria blames Boyle, rejecting his pleas.

In a bar, the drunken photojournalist meets Cathy Moore. It's Christmas, and she affectionately gives him an Irish whiskey gift, then leaves to pick up some nuns flying in from Nicaragua.

Outside, Boyle is surrounded by Smiling Death and his toughs. He pulls a switchblade, but is beaten up. Cassady and Rock manage to keep the toughs from killing him, Cassady photographing Smiling Death.

Driving back at night, Cathy Moore and her nuns are forced off the road by a truckful of thugs, who pull them out. "I am a good friend of the American ambassador. . . . You are going to be in a lot of trouble." But the men rape and then kill them.

In the brush, the bodies are exhumed. A shaken Boyle and Ambassador Kelley look on, the bodies rigid and decayed, journalists taking pictures. The frightened doctors won't do an autopsy. They don't have surgical masks, they claim. Kelley: "Fuck it, I give up! I'm going to recommend to Washington we cut off all aid—military and economic, as of now."

Boyle and Cassady visit the guerrilla mountain camp. The fighters are proud, defiant people of all ages, dressed like cowboys, native music playing softly.

At the embassy, Boyle tries to trade unrevealing photos and intelligence of the rebels for a *cédula* for Maria. But it's not much, and Hyde and Morgan don't trust him. Boyle mocks their lies: about Soviet subversion, Red advisors, aid money going for weapons. Boyle wants "a constitution for human rights for the whole world, and not just for a few people on the planet." Hyde tells him he hates the species he belongs to, and he'd better get out. Boyle tells the U.S. military advisor he fits right in, just another gangster.

The rebel offensive starts, and Cassady wants Boyle to cover it with him. Boyle stops at Maria's shack, the two embrace.

The MG races toward a roadblock, as cars and refugees flee past. There's artillery and small-arms fire. The two move up on foot to the central square. Ahead, National Guardsmen are trapped, firing back.

Waving a white flag, they dash ahead. The rebels attack, the photojournalists' cameras busy. Suddenly, the rebels make a cavalry charge, Cassady exposing himself to get pictures, the guardsmen cowering. Boyle finally pulls Cassady to safety: "You're not that lucky!"

Elsewhere, Smiling Death is directing troops from a command post. The rebels break in, leveling their weapons, killing him.

At the embassy briefing room, crowded with maps and computers, a tense ambassador is told the country has been cut in half, the situation deteriorating. Military aid must be restored:

"Listen, Ambassador, we all know you're going to be out in a few days, that's not the issue here, the issue is—do you want to go down in the history books as the man who lost El Salvador?"

The government troops are pinned down, the rebels hold the town's police headquarters. A runner shows up: the government is advancing!

Desperate, the rebels start executing their helpless prisoners.

"You've become just like them!" Boyle cries.

Figueroa and his government troops, resupplied, advance. The rebels try to rally. But helicopters appear, machine guns chewing up the rebels.

In the town's streets, civilians flee, die. Boyle and Cassady keep photographing the furious battle.

A U.S.-made fighter appears in the distance, coming in.

Cassady resets his telephoto, Boyle's camera jams. Cassady is in the street, lining up his shot. The strafing plane hits him, and Boyle is also shot. Bloody, Boyle performs a tracheotomy, but it's not enough. Cassady gives him his film and dies, smiling. Infantry swarm through, finishing off the rebels.

As Boyle recovers, Doc Rock provides false documents—he's found a girl and is staying. But at the border customs shed, Boyle's papers are found phony. He's pistol-whipped, the films are exposed.

Desperately, Rock tries to reach the ambassador, as Boyle is dragged off by the slovenly border guards to be shot. Luckily the rifle misfires, and a minute later Kelley's call leads to Boyle's release. The real films were hidden in a hollow boot heel. Boyle gets Maria and her kids across the border, posing as a family: "Oh, just took the wife and kids to Nogales for the afternoon."

But their bus north is overhauled by INS men. The border guards, wearing dark sunglasses, walkie talkies, and with guns on hips, discover Maria has no papers, pull her and the kids off the bus.

Boyle goes crazy, yelling: "If you send her back, they'll kill her! You don't know what it's like in El Salvador!" He attacks the cops and is himself arrested.

Maria and her kids are put into a car, and taken south.

A final title says Boyle continues to search for Maria in refugee camps. Cassady's pictures were published, Doc Rock returned to the U.S.

In his first film in years with relatively full artistic control, Stone once again creates a protagonist cut off from but fully aware of the world around him, but it's an amazing new version—a tormented but also comic rascal energetically surviving in a madcap version of the familiar Stone crazed amoral universe. From the very outset, Boyle is shown hilariously stripped of family, work, love, and social support, but instead of turning in on himself, seizes the opportunity to plunge ahead into a sort of comic chaos, the capricious nightmare of a Latin American revolution. Still, as Pauline Kael points out, Boyle's little different than Stone's other caring if doomed chaotics: "It wouldn't seem out of place if he spoke Mickey Rourke's line in *Year of the Dragon* 'How can anybody care too much?' He might even deliver Al Pacino's line from *Scarface:* 'Say goodnight to the Bad Guy.'"[13]

Yet critics are wrong to attack the Boyle character as himself sinister. He's irresponsible and a con man largely because he's helpless, and more often innocent and moral, a politicized Huckleberry Finn on a Mississippi where the Aunt Pollies are ineffectual and the Dukes and Dauphins carry Uzis and are eager to use them.

Despite critical complaints, as political and social analysis *Salvador* is extremely weak. The key fact about Latin American policy, as Noam Chomsky notes, is that the wealthy classes and foreign investors get rich because the government, with U.S. support, de-

clares war on those working for the peoples' interests—labor orga-
nizers, students, priests, peons.[5] With this left out or obscured—
we see no multinational sweatshops, rich landowners and peons,
etc.—society is reduced to victims and clowns—macho right-wing
killer clowns, apologetic policy-following State Department clowns,
careerist journalist clowns, and vaguely idealistic but potentially
rotten rebel clowns. Why do they act that way? Don't ask! An unwillingness to show economic relationships seems to be the flip side of
Stone's romantic individualism, and a persistent problem.

Critical responses to *Salvador* were, as one might expect, cool.
Walter Goodman in the *New York Times* appreciated but in the
end was skeptical of Stone's film: "The movie's Richard Boyle is a
freeloading boozer with a scrambled life but intact conscience, who
manages to be wherever the action is from military headquarters to
right-wing hangouts to guerrilla camps to the U.S. embassy. . . .
James Woods puts nervous energy and self-mocking wit into the
part, and it is not his fault if the qualities of scrounger, scoop seeker,
friend of the common man and sharp political analyst don't quite
stick together. . . . But Stone has more than action on his mind.
Taking his cinematic as well as historical leap from the work of Costa-
Gavras, he offers an interpretation of history, laying blame on the
conservative forces in the U.S. for abetting the horrors in El Salvador. . . . The realistic settings are put to the service of improbable
people doing implausible things. . . . For a movie with pretensions
to laying out political realities, the colorful *Salvador* is black and
white. . . . There is no acknowledgment here of any political position between the murderers on the right and the Marxist-led young
agrarian reformers on horseback. Too much reality might have gotten in the way of the show and the message."[10]

David Denby was more sympathetic: "The movie is in some ways
a piece of exploitation, its politics can't be taken seriously, [but] what
an impassioned, enraging, corrupt but all in all exciting piece of
filmmaking it is. . . . With his long boney face and strangely dead
eyes, James Woods can be hateful and almost spooky, but he's maniacally alive here as this rasping, insanely bitter egotist, a man always
sinning and always guilty. Trying to get ahead of the next curve,
Boyle is a jittery hipster version of a Graham Greene sinner . . .
you know him as you do few contemporary movie characters. Like
a hundred other movie heroes, Boyle is an instinctively antiauthoritarian and a defeated idealist. . . . As Boyle goes deeper and

deeper into Stone's film, *Salvador* begins to make a kind of sense. . . . There's a wide streak of nihilism in Oliver Stone's work that often seems indistinguishable from stupidity. . . . In everything he does Stone pushes things to the limit. He puts mounds of corpses on the screen and children with missing limbs, and he provides so little information and political context that the atrocities feel like high-minded exploitation, a way of showing off how bloody tough he is. Yet he has talent and has made a disturbing movie. Americans, of whatever conviction, can't simply shrug off the tough years in El Salvador as a bad scene. We're involved all the way, it's our bad scene. And the crumbum Richard Boyle, however infuriating, is our representative too."[8]

Pauline Kael also gave Stone qualified approval. "Oliver Stone expresses his pulp sensibility in *Salvador*. . . . He's probably aiming for a Buñuelian effect—a vision so intensely scummy that it clears the air. But if *Salvador*, with its grime and guilt, comes closer to suggesting a hyperkinetic, gonzo version of Graham Greene, that's still nothing to be ashamed of. . . . The Oliver Stone who made this movie isn't essentially different from the hype artist (of past films). . . . *Salvador*, too, is a self-righteous nihilist fantasy, and even more sensationalistic than the others. . . . He uses James Woods, perhaps the most hostile of all American actors as the hero, who is Richard Boyle, but represents Stone's convictions too.

Kael argues the film is biographical, not political. "The movie is almost all Boyle, hurtling from one emergency to another. It's not just that he stands in for both authors. He's really the only character. The movie is the story of his redemption. Salvador means savior, and Woods's Boyle is the one who needs to be saved. . . . The film's most memorable scene is of Boyle, after a gap of thirty-three years—Christ's life span—going to confession. . . [Woods] plays this scene very boyishly! Boyle tries to strike a deal with his confessor, wheedling, and trying to settle for a minimum of promises, because he genuinely doesn't want to break them. . . . 'If God gave me this woman,' he says to his confessor, 'then there must be a god.'"

Kael sums up: "*Salvador* has the tainted, disreputable, hardboiled surface we expect from Oliver Stone, and the sentimentality that goes with it. . . . The movie is as screwed up as its hero. As a revelation of a gifted filmmaker's divided sensibility, there's never been anything quite as spectacular as *Salvador*. . . . What he has here is a right-wing macho vision joined to a left-leaning polemic. . . . Oliver Stone's gaudiness drives the film forward. He writes and directs as if someone had put a gun to the back of his head and yelled: "Go!" and didn't take it away until he'd finished."[13]

Variety's review by Cart was its usual coolly professional box-office prognostication. "The b.o. road will not be easy. Contemporary political pictures in general, and those on Central America in particular, such as *Under Fire* and *Latino*, have not appealed to the public. There's plenty here to provoke discussion, enough to spark sufficient controversy to give the film a foot in the door of the specialized and art market. Designed to expose as many outrages, injustices, and human tragedies as possible . . . Stone seems anxious to straddle the political fence . . . to conclude by saying that Central America is such a chaotic mess that no coherent attitude is possible until a return to some basic human values is effected. Indeed, nothing in Stone's previous filmography would lead us to believe that he stands in the forefront of Hollywood's left liberal humanists. . . . The film's major problem as a story is such that its course seems determined by historical events, rather than the imperatives of good dramatic structure. . . . Despite the dramatic problems, Stone has gotten a great deal of visual and political material up on the screen, and it's all worth grappling with."[4]

Other critics also pondered *Salvador*, sometimes producing surprising insights. Lisa Jensen pointed out: "What is undeniably, unforgivably true . . . is the chaotic state of civil war to this very day, and the chilling American military presence that is only provoking more bloodshed. . . . What this means is a reign of terror where sudden death or disappearance—lurks around every corner. Those not caught in the crossfire may be shot for failing to produce their papers. . . . Stone succeeds . . . with his ambitious look at the effect of the war on every level of society, from the elite guests at the American embassy sipping cocktails and applauding the 1980 presidential election of Ronald Reagan to the corpses heaped up at the 'dump site' for death squad victims at the edge of town. . . . What exacerbates the situation is the American military, and this is where *Salvador* makes its strongest point. In the film's most disturbing image, a gun battle on horseback between rebels and government troops is suddenly invaded by U.S. armored tanks, helicopters, and a strafing plane; it's suddenly clear that whatever side such weapons are used on very little human life is likely to survive in their wake."[12]

Owen Gleiberman praises Stone's distinctive visual style in its emphasis on the handheld camera. "*Salvador* has a unique feverish look to it. The action is choreographed so that the camera becomes both our nervous, wavering stand-in and a kind of low-down omniscient observer, darting in and out of rooms and whipping back and forth to follow the motions of the jive-slinging characters."[9]

David Kehr was interested in *Salvador*'s antecedents: "The dispassionate journalist who's slow and objective pursuit of the facts leads him to finally embrace the political position espoused at the outset by the filmmakers has long been a staple of propaganda movies (*The Green Berets, Under Fire*). He makes life so much easier for the screenwriter. [The danger is] the film becomes a tiresome run through a rat's maze. . . . In *Salvador*, Boyle is a screaming baroque composition, assembled of equal parts Robert Capa, Hunter Thompson, and Bugs Bunny [with] antiauthoritarian heroes played by Eddie Murphy, Bill Murray and Tom Hanks. . . put in a realistic context. . . . Stone can't be accused of feeling superior to his characters, though it's less because he genuinely respects them than because, most of the time, he's just as confused about what's going on as they are. "Stone directs like a writer, with no sense of space to speak of and a very shaky understanding of how to shape the rhythm of a sequence. Though his scenes are strongly conceived, they're often executed with a jittery uncertainty that diminishes their impact. . . . Ultimately, the film's focus shifts from the ideological to the emotional, and Stone's epic vision of a country in torment collapses around the isolated figure of Boyle, helpless and seething with impotent rage. This too is a classic maneuver of liberal filmmaking—to substitute the romantic angst of the sensitive individual for the historical crisis of an entire people. . . . *Salvador* concludes with that old, strangely comforting fantasy of hopelessness."[14]

Indeed, the harshest criticism of *Salvador* has come from activists. Writing several years later, Robert Stone may be the most smilingly contemptuous. "There was . . . a lot in *Salvador* that marked Oliver Stone as a professional, in the Hollywood sense of the word . . . art is not what the moguls of Hollywood now propose to sell the Japanese, and it was apparent . . . Oliver Stone would not be a problem. The only thing really novel about *Salvador* was its timeliness. It's mildly druggy, anti-establishment buddy team—Woods and James Belushi—provided yuppie audiences the shock of recognizing the likes of Hunter Thompson. Scenes in which the hippies get to tell off flaky 'establishment' journalists and too handsome U.S. military industrial zombies took everyone back to the glory days of the sixties. *Salvador* is safely located in the traditional left liberal ethos of Hollywood. In spite of his headlong pace and verismo, the fundamental things apply and three little people don't amount to a hill of beans in this crazy world. . . . It's a true descendent of *Casablanca*, and even more of *Arise My Love*, whose lovely phony international sophistication makes it as much an artifact of its time as *Salvador* is of the eighties. It too had bohemian, antifascist journalists abroad, trading wisecracks in the face of danger, living for the moment. . . . It's completely accepting of every traditional movie method of keeping the message uncontaminated by irony or complexity (the message being that the U.S. in the name of cold war necessity, was associating itself with the violent repression of human rights)."[18]

Robin Wood, a more doctrinaire ideologue, perhaps clarifies the leftist's position: "In . . . *Salvador*, the protagonist declares at a key point . . . "I am an American, I love America," and we must assume he is speaking for Stone. But we must ask, *which* America does he love, since the American actuality is represented as . . . hateful. What is being appealed to is a myth of America, but the film seems . . . to realize that the myth cannot possibly be realized . . . hence the sense one takes of a just but impotent rage. . . . This is nowhere clearer than in *Salvador*, one of Stone's strongest, least flawed works and a gesture of great courage within its social political context. . . . Impotent rage is permissible, the promotion of a constructive alternative is not—Stone's films can be accepted, even popular, even canonized by Academy Awards precisely because their ultimate effect, beyond the rage, is to suggest that things *can't* be changed. . . . All the film can say is that the threat of a general 'communist' takeover is either imaginary or grossly exaggerated (if it weren't, presumably the horrors we're shown would all be justified or at least pardonable)."[22]

Conservatives also strongly criticized *Salvador*. David Brooks's critique is perhaps typical: "Stone's total nihilism makes *Salvador* one of the most rancid movies of this decade. . . . To Stone, everybody and everything is corrupt. . . . Stone conveniently ignores the democratic center that dominates El Salvador. These people are honorable, and Stone clearly has trouble understanding honorable people. So what we are left with are killers on the right, commies on the left (who turn out to be killers) and the U.S. embassy, which is staffed with militarists and preppy State Department stooges who spout a bastardized caricature of U.S. foreign policy. The Americans are pure cartoons, claiming there are commies under every bed and all that jazz. . . . Boyle is a sleazebag, but being a self-declared leftist, he has good intentions. . . . The movie crawls along, murdering peasants here, nuns there, journalists elsewhere. There are dozens of pointless, filthy episodes that don't mesh or make sense, all designed to further the numbing point that Reagan is causing murder in Central America. . . . Nothing is admirable, no virtue is applauded, nobody shines forth. For Stone, the world is a pile of sewage. Judging by the caliber of Stone's work, *Salvador* must be an autobiographical movie."[3]

Salvador was rejected for distribution in the U.S. on any terms Hemdale would accept. The company kept home-video rights to justify their investment—removing distributors' main reason for putting time and money into theatrical release. In the end, *Salvador* was badly and unimaginatively distributed by Hemdale itself according to Stone, with a very low budget. It did well in Los Angeles and a few other cities, but had no true national release.[7]

The writer-director admitted that a major weakness of *Salvador* is the two unlikable, sleazy main characters, destroying audience identification. Stone commented, "They're certainly a turnoff. . . . Reality dictates that two sleazoids would attract each other and the Rock-Boyle relationship was already in place. What was interesting, I don't know if it comes across, is that they didn't like each other. They go nuts just being in the same room together. Boyle is always trying to borrow money from Rock and Rock is always trying to borrow money from Boyle. If one of them fucks a chick, the other one goes crazy. I mean it's hopeless, it's a real Three Stooges situation, but that's what it was. I don't calculate the results of a movie. I don't think, well, this is going to turn off the audience. I go with what seems to me honest and right. Of course, I also like to turn the tables."

In terms of its politics, Stone feels the FMLN prisoners' execution scene is a distortion, but one he accepts. For "with all the Death Squad killings with what the National Guard has done in El Salvador—some fifty-thousand dead, murdered—if the FMLN came to power, I think they would be justified in executing the Salvadoran military command."[7]

Just for the reader's interest, ten years after the events depicted in *Salvador*, the U.S. continued to support ARENA, the party associated with the Death Squads, which won the 1994 elections.

4

Platoon

THE BASIS OF *Platoon* was hatched in New York City in 1969. But the writer-director felt that drugs, jail, and anxieties kept him from writing the first version of the script until 1976. The two "fathers," sergeants Elias and Barnes, were based on two real NCOs he encountered in combat. Elias was a dashingly handsome part-Apache; "He was a rock star but played it out as a soldier, real danger turned him on." Stone considered Barnes as "the best soldier I ever saw, except possibly for Elias . . . but unlike Elias, there was a sickness in him, he wanted to kill too much."[17]

Stone saw them as representing the essential conflict in the film: "The angry Achilles versus the conscience-stricken Hector fighting for a lost cause on the dusty plains of Troy." This in turn mirrored a sort of civil war among the U.S. troops: "On the one hand, the lifers, the juicers, and the moronic white element (part southern, part rural) against the others—the hippie, pot smoking, black, and progressive white element (although there were exceptions) . . . and I would act as the observer . . . then forced to act—to take responsibility, a moral stand. And in the process grow to manhood."

The first script was written in the summer of 1976. Stone was broke, had left his first wife, and was going nowhere. It came in a burst and he did it fast, twelve-hour days, four or five weeks, Chris walking. In the 1984 revision, he murders Barnes.

The four combat missions in the film also had their counterparts in Stone's real experiences, from the first-night ambush to the final skirmish—Stone thought it might in truth have been an attempt to draw out the Viet Cong.[5] Stone felt he went to Vietnam as a "budding artist ravenous for material in the raw," though he soon realized that "combat is totally random. It has nothing to do with heroism.

Cowardice and heroism are the same emotion— fear—expressed differently. And life is a matter of luck. Two soldiers standing two feet apart—one gets killed, the other lives.

His script, as noted, had at first been rejected everywhere, though it got him the writing of *Midnight Express*. Seeing Warren Beatty's unconventional film *Reds*, however, in 1981, got Stone's enthusiasm going for *Platoon* again.

The project was reborn in 1983, when Michael Cimino read it. Cimino and Stone persuaded Dino De Laurentis to make it in a sort of barter arrangement for Stone's work on the script of *Year of the Dragon*. In particular, Cimino felt the upcoming Stanley Kubrick film *Full Metal Jacket* would bring new attention to the Vietnam War, though both Cimino and Stone didn't really want their film compared to Kubrick's.

Stone cast *Platoon* and went to scout locations in the Philippines. But in summer of 1984, Dino De Laurentis reneged when no American distributor would agree to a commercial (approximately $3 million release). Reportedly, Stone had to sue to get back control of his script. He also rewrote it.

In the end, like nearly all the decade's Vietnam films, *Platoon* was financed by a foreign producer, Hemdale (*Salvador*'s producer), for about 6 million (as with *Salvador*). The U.S. distributor, Orion, put up 2 million.

The overturning of the Marcos regime forced a new set of deals with the Philippines' military for the use of their equipment (the U.S. Defense Department refused cooperation, deeming Stone's script "totally unrealistic"). Soon after about twenty-five mostly teenage actors of different races arrived at the main location; a jungle road was built, a stream dammed to create a river, and various sets were constructed.

Stone had his actors go through an intense two-week "training course" at Philippine jungle school under Viet vets, digging foxholes, eating cold rations, jungle marching all day, taking night ambushes complete with special-effects explosions. Stone: "The idea was to fuck with their heads so we could get that dog tired, don't give a damn attitude, the anger, the irritation, the casual way of brutality, the casual approach to death. What I remember most about being there and what a lot of guys remember is just the tiredness."[1]

Of Charlie Sheen's performance as himself, Stone said: "I saw myself as a young man . . . and it was sad. To see what I'd become

in Vietnam through him. I mean, certainly part of me became bad
or evil and I didn't have any realization of that at the time . . . that's
where the bottom line is. You find out if someone is moral or not.
That's what the film is about."

Shooting took fifty-four days, and about 15 percent of the script
was dropped in the editing.

On-screen "Rejoice, young man, in thy youth."—Ecclesiastes.

Sun and dust, a transport plane's hatch opens. New recruits out,
including Chris Taylor, twenty-one, tense, bewildered, innocent.

At once, plastic body bags are loaded, the ends held, middles
sagging.

Returning vets pass, faces pitying, eyes hollow. "Gonna love the
Nam."

Jungle images, titled: "December, 1967. Bravo company, somewhere near the Cambodian border." Chris is point, cutting their
path, clumsy, exhausted. The column snakes behind, bird and leaves
sounds. The jungle army, each man with his own style.

Barnes, the horribly facially scarred sergeant: "What's the matter
with you, Taylor?" The kind black medic and graceful sergeant Elias
help, lightening his pack. But Chris collapses.

The company sets up camp: clearing fields of fire, setting mines,
chowing down, lighting fires. A copter brings supplies.

Chris's letter to grandma, voice-over: "Somebody once wrote hell
is the impossibility of reason. . . . I don't even know what I'm doing,
a gook could be standing three feet in front of me. I'm so tired. . . .
Nobody cares. The unstated rule is a new guy's life isn't worth as
much because he hasn't put his time in . . . It's better to get it in
the first few weeks. . . . You don't suffer as much. . . . I think I 've
made a big mistake."

The leaders confer, Barnes running things. Chris and the other
newies are on watch. Elias counsels them, eyes smiling: "Sit tight,
we'll get to you."

At a night position, Chris and a newie set out mines, alternate
watch. The newie: "Don't catch no zzzs on me or I'll sling your ass!"

Chris voice-overs: "Mom and dad didn't want me to come
here. . . . I just want to be anonymous . . . do my share for my
country . . . with guys nobody cares about. . . . They're at the bottom of the barrel, and they know it. . . . yet they're fighting for our
society, and our freedom. . . . Maybe from down here I can start

18. *Platoon.* Tom Berenger as Sergeant Barnes, Willem Dafoe as Sergeant Elias, Charlie Sheen as Chris: "The unstated rule is a new guy's life isn't worth as much because he hasn't put his time in—" *(Copyright 1986 Orion Pictures Corporation. Courtesy Museum of Modern Art Film Stills Archive.)*

19. *Platoon.* Charlie Sheen as Chris, Keith David as King: "Everybody knows the poor always bein' fucked by the rich. Always have, always will." *(Copyright 1986 Orion Pictures Corporation. Courtesy Museum of Modern Art Film Stills Archive.)*

up again and be somebody. I can be proud without having to fake it, maybe.

Insects, mist, dripping water, his heart pounding. Silhouettes approach, leaves on their helmets. Chris freezes. The others are asleep.

Suddenly rifle fire, grenades, yelling! Chris trips the mines, again, again, till the other hits the safeties. They blow, a V.C. flies up, everyone's firing.

Another man's hit, Chris is scratched. "Don't give up. Help me." But he dies, blood-covered, as the others look away.

At base camp, Chris and the cheery black King pull the outhouse barrels. Chris has 332 days to go. He "dropped out of college and told 'em I wanted infantry, combat, and Nam." Why should just the poor kids fight and the college kids get away with it?

The black druggie tells him: "Sheeit, gotta be rich in the first place to think like that. Everybody knows the poor always bein' fucked by the rich. Always have, always will."

King shares his joint. We hear "Go Ask Alice." A dugout hutch on the base's edge holds a red-lit cabaret: candles, fans, tape decks, beers, dope, shirtless young GIs in headbands, medallions. King introduces: "This ain't Taylor, Taylor's been shot. This is Chris, he's been resurrected." Elias and the others greet him, happily, Elias blows drug smoke down a rifle muzzle to him.

In the barracks, to "Okie from Muskogee," the others play cards, trade insults: "Only way you get some pussy is your bitch dies and wills it to you—and then maybe." Lieutenant Wolfe visits, greeting them as at a frat house.

In the jungle, Chris is point, probing a bunker complex. It's abandoned. Elias scouts through the tunnels, smiling, invulnerable. But another man opens a documents box and is shattered by its booby trap. And a black soldier is gone. They're ordered to move on a gook village.

In the jungle, Chris's voice-over: "It was King that found him . . . not far from the village—it was the end of the mystery." He's dead, tied to a tree, throat cut, eyes staring, mouth open. Barnes: "The motherfuckers."

The platoon takes the village trail. Chris: "The village, which had stood for maybe a thousand years, didn't know we were coming. If they had, they would have run. Barnes was the eye of our rage."

It's thatched huts. The soldiers fan out among adults, kids, dogs.

In one part, Barnes forces three from a tunnel, throws a grenade—explosion! screaming!

In a hut, Chris finds a hole. Hysterical: "I'm sicka this shit, man, get outta there!"

Barnes stares at a weapons cache, rice to feed the enemy. "Burn it!"

In the hut an old woman and her retarded son climb from the hole. The murderous Bunny cries: "Do 'em, man, do 'em!" Chris, excited, fires into the dirt." "Dance, dance!" He stops, but Bunny advances, clubs the youth with his gun, again and again, blood flying: "Wow! You this, his fucking head come apart! Look at that!"

As kids scream, Barnes questions the headman. He had to hide the guns and rice. Barnes casually kills the headman's wife. A massacre is possible as Barnes grabs his daughter, gun to her head.

"Barnes!" Elias cries. "You ain't a firing squad!" The two struggle, are dragged apart. Lieutenant Wolfe has his orders. Torch the village, blow the weapons, round up the V.C.s. Elias asks why he doesn't do anything; he doesn't answer.

They torch the huts, blow the supplies, poison the well. Chris stops some from raping a child, shoves them off. As the village burns, Chris shoulders the child, the V.C. suspects are led on ropes, burning and explosions behind them.

Later the leaders huddle. Wolfe sides with Barnes. The captain needs all.

At night Chris and Elias watch the stars.

Elias: "Barnes believes in what he's doing."

But they're gonna lose the war. Elias: "We been kickin' other people's asses so long, I guess it's time we got our own kicked."

On a new mission. Machine-gun fire erupts from the jungle, hitting the point man. Gunfire and explosions as the men run forward.

Chris takes out an enemy with a pitched grenade.

Lieutenant Wolfe calls in artillery. Shouting over the shooting, Elias asks to take men to prevent a counterattack. Barnes joins them, Elias goes.

The artillery hits, too close! Their own are hit, Barnes digging sizzling shrapnel from the radioman. Retreating, two others hit a trip wire, exploding a satchel charge. Barnes rushes to Wolfe: "What the fuck coordinates you giving—you killed a bunch of people!" He orders a check fire.

Elias, Chris, and two others move fleetly through the jungle.

Barnes tells Lieutenant Wolfe that they must move back. He'll get Elias.

Chris's group see the enemy, Elias was right. Barnes comes up, tells them to move back. Ahead, Elias kills five V.C.s as Barnes stalks him. Chris gets the others back, goes after Elias.

Barnes and Elias see each other, Elias smiles, Barnes shoots him down. Chris appears, and Barnes tells him: "Elias is dead. Gooks all over the place!"

Choppers drop in, spraying dust, evacuating men. They blow ponchos off the corpses. But as the last chopper lifts, they see Elias exit the jungle running, shot, getting up, running, N.V.A. swarming behind. Elias to his knees, arms upward. Barnes and Chris exchange looks of guilt and revulsion.

In the hutch, the heads talk. Chris: "I know he did it. I saw his eyes. . . . I say we frag the fucker tonight!"

"Elias didn't ask you to fight his battles."

"Barnes has been shot seven times and ain't dead—that tell you something?"

Barnes appears: "You pussies gotta smoke this shit so you's can hide from reality. . . . Me, I don't need that shit. I *am* reality. . . . I got no fight with a man does what he's told, but when he doesn't the machine breaks down, and when the machine breaks down, we break down. . . . You loved Elias, want to kick ass, I'm here."

Barnes turns, contemptuous. Chris rushes him, pounding him. But Barnes overwhelms him, is ready to knife him—"Ten years for an enlisted man!" he's told. Barnes: "Death? What do you guys know about death?"

Choppers return them to the massacre village. Chris: "They sent us back into the valley. We knew we were going to be the bait to lure them out."

The camp is heavily sandbagged, dug in, barbwired, jungle encircled.

King and Chris share a foxhole, Chris, touchy: "We just sit around in the middle and suck on it!"

King's got orders—he's going home! The other pairs wait. Night. The ambush patrol is attacked, a young voice screaming over the radio: "Hundreds of 'em. I can hear 'em talking gook!"

In the jungle, the N.V.A. moves forward. Flares illuminate the night. A scared soldier leaps from the jungle: "Hundreds of 'em, comin' this way! You guys get outta here!"

Figures run forward—sappers! One runs into the command bunker, satchel charges on him—they explode the bunker!

Chris explodes his mines, there's return fire, voices. Chris and pal leap out, just as the hole takes a hit! Then Chris attacks, firing like a madman!

The rest of the platoon members fight, flee, die. There's no place to pull back, enemies all over. The air strike is ordered to dump all they have in the perimeter!

The N.V.A. sweeps in, firing. Wolfe is killed, one hides under a corpse, Barnes kills and kills. Barnes and Chris see each other, Barnes points his gun. Then, overhead, the jets unload their bombs, which detonate.

Chris wakes. It's dawn in the jungle. He rises, bloody, filthy, tattered. Around him endless bodies, sandbags, craters. He takes a dead N.V.A.'s weapon.

He finds an injured Barnes. They stare at each other. "Do it," he says.

Chris shoots him, twice. Barnes is dead.

New soldiers and a personnel carrier appear. A few others survived. Chris's black hole mate stabs himself, the hider emerges, a third takes cigs from a dead V.C. A great pit has been dug, and a bulldozer pushes in N.V.A. bodies. Chris is choppered out. He looks down at the battle site, the jungle.

Chris's voice: "I think now, looking back, we did not fight the enemy, we fought ourselves, and the enemy was in us. . . . The war is over for me now, but it will always be there, the rest of my days. As I am sure Elias will be—fighting with Barnes. . . .There are times when I felt like the child born of those two fathers . . . but be that as it may, those of us who did make it have an obligation to build again, to teach others what we know, and to try with what's left of our lives to find a goodness and a meaning to this life."

In this autobiographical film, Stone works harder than ever to cut his hero off from the world—in its first moments, he even sees his place in the transport aircraft taken by a body-bagged dead soldier. Early dialogue also has "the Nam" and "the world" used as opposites, (as soldiers there in fact thought of it). In his first voice-over letter home, the protagonist also says he must start over, not "faking it" this time, to become someone he's proud of. He does survive, perhaps makes friends, shows courage, and does both good and evil in the village raid and against Barnes, but remains largely isolated and opaque to the end. In his final declaration, he doesn't speak of the good and bad he did, just that he's aware of good and evil in himself. What will he build and teach—hope or resignation or ruthlessness, all of which he's shown? Finally, while he speaks of his fellow survivors, there's little sense of a society, of a "we," as if he has no real wish even to see any of them again. (In an interview, Stone admitted he had no idea what happened to the real platoon.)

Stone's view of society in this autobiographical film is also very revealing. He's repeatedly been quoted as saying he wanted to show young people what war was really like.[14] He does give us an extraordinary view of the day-to-day life of a combat soldier, but at the same time a very partial, sanctimonious and self-censoring view of the military. America's wealth-biased draft, for example, is slyly shrugged off in Chris's letter where he smugly admires the "poor ignorant soldiers fighting for their society," then, in an exchange with a black when he claims he volunteered because the rich didn't fight. The handsome black laughs this off as inevitable, and survives untouched, while one that it angers is cowardly and wounds himself to escape combat—the oldest sort of Hollywood morality, though elsewhere Stone calls sending the poor and uneducated to Vietnam "the ultimate corruption."[16]

In the same article he describes the large-scale thievery and crime in the ranks—PX supply rip-offs, prostitution, and other luxuries enjoyed by noncombatants, particularly lifer sergeants—yet there's no rottenness in Stone's war, rather he makes his good and evil sergeants tragic superwarriors corrupted by their noble excesses.

Finally, the Vietnamese people and U.S. policy are accepted without question— *Platoon*'s plot could be that for a good ghetto cop/ bad ghetto cop/new recruit thriller in the U.S., or even for that matter a good Auschwitz guard/bad Auschwitz guard/new recruit film about the World War II concentration camps. Stone chooses to omit all political and military context—presumably they are no concern of youthful warriors (Stone himself briefly plays a combat major, sacrificed by the final sapper attack). This omission is notable in particular light of the recent revelation[13] that while Nixon, Kissinger, and Haldeman made policy, 1969-72, and 20,442 Americans died in Vietnam, a troop pullout was prevented because it might hurt their future reelection chances. It seems unlikely that any of them thought of asking a Viet vet to execute them for this decision. But imagine if such White House meetings had been *part of the film* . . .*(!)*

In fact, reviewers' positive responses to the film focused on their surprise that a serious movie about Vietnam had been made, despite its limitations. Vincent Canby of the *New York Times* commented that "*Platoon* . . . is possibly the best work of any kind about Vietnam since Michael Herr's book *Dispatches*. . . . This vivid tense moving new film deals with the immediate experience of the fighting. . . . It's meant as praise to say that the film appears to express itself with the same sort of economy [as] B-pictures in which characters are largely defined by what they do rather than what they say." Canby goes on to praise the narrative order in a film that, at its heart, "is a dramatization of mental, physical and moral chaos. . . . *Platoon* seems to slide into and out of crucial scenes. . . . It's less a work that has been written than one that has been discovered . . . a major work, as full of passion as it is of redeeming scary irony."[2]

David Denby commented that "Oliver Stone's impassioned, mournful *Platoon* is the kind of Vietnam picture that many of us have longed for and also, in secret, dreaded. . . . Stone has told the familiar young soldier's story without copping out on the ineradicable bitterness and confusion of the Vietnam war. . . . *Platoon* has some obvious flaws: the hero is too straight and good, he finds his courage too quickly, he announces his perceptions in an overly sincere narration . . . and the lessons he enunciates at the end don't match the awfulness of the experience. . . . Still, this is a great American movie."[7]

Jay Hoberman comments that *Platoon* is "a guilty corrective to the fantasies of bellicose noncombatants Milius and Stallone (*Apocalypse Now, Rambo*). The film's power resides in its details. . . . *Platoon* is often crudely lyrical . . . [smoking a joint to Jefferson Airplane] and often just crude [cutting from dopers listening to Smoky Robinson to a redneck singing "Okie from Muskogee"]. . . . Combat is a mixture of incredible confusion—mines and shrieks and men dying with their eyes open—and shrill hyperexcitement. . . . *Platoon* isn't as wild as *Salvador*, but it's subject to the same sentimentality and simpleminded moral schema. . . . The film is so monumentally an unburdening, it's nearly lightheaded when Stone scores a long shot of the torched village. The effect is akin to the distancing that comes with traumatic shock. *Platoon* is as tactile as mud, but it's also dizzy with grief."[10]

Richard Corliss's *Time* article sees it as a slyly equivocating personal work with something for everybody: "Jean Luc Godard once wrote that when a good film is also a popular film, it is because of a misunderstanding. *Platoon* could very well be misunderstood into superhit status. The army of Rambomaniacs will love the picture because it delivers more bang for the buck; all those yellow folks blow up real good. Aging lefties can see the film as a demonstration of war's inhuman futility. Graybeards on the right may call it a tribute to our fighting men, in whatever foreign adventures. The intelligentsia can credit *Platoon* with expressing, in bold cinematic strokes, Stone's grand themes of comradeship and betrayal. And the average youthful moviegoer—too young to remember Vietnam even as the living room war—may discover where Dad went in the 1960s and why he came home changed or came home in a body bag. . . . The nearly 1 million Vietnamese casualties are deemed trivial compared with America's loss of innocence, of allies, of geopolitical face. And the tragedy of Viet Nam is seen as this: not that they died, that we debased ourselves by killing them. . . . [Chris]—a good man, and a murderer? It is a tribute to *Platoon*'s cunning that it can sell this dilemma both ways, and a mark of Stone's complexity that he can argue either side and believe both."[5]

Cart's industry-wise review in *Variety* makes a simpler evaluation, if in less wise-guy phrasing. "Intense but artistically distanced . . . Stone seeks to immerse the audience totally in the United States misguided adventure. In form it resembles the taut, close-in army films of the fifties (*Men in War, Attack, The Steel Helmet, Fixed Bayonets*). Stone implicitly suggests the U.S. lost the war because of divisions within the ranks, and an unwillingness to go all the way."[3]

Disapproving critics often saw the film reducing the war's complexities to irrelevant adventures of a semipsychopath. Pauline Kael: "The film is about victimizing ourselves as well as others, it's about shame. That's the only way in which it's political; it doesn't deal with what the war was about—it's conceived strictly in terms of what these American infantrymen go through.

"[Stone is] a filmmaker, all right, but he lacks judgment. Just about everything in *Platoon* is too explicit, and is so heightened that it can numb you and make you feel jaded. Stone's moviemaking [suggests] he was a romantic loner who sought his manhood in the excitement of violent fantasy. The key scene in the movie [has] Chris calmly deliberately shoot a fellow soldier . . . an unambiguous, justified execution. . . . Oddly weightless pulp revenge fantasy."[11]

Owen Gleiberman criticizes the film aesthetically. "Stone is . . . a simplistic moviemaker. Trying to make his statement about the war, about the forces that tore the American side apart. . . . There's something too obviously schematic about Elias and Barnes. It's impossible to forget *Platoon* has been rigged as a modern morality play. . . . It doesn't hold that the good cop/bad cop duo are holding out for the soul of a blank slate. . . . Chris Taylor is Stone's surrogate, and like a lot of autobiographical stand-ins . . . he comes off as an observer. [Sheen's] incessant blank-eyed staring accentuates the worst aspect of the script, Stone's tendency to foist 'bad' impulses on the other characters so his hero can stand back aghast. . . . Stone seems almost scared of soiling him."[10]

Sydelle Kramer points out a moral trick of the film: *Platoon* develops an ethic based on the distinction between those who fight well and maintain a sense of decency, and those who fight bravely but lose all sense of justice. "The moral landscape of the film is soon revealed to be a stunted one. We are given a battlefield that prohibits real extremes: the dichotomy between good war and bad war does not allow for no war. [Stone makes a movie about good and evil] without reference to the origins of the war that inspired him, its motives, or its moral ambiguities. . . . A war that should never have been fought, only he's left that part out. . . . We watch events unfold in a historical vacuum, shaped by men who are unaware of the past. . . . [These soldiers] never allude to whether they should be fighting or not. . . . It's as if he made *Platoon* while a black hole sucked up history. . . . Oliver Stone wants us to feel good about ourselves despite all the murder, the napalm, the rot, because, after all, we tried."[12]

A very perceptive critique of *Platoon* was written by Leo Cawley, an ex-marine rifleman now teaching. He has high praise for the film's lonely grunt's eye view of the world, faithfully presenting each mission's mechanics, such as the V.C.'s staying too close to use fire support and air power, the use of troops as "bait" as if in a kind of video game, and the emphasis on economically and socially expendable poor, ethnic, and dropout teens as troops. The black's statement that the rich have always taken advantage of the poor he feels suggests the American truth that "you might be able to save your own ass with luck and fortitude, but it will be the only one you can save. It is a place where sympathy and pity are the psychological luxuries of the rich." The "almost massacre" of the village suggests to him "a hidden history lies submerged like a lost continent under the waters of network coverage."

What Cawley faults are the two adored, unreal supertroopers: "As everyone in combat soon learned, modern war kills very very tough guys much like it kills everyone else. . . . In every unit tough capable guys got killed and everybody knew it. . . . When you see tough guys die, it creates a kind of skepticism about toughness. . . . [Oliver Stone] has concocted these two all-too-symbolic lovers of war for an unclear purpose, and with them he betrays the authenticity of the rest of the film. . . . The few people with the motives of Stone's heroes are more often incompetent, dangerous and revolting or at least one of these. In Stone's world, the war lover is a paragon of the military virtues who attracts. Why? . . . The fact that Stone/Taylor is possessed by the romanticism of a middle-class adventurer explains the flaws in the film, but also explains why there was a movie at all."[4]

Stone was pleased with *Platoon,* commenting after its release, "I think *Platoon* shows kids . . . what combat is really like, and what war really means. They fire back. The N.V.A. were good soldiers. They killed a lot of us, and we forget that. I hope a lot of kids who see *Platoon* will think twice. Maybe they won't make the same mistake I made."[1] Interestingly, Stone says he got as much mail from people who said they thought he was supportive of the war as from people who thought he was against it. "That's part of the appeal of *Platoon*—and the controversy." Stone feels his film was meant to oppose the mythology of the war. "There was no moral purpose. There was no geographic objective. There was no defined goal. There was not even a declaration of war. There was no moral integrity in the way it was fought."[14]

The Elias/Barnes conflict seems to be the counterpart of this in the film. Stone told Richard Corliss: "You have to fight evil if you are going to be a good man. . . . That's why Chris killed Barnes, because Barnes deserved killing. . . . I also wanted to show that Chris came out of the war stained and soiled—all of us, every vet. I want vets to face up to it and be proud they came back. So what if there was some bad in us. That's the price you have to pay. Chris pays a big price. He becomes a murderer."[5] Or as another writer-director, Mike Nichols, put it: "Moral problems are so much more fun than real problems."

Platoon was initially sold with "reader ads" that told of Stone being wounded twice and winning a bronze star, and his "making a movie about men he knew and fought with." There were also some Polaroid shots of Stone in uniform. The ad legitimized the picture, said Orion's head of marketing.

By February 1987, *Platoon* was the top-grossing film in the country. Ashley Boone, Vice President for marketing and distribution, commented: "If *Platoon* had been released ten years ago, people would have said 'Don't remind us of our mistakes.' . . . No one would have watched the movie or cared. A lot of things with historical background are too painful to address when they're fresh." In time, *Platoon* took in $136 million at the U.S. box office, a Director's Guild of America Best Director Award, eight Academy Award nominations, and four Oscars, including Best Picture of 1986.

5

Wall Street

OLIVER STONE'S FATHER worked on Wall Street, and Stone apparently had always wanted to do a movie about "the street." In the film's production notes, he acknowledges the influences of *Executive Suite* (director: Robert Wise) and *Sweet Smell of Success* (director: Alexander Mackendrick), commenting: "There is no physical violence on Wall Street. But tension and mental violence are a way of life down there. These men and women really live on stock-and-bond high-wire acts—taking over companies, structuring the capital of the country, and shaking the global economy."

Stone has said the idea for *Wall Street* occurred to him while writing *Scarface*. "His get-rich-quick Miami mentality had certain parallels in New York, where an acquaintance of mine was making a fortune in the market. He was like some crazed coke dealer, nervously on the phone nights trading with Hong Kong and London, checking the telex, talking about enormous sums of money to be won or lost on a daily basis. His lifestyle was *Scarface* north. He had two Gatsby-like houses . . . several dune buggies, cars, jets, a private seaplane company, an art collection, and a townhouse in Manhattan. Then he took a giant fall."

Stone wanted to "concentrate on the ethics of the characters and see where they lose their way. . . . I think they are perverted right off the bat. . . . Ultimately, it's not about money, it's about power. . . . We deal with these issues by staying inside a very small story, one fish in one Wall Street aquarium and what happens to that fish."[1]

The script apparently went through a number of changes. In the first draft, the protagonist is Jewish, but Stone later wanted to use the clearly "non-Jewish" Sheen, and also decided to avoid feeding what he feels is a common belief that Wall Street is all run by corrupt Jewish gangsters. The story line also seems to have grown less sentimental. An April 1, 1987, third draft has the love interest Darien tell off the financier Gekko, and despite, rejection, meeting the protagonist as he's about to go to jail: "I figure a guy who's made some mistakes should be able to understand a girl who's made some of her own." This idea is dropped. On the other hand, meetings with consultants on the project[6] led to "more realism" including an added corporate stockholders' meeting and a boardroom scene showing the breakup of Blue Star Airlines. Much of the dialogue and the sense of what happens behind the closed doors only came about through talking to people who were inside those closed rooms. Finally, numerous critics have pointed out the similarities in plot structure to *Platoon* (good father/bad father/redemption), enriched by the fact that the good father is the protagonist's actual father and family head.[6]

Stone first brought the script to John Daney of Hemdale (producers of *Platoon*), who didn't think that audiences would be sympathetic toward characters making millions of dollars. Its high production costs may also have been discouraging. Stone, however, found a studio, Twentieth Century-Fox, for whom its fifteen-million-dollar budget would be only a "medium budget," and an enthusiastic producer, Edward R. Pressman, who produced *Conan the Barbarian* and *The Hand*. Coproducer was A. Kitman, also coproducer on *Platoon*, while director of photography Robert Richardson and editor Claire Simpson had the same jobs as in *Platoon* and *Salvador*.

In researching "Bud Fox," Charlie Sheen spent six weeks visiting brokerage houses, including several days with David Brown, a former trader who pleaded guilty to insider trading. Sheen: "When you get this overloaded mentality, it's tough to find ways to relax yourself, so in many ways the portrayal was more difficult than *Platoon*."

Stone cast Sheen as his lead because he felt there was a "devilish side to him . . . a strong streak of rebelliousness combined with an inner grace." Only twenty-two, much younger than the real crooked brokers, Sheen was aged by Stone with good suits, a haircut, and enough food to put on weight and jowls.

Daryl Hannah was cast as the type of beauty who associated with the big-money types, though Stone saw her as a natural simple person who hated and feared her completely artificial character.

Stone worked hard to reduce what he called her wanness and passivity.

Michael Douglas, who had never played a bad guy (his character in *Fatal Attraction* is arguably simply "weak"), proved professional and easy to work with. He supposedly loved his first chance to play a "heel," a role more toward his father's.

Consultants also helped fine-tune the performances. Ken Lipper, a former Saloman Brothers partner, helped Stone with such details as how brokers deal with sales, write up orders, hold a phone, pace conversation, and other aspects of body language.

The film used outside locations exclusively, no studio sets, hoping for better, more realistic performances. The hundreds of SAG actors came to work Monday through Friday, riding up real elevators to real offices. Then they worked fourteen hours in front of cameras and lights as brokers, traders, messengers, secretaries, and executives. Both Gekko's offices and Jackson Steinham where Bud works were shot at a vacant downtown high-rise, 222 Broadway. Gekko's office, formerly a company auditorium, was transformed into a suite for a Wall Street aristocrat: palatially redecorated and hung with original art by Picasso, Miró, and Nevelson. The Jackson Steinham set involved an elaborate computer-video-telephone complex created for its sequences. Bud's redecorated condo penthouse was specially decorated in the latest "demolished" look—textured, archaeological, and very objet trouvé—a chic dilapidated ruin. Another location was Gordon Gekko's oceanfront mansion. The moneyed, fashionable world was deliberately contrasted with Bud's first apartment and his father's shabby airport bar hangout.

Costume design was likewise carefully planned. Gekko's wardrobe has extravagant style recalling classic movie stars—his money supposedly allows him not to worry about "fitting in." Bud's clothes move from presentable business suits to a protégé's emulation of Gekko's outrageousness to following his own plutocrat's whims.

To facilitate shooting, Stone came up with a number of innovations. To forestall difficulties with onlookers, for example, Stone hired two hundred extras who "froze" between the cues for action—a sight pedestrians apparently found so disturbing it kept them from lingering.

In his rehearsal period, Stone tried to outline the characters' contexts: their backgrounds and inner lives, giving the actors suggestions and getting them to run with the ideas. Then there were

20. *Wall Street.* Charlie Sheen as Bud Fox, Michael Douglas as Gordon Gekko: "I want guys that are poor, smart, and hungry—and no feelings!" *(Copyright 1987 Twentieth Century-Fox Film Corporation. Courtesy Museum of Modern Art Film Stills Archive.)*

21. *Wall Street.* Charlie Sheen as Bud Fox, Daryl Hannah as Darien Taylor: "You got it, a great spender of other people's money." *(Copyright 1987 Twentieth Century-Fox Film Corporation. Courtesy Museum of Modern Art Film Stills Archive.)*

readings, so Stone could see how his actors actually interpreted the roles.

Wall Street was filmed over a twelve-week period all over New York City. The filming relives the rehearsals seven or eight weeks before—often the results were different, since the material had been "marinating" in the actors' subconsciouses.

Stone: "I clear the set except for the actors, so that we keep it quiet. The rehearsal itself can take anywhere from thirty minutes to six hours, in which it should become clear what everybody is looking for in the scene and how to play it. Whether they succeed doesn't interest me. . . . I always try to encourage spontaneity. I like to be surprised. Astonish me! . . . That is the hardest thing a director has to face; he has to stay fresh. . . .

"[When a scene isn't working] I often deal with it by rewriting extensively on the spot. Part of that process includes listening to the actors. Some actors just can't say certain words, or they will feel uncomfortable with a speech. They will say, 'Gee, Oliver, do I have to say that line? Can't I just do a look?' Or I try to use the camera to respond to a mistake. You shoot the scene in such a way that you can cover the blemish. You change the angle, you move the camera. We did enormous amounts of moving the camera in this film because we are making a movie about sharks, about feeding frenzies, so we wanted the camera to become a predator. There is no letup until you get to the fixed world of Charlie's father, where the stationary camera gives you a sense of immutable values."[1]

Stone shot *Wall Street* in fifty-three days, coming in seven days ahead of schedule and two million dollars under budget. He said he usually does only six or seven takes—the most used in a shot on *Wall Street* was nineteen takes.

Stone saw *Wall Street* as typical of his films—three hours of film material edited down to two hours. His scripts are long, and some shot scenes never get into the final film. Of the eighty speaking parts in *Wall Street,* he expected to cut twenty. Stone: "Editing to me is like a tremendous retreat, a march back from Moscow. When you are writing and directing, you feel like you're on a perimeter, expanding. When you are editing you are withdrawing your perimeter as quickly as possible and trying to maintain the CP, the command position."[1]

A burning red Manhattan dawn. Rush-hour crowds swarm the Wall Street area. A jammed subway. A young man, face ambitious yet unformed, Bud Fox rides a chromed escalator, jammed elevator to his job at Jackson Steinham. He tells the receptionist: "If I was doing better, it'd be a sin."

He pushes through rows of trading desks with phones, computer screens, greets next-desk pal Marv, kindly older broker Lou, overbearing office manager Lynch: "It's 9:30. Let's go to work!" The market ticker rolls.

Bud's a cold caller, his repeated spiel: "We are in the biggest bull market of our generation. If I could have five minutes of your time. . . ."

Later, Bud's in trouble. A customer wants his money back. His manager takes over: "If he doesn't pay, you pay!" Marv reminds him of a call.

Bud calls big-time trader Gekko (Marv: "It's big-game hunters that bag the elephants").

Bud just wants five minutes. "Yes, I shall give him your message."

A glimpse of Gekko in his palatial office.

La Guardia, tract houses, a bar. Bud meets his father, a gruff supervising aviation mechanic, pleased with his glamorous son, but he could have been a doctor or a lawyer: "You get on the phone and ask strangers for their money. You're a salesman."

Bud makes fifty thousand dollars, just enough "to be in Manhattan, to be a player." He borrows three hundred. Dad: "I always say money is something you need in case you don't die tomorrow." There's big insider news; his airline, Blue Star, is having a suspension lifted, will acquire new routes, compete with the big boys.

Next morning, in Bud's workaholic decor apartment, his computer screen blinks: Gekko's Birthday. At least there's a naked girl in Bud's bed.

Package under his arm, Bud enters Gekko's penthouse offices, talking his way in. He saw GG's birthday in the Bible (*Fortune* magazine), his gift is his favorite Cuban cigars. He waits two hours, is given five minutes.

Hypermodern furnishing, art, and gadgets fill the enormous room. Gordon Gekko, fortyish and tigerish in a custom English suit, is on multiple calls: "I'm looking at two hundred thousand shares. . . . Raise the sperm count on the deal. . . . The kid called me fifty-nine days in a row, would be a player . . . in the kill zone, lock and load. Lunch? Lunch is for wimps."

Gekko regards Bud: "Why am I listening to you?"

Bud has briefs on deals that Gekko hears while working ("If that guy opened a funeral parlor, no one would die").

Gekko rejects Bud's ideas. Desperate, he gives the inside dope of Blue Star's expansion. "Interesting."

At his desk, Bud gets a call—it's Gekko! He wants twenty thousand Blue Star shares! To Marv: "I just bagged the elephant!"

Gekko and Bud lunch, Gekko congratulates him, asks if he's bought stocks mentioned during his visit. Bud: "No sir, that would have been illegal." Gekko gives him a six-figure check, tells him: "You do good, you get perks, lots and lots of perks."

At night, a first-rate hooker is at his door; they're going out. In a stretch limo, Bud starts to give stock tips, her skirt slides up, the cocaine and champagne come out, his fly's unzipped, she's on top.

Coming in to work: "You look happy!"

Later Bud frantically plays racquetball with Gekko: "You have to fight harder!" Gekko knows about his Blue Star connection. "The most valuable commodity I know of is information. . . . I want guys that are poor, smart, and hungry . . . and no feelings." Bud's desperate. "You want another chance. Then stop sending me information, and start *getting* me some."

In his limo, Gekko explains. Sir Larry Wildman—his "mole" in his employ—was fired. Something big is about to go down: "I want to know where he goes and who he sees."

Bud says he could lose his license, go to jail—that's inside information. Gekko says the Blue Star tip was inside info. Without such connections, the two have no business. Gekko: "You work hard . . . and where's it get you? Wake up, pal, if you're not inside, you're outside—fifty million, a hundred million—a player or nothing."

Outside, a top executive stands tall near a shopping-cart bum. "You really think the difference between this guy and that guy is luck!"

Let out, Bud faces Gekko: "All right, Mr. Gekko, you've got me."

Helmeted, on a motorcycle, Bud trails the authoritative fiftyish Sir Lawrence Wildman to a brokerage, an exclusive restaurant, a private jet flight to, he slyly learns, Erie, Pennsylvania. He passes the info to Gekko, who concludes he's buying American Steel. Gekko gives him buying orders.

At work, Bud calls in the orders, we see the stock exchange boiling with activity. Bud leans in to tip the kindly "old values" Davis, who scoffs: "Not a good company anymore. What's going on Bud? There are no shortcuts."

At dusk, Gekko's Bridgehampton home is a vast modern space full of art objects, floor-to-ceiling windows, expensive furniture, and people. Bud comes out with the options for Gekko's signature.

Gekko introduces Bud to the guests, including a tall exquisite blond young woman, Darien Taylor: "I'd like to do for furniture what Laura Ashley did for fabrics."

"I gather you're a decorator."

"You got it, a great spender of other people's money."

Sir Larry Wildman arrives to confer with Gekko, Bud, and staff. Wildman is angry: "You're getting a free ride on my tail. With the money I'm paying you I could modernize the plant."

Gekko recalls several companies Wildman bought, followed by layoffs of thousands. Gekko asks Bud for an estimated share value, which he ruthlessly makes. Wildman calls Gekko a two-bit pirate and greenmailer. Angrily, the two come to terms. Gekko later says he had to sell. Bud quotes Sun-tzu: "All warfare is based on evasion." Gekko: "You're learning!"

Returning home, Gekko calls. He's giving him eight hundred thousand dollars to work with. "Astonish me, new info, I don't care how or where, you get me. I'm gonna make you rich, Bud Fox. Rich enough so you can afford a girl like Darien."

Bud enters the law offices of cocky young old-money attorney Jim Barnes, a classmate. He passes on a stock tip, asks about a merger. "You want to get me disbarred?" He leaves, noting the cleaning force.

Bud visits the cleaning company. Bud, in janitor coveralls, joins the law-firm night cleaning crew, going through files, copying reports, passing on the info. He visits other offices, doing the same.

At Gekko's home, his lawyer explains for protection Bud will sign a power of attorney. "The trail stops with you."

Darien emerges, blond and perfect, in a wetsuit from the Sound. To Bud: "If I could have anything: a Turner . . . a perfect canary diamond . . . world peace."

At the office, an old fat broker pleads to Lynch: "When you fire me, I'm finished." Marv to Bud: "Didn't make quota." "Old Values" Lou tells Bud: "You're on a roll, kid, enjoy it while it lasts."

Bud buys an eastside condo, Darien supervising its transformation: mural, columns, fantail chase, moldings, found objects. The two dine together: beautiful food, people, decor. Bud: "It's too perfect. Let's just watch it."

The two go to bed. At dawn, Bud faces the sky: "Who am I?"

Leaving an auction, Darien tells Gekko she's fallen for Bud. Gekko: "Told him about us? We're the same. We're smart enough not to buy into the oldest myth going . . . love."

At work, Bud puts in more orders. They're executed. But at Stock Watch, two investigators are tracking his transactions.

Teldar Paper's stockholders meeting is held in a large room crowded with four hundred stockholders, including Gekko. The executives are on a platform before them.

The CEO announces: The company is under siege from Gekko.

Gekko responds: "America has become a second-rate power. . . . Today management has no stake in the company. You own it, and you are being royally screwed over. . . . Teldar Paper has thirty-three vice presidents, each earning over two hundred thousand dollars a year. This paper company lost 110 million dollars last year, and I'll bet half of it is in the paperwork. The new law of evolution in corporate America seems to be—survival of the unfittest. In my book, you either do it right or get eliminated. I am not a destroyer of companies, I am a liberator of them. The point is, ladies and gentlemen, that greed is good. Greed is right. Greed clarifies, cuts through, and captures. Greed has marked the upward surge of mankind—and will save not only Teldar Paper but that other malfunctioning corporation, called the U.S.A." Frank Sinatra singing "Fly Me to the Moon" comes up on the sound track.

At home, at night, Bud crouches over his computers, Darien lounges in bed. Bud: "I'm going to be a giant, Darien!"

Aboard Gekko's jet, Bud sells Gekko on a Blue Star Airlines takeover: "An unpolished gem . . . capital reserves . . . 75 million cash. . . . I want to be your copilot . . . I'm gonna make us a fortune . . . I worked there."

At Bud's condo, his father greets him, Darien introduces herself. Also present are Gekko, his lawyer, and a handsome pilot and a tough, happy flight attendant, the other two Blue Star union representatives besides Bud's dad.

Gekko speaks: He sees Blue Star Airlines as doomed, management breaking unions and contracts. Gekko's answer: 20 percent wage cuts and seven more work hours a month. Bud's plan to return Blue Star to profitability—modernize, advertise and reorganize—

expanding. Pilots and flight attendant reps like it. His father smiles: "The only difference between the pyramids and the Empire State Building is that the Egyptians didn't have unions. This guy's in it just for the bucks and he doesn't take prisoners. The 'scum' built this company up from one plane in thirty years." He leaves.

In the street, furious, Bud attacks him: "Save the workers of the world speech, I heard it too many times growing up!" Bud presses him to present the facts not his opinion: "Don't destroy their lives, let the membership decide for themselves." His father won't lie.

Bud asks: "All your life your men have been able to count on you. Why is it you've never been there for me?"

At Stock Watch, the two investigators report: "Looks like that guy at Jackson Steinham is buying large amounts."

At his rich young lawyer friend's offices, Bud is told they've had calls from the SEC. "Don't worry, I'm the invisible man." He's asked to a meeting on Blue Star—you're just the president!

In a conference room lawyers and bankers confer. To pay back the buyout loan, the company will be liquidated—condos built where the hangars are, planes and routes sold off, employees getting minimum annuities, Gekko getting the rest. Bud's shocked—"Your boy did his homework!"

Bud bursts into a Gekko conference. "I found out about the garage sale at Blue Star! I gave my word!"

Gekko: "You're still going to be president. When the time comes, you'll parachute out a rich man—your father won't have to work another day."

Gekko proudly defines himself: "Money isn't lost or made. It's simply transformed from one perception to another. . . . That painting cost sixty thousand dollars ten years ago. . . . I could sell it today for six hundred thousand dollars. The illusion has become real. The richest one percent owns half the country's real wealth. Ninety percent of the American people have little or no net worth. I create nothing. I own. We make the rules. The news, war, peace, famine, upheaval, the price of paper clips. We pick that rabbit out of the hat while everybody stands around wondering how the hell we did it. Now, you're not naive enough to think we're living in a democracy, are you, buddy? It's a free market—are you with me?"

"I'm with you."

In his condo, Bud slumps, drunk, disheveled. Darien tells him:

"It's not your fault—don't provoke Gekko, he'll crush you. If he doesn't buy Blue Star, someone else will." Bud says they can survive. Darien: "If you're going to make an enemy of Gekko, I won't stand by you. . . . You're not exactly pure. . . . It was Gordon who helped me—you may not believe it, but I really do care for you. I think we could've made a good team."

Bud sells the condo. His father has a heart attack. At the hospital he tells the sick man: "I love you, Dad. . . . I got a plan, I can save the airline." He gives the pilots and flight attendant reps stock-buying orders, meets with Wildman: "What would you say to owning Blue Star Airlines? There would be an ironclad contract agreement."

At work, Bud watches the airline's quotation rise. Gekko calls, telling him to buy all he can. In his office, Bud tells everyone to sell.

At Gekko's offices, the union reps appear, all knowing the deal: "I hope you have your pilot's license . . . wouldn't let the engines fall out, but reservations can get awfully screwed up . . . and baggage."

Gekko warns them of other takeovers. "We'll take our chances."

Gekko sells. And Wildman begins buying, but not enough to stop the disaster. Gekko, cursing, calls Bud, swearing horribly, telling him: Dump it.

A newscast reports the stock's rise, fall, and buying up by Wildman.

At work, Old Values tells Bud: "I like you, just remember—man looks into the abyss. There's nothing staring back. At that moment, he finds his character, and that's what keeps him out of the abyss." A moment later, police and officials arrest Bud for securities fraud and inside trading, and lead him out, weeping.

In an empty Central Park Sheep's Meadow, a storm breaking, Bud and Gekko face each other: "You think you could have gotten this far this fast with anybody else. . . . I opened doors for you, showed the value of information, showed how the system works. I gave you [those companies]. I gave you Darien, your manhood, everything. You could have been one of the great ones." He bashes him.

"I guess I just realized I'm just Bud Fox."

In a nearby tavern, investigators remove the concealed tape re-corders he carried: "You did the right thing."

Bud's parents drive him through the city: "You told the truth and gave the money back." Bud tells his father he's going to jail.

"In a crazy way, it's the best thing . . . create instead of living off the buying and selling of others." Bud goes up the courthouse steps. The camera zooms up to show the surrounding office towers and we see THE END. The film is dedicated to Louis Stone, stockbroker.

Once again Stone chooses, here in the midst of a teeming metropolis, to create a protagonist almost totally cut off from humanity. Bud's job is the selling of stocks by phone, the creation of momentary monetary illusions, his own preoccupation the dream of wealth and success. Perhaps his single deep relationship, to that with his father, is highly uneasy, the older man disapproving of his career, while his association with his "second father" Gekko depends on constantly showing new prodigies of cleverness, craftiness, treachery, and betrayal. His links with society are frail; all he does is work and spend money on status symbols. His romantic relationship is itself with a beautiful object, Darien Taylor, who sadly seems to care only for other beautiful objects (and whoever provides them). After intimacy with her, his response is: "Who am I?"—No response. The story tries to show Bud rejecting this way of life by becoming furious when Gekko's plans to make him airline president are revealed as a ruse to dissolve it. But he has repeatedly shown his love of money, and has become a ruthless betrayer, thief, and trickster to get it. Moreover, Gekko explains that he and his father will exit rich men. Bud's fury at being "used" is a plotting gimmick; he's made his deal, he's even attacked his dad's "dignity of labor" viewpoint. If Gekko had explained the plan at the start, he'd have surely accepted it. There's a similar plot trick in the film *The Spy Who Came in from the Cold*—the spy, a longtime assassin and betrayer, used as a dupe in a double cross, is suddenly morally outraged. Perhaps the real point is that at the end, despite his father's approval of his sellout of Gekko (all legalities left vague),and vague hopes of a "creative" career, Bud seems lonelier and more isolated than ever as he goes off to prison, and the camera pulls back, making him just one more struggling ant in the ant heap of a society "where the enterprise is free, but nothing else is."

Stone's vision of society in *Wall Street* is also revealing in its careful limitation of viewpoint to stockbrokers' offices and their lives. Considering the effects of Wall Street decisions on ordinary jobs and workers, it's as if Stone decided to make a movie about the world napalm, land-mine, and weapons trade that limited itself to scenes and conflicts in the offices and boardrooms, avoiding all human consequences for good or ill. Indeed, we never really know the "truth" or "facts" about the major characters or situations; the "old values" guy suggests a past idealistic market; the raider Gekko justifies a ruthless greed that will "save" America if not all companies; the aristocratic Sir Wildman may want to save jobs and industries, but we're never sure about anybody (or cynically, Stone lets us believe what we wish). Only Bud breaks the laws, is caught, and goes to jail. What happens to Gekko is left out (if anything does happen to him). We do, however, see that the conventional stock brokerage is a place of dissembling and ruthlessness—when Bud triumphs his supervisor says, "I always knew you had what it takes"; when he's arrested he says, "I always knew you were no good." A man who fails to make his quota is sacked. Stone may call *Wall Street* the story of a lost soul reclaimed, but there is little room for souls on Wall Street. Gekko in fact seems to be a vision of the "next" stage of global economic progress—in fact his "greed is good" speech seems arbitrarily placed, as if Stone had wanted it as his ending, but realized that would have gone "over the top."

Despite my comments, a number of critics received *Wall Street* with enthusiasm. Vincent Canby gives it credit for "having its heart in the right place," only finding it dramatically unbalanced: "a gentrified everyman, an upscale morality tale to entertain achievers who don't want to lose touch with their moral centers, but still have it all. . . . The movie crashes in a heap of platitudes that remind us that honesty is after all the best policy. . . . *Wall Street* isn't a movie to make us think. It simply confirms what we all know we should think, while giving us a tantalizing, Sidney Sheldon–like peek into the boardroom and bedrooms of the rich and powerful. . . . The film's subject is a potentially great one that demands the sort of brainy, brazen, unsentimental common sense that illuminates "*Major Barbara* and *Heartbreak House.* Shaw could write heroes and heroines that are a match for brilliant villains. Even at its best, *Wall Street* . . . is an uneven struggle. At its worst, it's a muddle."[4]

David Denby praises the film more highly: "A sensationally entertaining melodrama about greed and corruption in New York. . . . The writing is expansive and somewhat overexplicit, like late Chayefsky, though without the great blowhard's manic self-righteousness. . . . The romance he's celebrating (satirically) is the romance of money and power. These men and women love beauty in a special way: Big success fills them with a swelling new appreciation of sunsets, art, and food, lovely things whose aesthetic worth they quickly calculate as investment properties. *Wall Street*, a gleeful send-up of the culture of money, rarely averts its rapt attention from the gross yet also mystical and delicate issue of dollar value—not just of stocks but of paintings, decor, and even personal relationships. . . . Gekko, the soul of contemporary finance, expresses the profoundest contempt for people who labor; he intimates that making money through mere stock manipulation is a form of exquisite larceny, a great joke on the working world that he and a few others are qualified to enjoy."[7]

Carrie Rickey sees the blending of the film's economic and familial conflicts as the film's real strength: "It is a brazenly entertaining melodrama, festering with greed, bilious with revenge, and positively reeking with the sour stench of success. . . . There seems to be but one conflict in Stone's naked city. Though in *Wall Street* he promises to show us the anatomy of greed, he delivers yet another dissection of the Oedipal conflict. Why *Wall Street* finally succeeds is that the Oedipal drama becomes a motif in the tragedy of speculators who place monetary values over moral ones."[15]

Academic Jack Boozen in fact found the film valuable as a carefully realized view of the world's economic future: "The story of Gekko and his seductive power serves as a metaphor, a new version of the American Dream. . . . Unlike Gatsby, who at least dreamed of a future, Gekko sells the future into debt for cash returns *now*. . . . He is interested mainly in manipulating the valuation system and not in the things to be valorized. . . . Distinct categories of personal experience—occupational, political, psychological, and historical—like cultural economic boundaries, have begun to crumble into one great pastiche of commercial semiotics, one grand 'free' market of consumer language and signs . . . greed is only good when one can get away with it by passing negative repercussions on to someone else. This is Gekko's art. . . . Gekko's world of speculative capitalism has no interest in products or people—it battles in the name of control over perception and desire. . . . The narrative clearly privileges Carl at the expense of Gekko on the ethical level. . . . Yet Carl continues to have faith in the formal justice of a system that has almost killed him and nearly destroyed his son. . . . And although Gekko may eventually be forced to serve a term in prison because Bud turns State's witness, the law seems little more than a technicality in an issue that goes to the heart of the pervasive ideology, an ideology inseparable from the relentlessly projected images of the 'good life.'"[2]

Those who faulted *Wall Street* found a variety of grounds for their displeasure. James Gardner found the script and story and leads simply unthought out and unbelievable: "The computer was given its instructions: Oliver Stone is turning from the jungles of Vietnam to the jungles of Wall Street, and he will need a script. After a three hundred millionth of a second or so, the computer spat out a story. . . . Had there been a human monitoring the system, questions might have been asked: Would any young Wall Streeter, however naive, try to approach Gordon Gekko—the Gordon Gekko—with a series of ordinary stock tips culled from public documents? Would Gekko choose for his protégé a boy who stages a temper tantrum on first being asked to do something slightly illegal, and who has such a flimsy network of contacts that, in order to secure the information Gekko wants, he has to dress up as a night maintenance man and prowl the halls of a law firm specializing in takeovers? With thousands of aspiring young Wall Street felons to choose from, couldn't Gekko find a more reliable partner in crime than this lunkhead?"[11]

Others also found the story line just too crude and clumsy. John Powers notes: "There's no doubting the crudity of the conception. . . . Here, Bud Fox is little more than a board upon which Gekko and Dad play checkers for his soul. . . . *Wall Street's* hamfisted psychology is a disappointment, but it's hardly a shock. After all, Stone's a pulp filmmaker whose coarsest excesses are probably inseparable from his most flamboyant virtues. *Wall Street* has the jacked-up quality you find in Sam Fuller or Jim Thompson: the swatches of undergraduate dialogue ("Who am I?" Bud wonders aloud), the speed-freak camera style (Stone even uses whiplash pans for a conversation in an elevator), the stupefying incomprehension of women (Stone's usual assortment of tramps and bimbos). . . . Stone is fascinated and repelled by both attitudes to life—libido-mad acquisition, out-to-lunch honesty—and these unresolved feelings fuel his work. . . . All the [real world problems in the film] are papered over by *Wall Street's* focus on Bud Fox's personal moral crisis."[14]

Likewise, David Edelstein sees the film as equivocating and avoiding the true issues: "Stone wants to have it both ways, for the kid to be a crook and also be an innocent. . . . And Stone's own morality is a little shifty: the scheme Bud concocts to wrest control of his father's airline from Gekko raises questions of its own—like: What happens to all the smaller investors who get fried along with the big fish? In fact, Stone defines the whole sickness unconvincingly. The struggle for America's soul doesn't boil down to the dark fathers versus the white fathers. It's in the souls of the gray fathers— the ones who are ignorant, ambivalent, or just plain self-interested. If we all had spiritual leaders like Martin Sheen—who said 'Do what's right,' and not 'Do what will make you rich and comfortable, so that people will respect you more'—then the choice would be so easy. Wall Street is thrilling left-wing trash, and it's more or less disposable."[8]

Similarly, Variety's showbiz-wise editor saw the film as too dull and preachy: "Watching Oliver Stone's Wall Street is about as wordy and dreary as reading the financial papers' accounts of the rise and fall of an Ivan Boesky type arbitrageur. . . . Core problem with this filmed version is that it is too thoroughly a retelling of the impact of stock manipulation, more like a docudrama than a drama . . . diluting the human consequences such actions have on the targeted airline company and its employees. . . . Sheen comes off as a pawn in Douglas's game and as the easily duped sort doesn't elicit much sympathy since he is only remorseful once Douglas cheats on him and changes the rules of play."[3]

Indeed, a foreign reviewer, French saw the film as supporting ruthlessness: "Stone's j'accuse is confused at its very heart: is it the system itself or the abuse of the system that is wrong? Oliver Stone pretends to be a moralist, but at his best he's really a sort of Darwinist—what really interests him is the battle for survival."

Finally, Jeffrey Madrick saw the film as having little to do with the real problems and personalities of Wall Street: "What the movie leaves out is the banality of it all; the frequent ordinariness of these men's motives, and the pettiness of many of their faults. Gordon Gekko . . . betrays no aspirations towards social climbing, for example, an all-too-common but none-too-glamorous characteristic of those who have made it. He gives no hint of the personal insecurities that may be driving his passion for money. No takeover specialist I have known or met is as in control of his emotions as is Gekko. Some hide them reasonably well, but the effort always shows. And none parades a machismo and tough-as-nails cynicism with the pride and self-awareness of Gordon Gekko. Fear of failure is much more evident in these men than certainty of success.

"Mr. Gekko's now famous comment in praise of greed, a paraphrase of a speech Mr. Boesky made, was delivered with a self-assurance Mr. Boesky could never have mustered. . . . A good movie would have shown it for the bit of silliness it was, not a sign of a diabolical nature. . . .

What *Wall Street* so patently leaves out is that large middle ground of what can be called soft insider information. The hints over the telephone from banker to banker, and arbitrageur to arbitrageur that give an indication of the direction of a deal; the trail of trades that suggests how someone in the know was betting. . . . The banal of Wall Street went for the bucks. It was the ordinary course of events that produced illegalities and a host of bad business mergers . . . precisely what moved Wall Street history for a dozen years."[12]

At a screening of the film for real investment-banking "luminaries," Geraldine Fabrikant recorded a variety of responses, from "The film captured the mood of the trading rooms. They tried to capture something about the deal-oriented side of Wall Street and they succeeded" to "It was an accurate portrayal of a relatively small sliver of the Street. That odd .001 percentage is nuts" to "It laid bare the real motivations. People pretend they are doing something noble, raising capital to support America's businesses, but Wall Street is about making money" to "How can the image of Wall Street be hurt anymore?"[9]

Commenting on the film shortly after its release, Stone spoke of it as a project turned out relatively quickly for a number of reasons: "It appealed to me precisely because it is a lesser statement (than *Platoon* or *Salvador*). There is only so much you can say about yuppies. I know if I sat around doing a Hamlet number—should I give the world another film?—I would really drive myself crazy. I would rather turn something out fast, get it over with, give the gold crown to somebody else so I can get on with doing things that I really care about, which are ideas. I'm ready to take a fall. I'm not expecting the same critical praise or the same box office that I got for *Platoon*. . . . I think I have always been identified with 'lower case' films that take people by surprise. It is strange suddenly to be in a front runner position with *Wall Street*. I like being a dark horse. Celebrity can hurt the creative process if you let it go to your head.

You can start weighing your image of yourself instead of somehow keeping your head low down to the ground like a bulldog, telling a good story, and not letting your ego stand in your way."[1]

Discussing the film's specifically political content at release, Stone added: "It has an analysis of class structure that you don't see in mainstream movies very much. . . . It's about greed, about people who are somewhat more selfish—super rich people, really. I think that, at best, the film is in the *Network* genre."[6] Asked about his own point of view in the film, Stone commented: "McDonald's is good for the world, that's my opinion. . . . Nationalism and patriotism are the two most evil forces . . . and cause more wars and more death and more destruction to the soul and to human life. . . . The best way to [prevent war, to live in peace] is to bring prosperity to as many people across the world as you can. And when you spread McDonald's all over the world, food becomes cheaper and more available to more people. . . . The Pax Americana, to me, is the dollar sign. It works. It may not be attractive. It's not pretty to see American businessmen running all around the world in plaid trousers, drinking whiskey. But what they're doing makes sense."[13]

Though I prefer to have Stone have the final say on each of his films, his notion of U.S. business as a benevolent Pax Americana is hardly accurate. As *USA Today* for June 27, 1994, notes, the United States of America is the leading weapons-trafficking nation, in 1993 selling more than $36 billion worth of military equipment, more than three-quarters to undemocratic governments. Of forty-eight ethnic conflicts that were under way around the world in mid-1993, thirty-nine involved forces that had received U.S. weaponry. Such weapons were used against U.S. servicemen by Panama, Iraq, and Somalia.

Wall Street was a popular and critical success, and Michael Douglas got the 1987 Best Actor of the Year Award.

6

Talk Radio

IT WAS IN 1984 that an artist in Oregon first approached Eric Bogosian with the idea of the two doing a performance together based on talk radio. The incident led to his New York stage hit of the same name, much of its detail drawn from Stephen Singular's *Talked to Death: The Life and Murder of Alan Berg*, a real Denver talk-show host assassinated by a neo-Nazi hit squad on June 18, 1984. The main character was also strongly influenced by Howard Stern and Morton Downey, Jr.

Originally, Oliver Stone was brought in to supervise how *Talk Radio*, the play script, was turned into a movie.[1] Without a director chosen for the project, producer Ed Pressman asked Stone, a long-time collaborator, to monitor Bogosian's screenwriting efforts. At their first meeting Stone said simply: "Get to work. It's your movie."

The play centered on a call-in talk-show radio host, a "shock jock," on a particular crisis evening in his life—the possible national syndication of his program. In an interview, Bogosian said of his creation: "Barry really does care. If he didn't, he wouldn't have become a star. But he has put this genuine concern on the auction block and made it a product. And as he sells it again and again, it just becomes rote, the yelling and screaming just become an act. He's dealing in a currency that has become debased. But the audience demands it and keeps wanting more, they want blood."

Bogosian, working with Stone, agreed that plays and films had basically different dynamics. Bogosian: "A film should tell a story and has greater means to do so. A play can rely on the physical presence of actors where a film can't; on the other hand, a film can get so close as to seem inside a character."

Bogosian knew he wanted to preserve his character and crisis.

Telling the story and showing his emotions were left open—for example, there could be more characters, and the monologues about Barry's outside life could become visualized scenes.

Bogosian worked on the screenplay for several months under Stone's supervision, after which Stone decided to direct the film. Together they "punched up" Bogosian's second draft, Stone taking the script off for a week of work. The changes were then discussed. The two interviewed people from Alan Berg's life, including his widow, and hired his producer as technical advisor.

The two collaborators realized that they had complementary concerns and skills in developing the script. "I was aching to get Champlain as a character across," Bogosian said. "Oliver thought it was important to talk about the way this character fit into the social concerns he has. . . . Oliver is terrific in his sense of the story arc of the film. On the other hand, I am fairly rigorous about language and I have a good solid grounding in dialogue. I was the detail man and he was the big shape man. The area in between we would discuss at length."

Stone agreed: "I always saw it as Eric's raw vision. I helped mold it, and shape it, combining it with the new [Singular book] material."

Changes from play to film included a new section on the protagonist's marriage and the wife character, and a long flashback showing his start as a salesman and radio-show guest, the change to host, and its effects on his life. New character callers were also added, both Bogosian creations and transformed real people from the career of Alan Berg, including a Nazi and a serial rapist. The sequence in which Berg is booed at an athletic event is based on a real Berg experience, but his actual assassination was the result of an elaborate plot—not as appears in the film, a disturbed individual's impulsive act, recalling the death of John Lennon. Bogosian commented: "My feeling is that we know someone will come after Champlain, but we don't know who. The only certain thing is that sooner or later the fringe element will come after someone who works the way Champlain does."

Talk Radio was made by the same team that worked on *Wall Street*, producer Edward R. Pressman and coproducer A. Kitman Ho, Pressman purchasing the rights, Cineplex Odeon joining the project later, the film being made for $3.5 million. From the first, Pressman was sure Bogosian should have the Barry Champlain role, stating: "My commitment to Eric as a writer and actor was the basis of my first impulse . . . part of my commitment to the project was the commitment to have Eric play the role." In fact at least one media professional felt Bogosian had exactly what it takes to be an actual radio personality: quick on his feet mentally and spontaneous and outrageous, as well as possession of an amazing classic radio voice—deep and brassy, under very good control, as in his imitations of people. The cast also included Ellen Greene, John McGinley, Alec Baldwin, Leslie Hope, Michael Wincott, and John Pankow

The screenplay was finished in less than three months, whereupon Stone began shooting at once. (Casting had been carried out in New York and Los Angeles.) The director had already been locked into a fall start date for his film version of Ron Kovic's *Born on the Fourth of July*. Supposedly, there was just enough time to make *Talk Radio*—if nothing went wrong. Shooting, to be done entirely in Dallas, began in April 1988.

A production designer, Bruno Rubeo (*Platoon*'s set designer) had turned a local warehouse into a fully equipped radio station. Bill Abbott, a fourteen-year radio professional, had gone over the script line by line for technical errors—how specialists did their jobs, talked to each other, handled crises, etc.

To keep *Talk Radio* from becoming too static, it was decided, antirealistically, to have the Champlain character use a headset that allowed him to stand up and walk around while broadcasting. The "sound," or special ambiance, of the fictional KGAB—IDs, commercials, promos, newscasts—were all created using familiar Dallas radio voices, and a Dallas sound production house for the musical logos. Some of the commercials were comical, but all "wallpaper" for the drama was intended by Stone as real items keyed to current concerns.

Shooting involved realizing complex shots using advanced equipment. An amazing sequence had Bogosian strapped to a camera dolly as he delivers the climactic tirade, clinging to the moving device so the background spins slowly behind him, growing gradually darker, while he remains stationary (the "lazy susan shot").

Bogosian, in nearly every scene of the four-week shooting schedule, recalls: "I just remember a blur of very long days, and being tired, very tired, too tired on Sunday to even get out of bed. . . . For being an actor playing a strong role, you can't do better than Oliver. I looked at his record, I saw what he'd done with other actors, and told myself, I'm going to do whatever he tells me. The

22. *Talk Radio*. Eric Bogosian as Barry Champlain: "You better have something to say. I know I do—" *(Copyright 1988 Cineplex Odeon Films, Inc. Courtesy Museum of Modern Art Film Stills Archive.)*

23. *Talk Radio*. Leslie Hope as Laura, Eric Bogosian as Barry Champlain: "We work together, we sleep together, that's the deal." *(Copyright 1988 Cineplex Odeon Films, Inc. Courtesy Museum of Modern Art Film Stills Archive.)*

main thing I remember about his style of working is his coming to me at the beginning and saying don't ask me how you did after a take. If I don't say anything, it means you were good."

But at one point, Stone took Bogosian aside and whispered: "I've been looking at the rushes and uh, the film's just not working, it's not coming together." Bogosian's fatigue was replaced by fear, and nothing could stop him: "Stone may not believe in this film, but I do!" Months later, he realized he'd been a victim of Stone's "psychology."

Night scenes of long shots of a great modern city, Dallas, its office and apartment towers enormous abstract grids of lights, reaching skyward. A smooth announcer's voice gives the weather, introduces "Night Talk" with Barry Champlain.

Champlain is a slender thirtyish man with a long intense face, great eyes, tight mouth, a sarcastic yet somehow vulnerable manner. He works in a shadowy modern radio studio, isolated, glass walled off from his bearded engineer and taller young woman producer.

Champlain: "The worst news is three out of four people in this country say they'd rather watch TV than have sex with their spouse. The second worse news is some kids needed money for crack, so they stuck a knife in an eighty-year-old grandmother's throat. . . . A country where culture means pornography, ethics means payoffs, integrity means lying . . . this country is in deep trouble, people, this country is rotten to the core. . . . Tell me what to do about the mess this country's in!"

His callers: a transvestite saving money for an operation (cut off); a man claiming U.S. problems are due to third-world exploitation (bleeding heart liberal, cut off); a young woman, Debbie, who does nothing (you just want someone to take care of you, cut off). We see how Barry can choose which caller to speak to. Through the studio window, his station manager and another executive type observe him, faces opaque.

Callers: the government shouldn't give away needles (the drug program's a joke, legalize drugs, tobacco's the biggest killer, gangsters and politicians are the winners).

The studio manager introduces Chuck Deitz, vice president, Metro Wave, Chicago. They want his show for national distribution—we're talking Larry King!

Barry tells his audience: "They asked me if I wanted to soften my touch, go easier. I told them take it or leave it. Monday, we begin national broadcasting. You better have something to say, I know I do."

Caller: How come you're always talking about drugs, muggers, homos, Jews, are you really Jewish, who're the people behind the show, who pays the bills? Champlain says he visited a Nazi concentration camp, picked up a tiny star, holds it to give him courage (he holds only a coffee cup), to face cowardly spineless gutless people who make him puke.

Caller: Nineteen-year-old Kent, a druggy voice telling how he and his girl party, take drugs, drink—now she won't wake up! (Barry wants to call a doctor, Kent hangs up. He's a hoax!) Angrily, to his engineer and producer: "Give me some stuff I can work with!"

Barry stalks into the manager's office to attack the exec: "I can't work with him breathing down my neck. I want him out of here now, I feel like I'm auditioning for my own job!" His manager won't apologize for getting him a national radio slot—he's good and he'll blow them away everywhere.

Outside, the engineer tells the producer: "You get used to it or you leave. That's what his wife did. So did two producers before you."

A sweet disabled caller babbles clichés (Barry matches them, then—gotta run—I know that you can't!); a dignified black defends the Jews (Barry mocks him—I like you blacks, I think everyone should own one!); Debbie the do-nothing calls in despair (Barry cheers her up); racist Chet claims to have mailed him a bomb (Barry opens it—a dead rat [what you look like!]); a tearful Debbie calls, scared of everything—her disposal grinding her hand, bad air. . . . Show over, Barry introduces a psychologist radio host. His theme, "Bad to the Bone," commences.

Barry and the woman producer at a Dallas auditorium basketball game; "When I talk to you as a producer, you treat me like your girlfriend; when I talk to you like a girlfriend, you treat me as your wife."

"We work together. We sleep together. That's the deal."

An autograph seeker insults him. He's introduced to the crowd but is booed by the mass of people. He waves his arms: "They really love me."

In his apartment, his sleep-in producer takes a call. He's got a meeting with the Metro Wave man, he wants ground rules.

"I do *my* show or I don't do a show!"

He picks up his ex-wife, whom he desperately asked to come to talk about it. Ex: "I spent so much time taking care of you, Lou takes care of me. You've got to start loving yourself."

In a flashback, young Barry works in an upscale men's shop, a slick salesperson. Introduced to an older man with a rich announcer's voice, he's soon a guest on "Talk of the Town": "It's time to confess—Jeff Fisher and I are lovers, we're holding hands right now."

A caller thinks they're nigger lovers! Barry: "Do you know how much white Americans spend on suntan lotion—because they want to feel black."

Jeff Fisher angrily tells him: when I cut you, stop talking! But his boss calls up, wants to meet Barry.

Barry soon has his own show. He hustles his wife into the men's room, she could be his producer. "Fuck our marriage!" They make up, but when she comes home from a trip, there are naked girls and a party in their home. She walks out.

In the present, at the studio, the national feed is delayed. Barry at once tells his audience: "Just business as usual . . . this show is about saying what's got to be said."

Callers: the holocaust didn't happen, Zionists use it and guilt to extract U.S. tax dollars (Barry names a dozen social fears: "It's my gripe theory of history—always blame someone else!); an old woman has nothing to say (what about lesbian priests? masturbation? Barry hangs up); Kent, the druggy youth, wants to be on the air (Barry agrees, his staff disapproving).

Barry's manager: "There's too much riding on what's happening tonight. . . . If they think you're undependable . . . don't blow the deal. It's a job, that's all it is. It's a job you didn't know how to do. You hang up on people, that's your job. You're good at it. But you work for me, I'm your boss. You fuck up the deal, and you go back to selling double-knit suits. . . . I'm glad you take it all so seriously, but you've got to know when to stop."

Callers: a cabdriver says young Kent needs to be hit (Barry says the way you hit your little girls, your brother's a pimp, your wife's a hooker); a listener calls him a jerk-off loser (cut off); a confused lady wants new "Lucy" programs (no one can be that stupid!); a three-time rapist chillingly says he's compelled again (Barry gives his word to get help; a tracer fails).

Kent, a druggy, foolishly smiling aging teen with long blond hair, arrives.

Barry: "We've brought Kent on board to get an inside view of the future of America. Kent is the classic American youth; energetic and resourceful . . . spoiled, perverse, and disturbed. . . . Are you on drugs now or is this your natural moronic self?"

Kent gives a rocker howl to his friends. Kent isn't political or nothing, he likes Bruce Springsteen, he's from New Jersey, he's got that foxy babe. Kent: "You're a fancy star . . . got that foxy babe (nod to producer). If you've got some cash and you're cool, you get yourself a model. . . . Revolution's the important thing. . . . Saw a show about how people will have two-way televisions and then they won't be able to stop the revolution . . . Freedom's the important thing."

"Kent, you're an idiot. If you represent the future of this country, we're in sad shape."

Kent laughs, drools: "Barry, you're so funny . . . it's *your* show!"

Callers: A woman loves Barry and hearing him talk, doesn't know why (it's to feel superior to the other losers!); a young woman soothingly says he's an intelligent man hurting others, because he's so lonely and doesn't know how to love (no response).

His woman producer: "He's going down in flames."

The manager, opaque: "Let Barry do Barry's show."

Callers: A man repeats the day's news, adding I don't get it (Barry: How do you dial the phone wearing a straightjacket?).

Kent's response: "Buy a box of razor blades and slash your fucking wrists, pinhead!" He pulls out a clicking device, a flashing camera, and is dragged out.

Caller: a woman speaks of her ex-husband (it's Barry's ex): "I still love him, I want to take care of him, I want my old life back."

Barry tells a story, a dog with a bone sees his water reflection, barks, loses both bones. Women like her are never happy—your ex doesn't want you. . . . You're a sexually unsatisfied woman . . . go out and buy yourself a heavy-duty vibrator—we reap what we sow.

Caller: a bitter crone's voice tells him: "There will be a reckoning. . . . You are responsible. . . . The whips will strip your back bare. The Jews will hang high over the streets. . . . The day will come."

Barry now speaks in a rising curve of horror and self-destructive fury, as the studio spins and darkens: "I'm a hypocrite. . . . I ask for sincerity and I lie. I denounce the system and I embrace it. I want money and power and prestige. I want ratings and success and I don't give a damn about you or the world. Who the hell are you anyway? The audience—you're on me . . . because you can't stand facing what you are and what you've made. . . . Yes, the world is a terrible place. . . . Everybody's screwed up, and you like it that way! You're fascinated by the gory details, you're mesmerized by your own fear. . . . That's where I come in, isn't it? I'm here to lead you by the hand through the dark forest of your own hatred and anger and humiliation. . . . You fear your own lives have become your entertainment. . . . Marvelous technology is at our disposal, and instead of reaching up to new heights, we're going to see how far down we can go. . . . I despise each and every one of you. . . . You've got nothing. No brain, no power, no hope, no god. All you believe in is me. . . . I'm not afraid. I come here every night. . . . Go away! Stop talking! A bunch of obscene phone callers! The hell with you. Pearls before swine!"

Callers: You're just jokin', I've been listenin' for years—(cut off): About loneliness, I'm an electrical engineer—(cut off). Why call homos normal?—(cut off); I'm at home . . . come over . . . I'll wait (dead air . . . pure silence . . . through the show's last thirty-five seconds.

"I guess we're stuck with each other. . . . This is Barry Champlain."

The "Bad to the Bone" theme comes up.

The producer and the network vice president meet him. The network man says "very good," in a solemn tone. His manager tells him: He pulled it off! He'll come in tomorrow, he always does.

His ex-wife left. Barry says her best line was: "Barry Champlain is a nice place to visit, but I wouldn't want to live there."

He asks the engineer, if it's not that important, why's he doing it?: "If you don't like the heights, Barry, don't climb the mountains."

He walks the woman producer out, saying he's too old for her. His greatest fear: "Being boring. . . . I'm afraid the audience will get up and leave."

"I don't think you're the bad guy you think you are."

"Oh yes I am."

Champlain walks to his own car. A fat middle-aged man with bad teeth asks for his autograph, shoots him several times. Collapsing, blood-splattered, he seems to white out, going angelic, or onto the info highway, the camera rising up the big transmission antenna. More night shots of lit apartment towers, and a call-in farewell: "My life is different. I'm kinda blessed. . . . I miss him . . . like a fudge sundae with pecans. . . . He had problems with his wife. . . . Why would anyone do such a thing?. . . I was in love with his voice. . . . He was in love with his own voice . . . like a little dick, flapping in the breeze, now they cut it off, he's dead."

Once more, Stone has gone beyond himself to create a still more isolated protagonist—unlike *Wall Street*'s hero, alone and unbelieving at the economic focus of a money-driven society, Barry Champlain is actually cut off from all his intimate myriads of fans by his special unique role in the communications process—an individual for whom all such relationships must become "entertaining" antagonism. People, people, everywhere, but never a friendly voice. He has no relatives, turns on his ex-wife, cuts himself off from the people at work. Feelings and ideas become only tools and tricks to use on callers to keep the show going—climaxing, as all of Stone's heroes, in a final hysterical self-destructive, self-justifying monologue. In addition, he creates lies and fantasies (e.g., the concentration camp star) to sustain himself. Like Stone's other artistic character in *Seizure*, if only an entertainer, he suggests a nightmare view of the creative individual as a sort of Dr. Frankenstein, twisting and tormenting self, aides, and audience to produce his creations. "Why can't they give me something to work with?" he cries to the call-forwarder at one point. His "creation"—Kent—is a sort of Champlain doppelgänger—selfish, sly, silly, irresponsible, mindless, and vicious by turns, without his flashes of compassion and empathy.

Talk Radio's view of society is a sophisticated if bleak vision—we see endless skyscrapers and apartment towers, lit but symbolically lifeless except for their telephone voices, and see only the talk-show team—society is a great technologized void, real feelings and personalities erased and isolated into faint abstractions, as well as made secret, shameful, and cruel. What a hypocritical farce is progress! And what's available to deal with this desperate situation? Only a half-contemptuous, half-terrified isolate straightjacketed by economics. The drama indeed suggests our mental health crisis, where mild cases buy dulling therapy (the film?), while the suicidal and maniacal get barely qualified hot-line volunteers. The protagonist's superiors see it all as only "a job" of course, from which is to be extracted the maximum profit.

Several critics received the film with great enthusiasm. David Denby in particular, saw its strengths and limitations: "*Talk Radio*'s

exciting and nerve jangling—without doubt one of the most complete expressions of paranoia ever put on film. . . . 'This country is in deep trouble,' he begins, as if he had something urgent to
say. But the material of his show is mostly lurid barroom/tabloid
rage, a farrago of jeering racial and sexual attitudes. . . . He's very
smart, but he doesn't think, he *talks*, so what comes out may be
mawkish blather. . . . His voice, taunting, comforting, selling, ad-
vising, is all that he's got, and he sacrifices everything to it, saying
nasty things because he's afraid to bore the audience with common
sense. . . . Emotional extremes are his medium.

"Stone is a master of unease and loathing. *Talk Radio* is a scary
ride on a roller coaster that goes faster and faster until it finally flies
off the rails. Yet. . . the movie feels irresolute. . . . What is Bogosian's and Stone's take on Barry? Do they mean him to be merely
a show-business creep and megalomaniac? Or do they think he's
serving willy-nilly some higher function—drawing the poison out
of the body politic and taking it into himself, sacrificing himself to
the manias, the collective sick psyche of America? At times he seems
to be both things—a creep who is also a suffering American
saint. . . . Bogosian and Stone are a dreadnaught combination: they
produce enough anxiety to throw a ten-ton tank into a depression.
And *Talk Radio*, though exciting, isn't really exhilarating. It's too
overwrought to give much pleasure."[5]

J. Hoberman entertainingly evaluates the film as psychopathology.
"It has terrific velocity—watching talk radio is like being harassed
by a brilliant street crazy with a dervish twitch. . . . Bogosian's one-
man shows are closer to psychodrama than to stand-up. . . . He
gives the impression of being inhabited by demons; his ultrasuede
baritone belies the rude monsters within . . . conjuring fawning
spirits from the great smile button void playing devil's advocate. . . .
Champlain flits from one persona to another, juggling hate mail,
death threats, and packaged bombs all the while. . . . He's meant
to be a curdled creature of the Sixties—a mediawise posthippie,
telling it like it is for fun and money, perhaps Stone's rancid self-
parody. . . . The filmmakers have set him up as a sort of Antichrist—
or at least another Lenny Bruce. 'Your fear, your own lives become
your entertainment,' he howls into the great out there. 'I tell you
what you are, I have no choice, you frighten me.'"[7]

An interesting variation on this view is offered by Jonathan Rosen-
baum, noting Champlain is based on several real broadcasters. "He

is not so much a character as a brilliant theatrical conceit, and the movie's biggest mistake—damaging but not fatal—is to try to make sense of him as a character (i.e., the flashback of his past). . . . An unfortunate bias of conventional American movie taste is its preference for bogus psychology and perfunctory motivation over no psychology or motivation at all. . . . Yet the strength of certain fictional worlds rests in their refusal to offer the bromides of easy explanations. The tortured letters included in Nathanael West's novel *Miss Lonelyhearts* and the blighted lives in his later novel *The Day of the Locust* are terrifying precisely because they suggest that certain human miseries have no solution or explanation. A similar terror is conveyed in some of the crank calls of *Talk Radio*—as well as in Champlain's brutal responses. . . . The film's truly disquieting message . . . is the seductiveness of Champlain's sadomasochistic style of radio, which the film asks us both to experience directly and worry about from a certain reflective distance."[10]

A subtle analysis of that sadomasochism is made by Owen Gleiberman "[Champlain] holds court like a demonic pied piper, leading his listeners and himself through a swamp of invective . . . yet the key to his appeal is his ability to get on the wavelength of whoever's calling him . . . His technique is to involve these people—to share their fantasies—and then to outtalk them. . . . Barry doesn't play fair, and that's part of his appeal. He cuts people off at will, not just to keep the show moving, but as a ritual demonstration of power. He's like a lightning rod for the listener's obsessions, and the whole movie revels in the fake but seductive intimacy that talk radio encourages. . . .

[Bogosian] is a dazzlingly accurate satirical mimic . . . yet he's driven to showcasing the most reprehensible side of people. . . . The film is a bit of a stunt, really, but then so is the new trash media culture, which revels in an outrage that's part show biz, part pure American innocence: the parading of everyday madness. . . . In essence *Talk Radio* is the movie *Scrooged* wanted to be; it's about how a hippie turns into a young successful curmudgeon. . . . Barry is destroyed by forces beyond his control, but they might as well be of his own devising (in spirit, they are). The whole premise of abusive talk radio (and TV) is based on a kind of apocalyptic self-loathing— both the host's and the culture's. . . . Barry's big monologue . . . is a hate letter . . . to a world where we can instantly be linked up to another's ugliest sides."[6]

Robin Wood, the leftist film theorist, proposes that considered in this way *Talk Radio* was up to then Stone's most completely successful film: "We can credit Stone with firmer personal integrity and higher ambitions than are evidenced by Barry Champlain. . . . But, that allowance made, Stone has found here the perfect objective correlative for his own position, his own quandary. Champlain's rage, toppling over into hysteria, parallels the tone of much of Stone's work and identifies one of its sources, the frustration of grasping that no one really listens, no one understands, no one *wants* to understand. The sense of addressing a people kept in a state of mystification so complete, by a system so powerful and persuasive that no formal brainwashing could improve upon it."[12] Wood's own, presumably unclouded view, is not detailed.

Finally, *Variety*'s industry-wise reviewer saw *Talk Radio*'s primary appeal to "serious" upscale filmgoers interested in Stone and the issues in question, but the film could break out to wider audiences."[3]

A number of major media critics were impatient with *Talk Radio*. The *New York Times*'s Vincent Canby gave an unsympathetic if precise critique, starting by comparing play and film unfavorably: "Taking *Talk Radio*'s compact piece of Americana, less a drama than a small slice of bizarre life, [the two writers] have made a mess of a movie that comes complete with a conventional beginning, middle and end, and long spongy flashbacks. . . . Mr. Bogosian repeats his stage performance as Barry with a lot of furious energy but no real payoff. He keeps being interrupted by the dopey demands of the dreadful screenplay. . . . [Tension] is reduced to zero by the introduction of a wife and by a series of flashbacks written to explain how he got his start and what happened to his marriage. . . . [It's] a nearly perfect example of how not to make a movie from a play [fancied up] with empty narrative asides [and] idiotic camera work. A lot of Mr. Bogosian's sharper lines remain in the script, but its nihilism now seems unearned. It is also at odds with the orderliness of the new narrative."[2]

Time's Richard Corliss likewise wouldn't go along with the film. "The play had a point: In America agony is just show biz, life and death issues are matters of style, even the most desperate night callers seek sleazy entertainment, not salvation. But Stone wants more. . . . He must invent tragedy to suit his spleen. He moves Barry from Cleveland to Dallas and appropriates the murder of Denver radio host Alan Berg. . . . Stone's camera closes in on Bogosian's face as if it were the cratered moonscape of the American mind, and the actor starts shouting into his megaphone mike. Finally, these two have become like Barry's listeners, shrill and unconvincing, weaving their own conspiracy theories in the bleat of the night. This is bag lady cinema."[4]

Stanley Kauffmann faults the film's concerns: *Talk Radio* has a theme deeper than its makers have grasped. . . . A hunger—the hunger in the callers' lives for someone to like or loathe who is actually *famous*, who is actually *on the radio*. . . . This hunger courses upwards to make the person in the studio feel he is the divine dispenser. . . . Stone has a liking for large subjects. . . . Here he has missed the point. The real subject is the talk-show host himself, not his topics or adversaries."[8]

A leftist critic, Richard Porton complained: "Bogosian's Champlain . . . has been viewed as a latter-day Lenny Bruce. While Bruce's high calculated form of a previously taboo form of scatological cant has come to be widely viewed as a fundamentally moral assault on American hypocrisy, Champlain's supremely cynical assault on his listeners' sensibilities is merely an essential component of a corporate scramble for ratings and money. . . . Champlain's ostensible frankness is simply a matter of shtick, a nihilistic willingness to say anything to shock. Bruce's abrasive nonconformism has been transformed into a slick conformism that retains only the surface venom.

"[Both film and play] present Champlain as an ex-hippie who has succumbed to cynicism . . . illustrated in both versions with a confrontation between Champlain and a stoned, barely coherent teenager named Kent [which] reveals the film's didactic epicenter. . . . Kent's obsession with heavy metal music, empty slogans, and most of all, Barry Champlain, is put forward as an indictment of a generation looking for an angry media fix, with the implicit proviso that *Talk Radio* itself is somehow exempt from popular culture's propensity to transform politics into "one big rock video." . . . The detached, almost clinical aesthetic of performance art clashes incongruously with the film's docudrama liberalism, and the result is an intermittently intriguing, if finally unsatisfying, film."[9] Porton's review also hints how the film anticipates the current yuppies-versus-Generation X conflict.

A scholarly discussion of talk media by Professor Frank Tomasulo also leads toward a negative evaluation. As Tomasulo points out:

"Implicit in the talk show format is the notion that problems can be solved merely by talking about them, a sort of national 'talking cure.'. . . [In fact] the crisis of capitalism is constructed as a near permanent one, with 'talking about it' as the only solution. This fosters indifference and a retreat into self, a 'crisis of narcissism' supervenes. . . . As Eric Sevareid has observed, 'The biggest business in America is not steel, automobiles or television. It is the manufacture, refinement and distribution of anxiety.' In a sense, the Barry Champlain character realizes this idea, although of course it's never explicitly acknowledged."[11]

To revise Tomasulo slightly: "The rephrasing of anxiety-ridden issues merely extends the pressures and contradictions of the administered world of advanced capitalism into the private sphere. As common consensual values decline, [the Barry Champlain character] searches for causes and finds them, not in the social world of alienated labor, monopoly capitalism, and corrupt political institutions, but rather in the breakdown of parental authority, in the family, 'failure to communicate,' and other personal values."

Otherwise put, despite all their titillating insults and innuendo, the only real message of Rush Limbaugh, Howard Stern, and Barry Champlain (and for that matter Phil Donahue, Oprah Winfrey, et al.) is: the world is crazy! Blame yourself for your troubles! Be glad you have a job at all! Laugh all the way to the bank because you're in this all alone forever, Mr. Consumer! In fact to make a shock comedy about this situation would of course be an interesting challenge, but would result in a very different film than *Talk Radio*.

Stone commented on his film: "I think Eric Bogosian really deepened as an actor on this film. He had this problem of being a writer acting out his own material. He had basically become a writer in order to act, and over the years, he had encrusted in his acting. For me it was interesting to watch him seem to loosen up as an actor as he ceased to be sole writer."

7

BORN ON THE
FOURTH OF JULY

SHORTLY AFTER THE FIRST favorable reviews of Ron Kovic's
book *Born on the Fourth of July* appeared, ICM agent Lynn Nesbitt
contacted the Vietnam vet, telling him that Al Pacino and Marty
Bregman were interested. The first screenplay effort didn't work,
and Oliver Stone was brought in for a rewrite.

Stone recalls that first meeting. "It was as if we had been linked
by destiny. Chosen as God's instruments to get a message, a memory
out about the war."[13]

Elsewhere the writer-director commented: "I never talked to another Vietnam vet until I met Ron in 1978. It was very important
to me to be able to speak with him about being there, about being
back. I didn't find hostility when I came home. What startled me
was people's totally implacable, merciless indifference. . . . Ron and
me, we're like brothers. . . . For ten years now I've grown to love
him as much as any man. . . . In a way, I merged Ron's story with
that of other veterans, including me. Ron had the radicalization
experience of the veteran's hospital, and I didn't. It took a lot longer
for me to turn against the war than Ron—and on that, the movie is
a lot closer to my experience."[4]

Later in 1978, producer Martin Bergman put a deal together to
make Stone's screenplay, with director Dan Petrie, and Al Pacino
set to star as Kovic. Four days before filming the project was can-
celed. The West German investors never came through with the
eight million, and Al Pacino went on to . . . *And Justice for All.*
Stone felt that "[Hollywood] lumped *Born on the Fourth of July*
together with *Coming Home*—you know, 'another wheelchair story.'

Because *Coming Home* didn't make a lot of money, we were dead in the water. . . . Al [Pacino] got cold feet. It was a heartbreak. I just wanted to hide."[16]

Hard times followed. Stone and Kovic would frequently run into each other and have recriminations, including one scene in a West Los Angeles parking lot where Kovic punched Stone over something neither can remember. Stone went off to Poland to drink himself into oblivion.

Stone continued to push his script over the next ten years, but despite his Academy Award for writing *Scarface* it was turned down everywhere. "People like Ned Tanen at Universal said, 'We don't care if it's Al Pacino or fucking Marlon Brando—it's not the kind of movie that can make a dime.' They will never tell you why, but you know they don't want to make it."

Finally, with the success of *Platoon*, Stone was a bankable director. Tom Cruise and Stone had the same agent, Paula Wagner, and Cruise contacted him about doing a movie together. She showed Cruise the script, and after ten pages, Cruise wanted to do it. Stone and Cruise would work for scale plus a percentage. The film was budgeted at $17.8 million.

Stone commented, "Tom has the classical facial structure of an athlete, a baseball player. He's a kid off a Wheaties box. I wanted to yank the kid off that box and mess with his image—take him to the dark side."[5]

Through filming, Stone focused on Cruise: "I put a lot of pressure on Tom, maybe too much. I wanted him to read more, visit more hospitals. He went to boot camp twice, and I didn't want his foxhole done by his cousin. At one point I talked him into injecting himself with a solution that would have totally paralyzed him for two days. Then the insurance company—the killer of all experience—said no because there was a slight chance that Tom would have ended up permanently paralyzed. But the point was, he was willing to do it."

Cruise spent hours questioning Kovic, the two men going shopping in matching wheelchairs. A highly unusual aspect of the filming was the presence of Kovic on the set, and his active participation.[14] When the terrible drunken fight scene between Kovic and his mother was filmed, the set was cleared except for Stone, Cruise, and Kovic, whereupon Cruise asked Kovic to relive it, reading his mother's lines. Kovic commented that he became very emotional, loud, and impassioned: "I gave every single thing I had, as if it were happening again."

A complete copy of Kovic's childhood home was constructed inside a Dallas warehouse, as were the shameful U.S. Veterans Administration Bronx hospital facilities. Stone had his extras, including children, shipped in from Kovic's real hometown. The Vietnam and Mexican scenes were shot in the Philippines to save money.

Cruise pushed himself, commenting, "Sometimes Oliver would say, 'Okay, we've got to move on to the next setup,' and I'd say, 'Wait, let's do one more take,' or I'd say to Oliver, 'Look man, I'm lost. You've got to help me. What would you or Ron be thinking in a situation like this?'

"I remember the scene in the coffee shop, where this girl was going on about Kent State, was pretty one-sided. I kept thinking that even though Oliver and Ron knew the war was wrong, they felt a certain anger that the protesters couldn't separate the warrior from the war, couldn't forgive a man for loving his country. How the whole country was going: 'Yeah, you're stupid, you killed babies.' People had *no* understanding. So Oliver wrote a line that changed the whole meaning of it.

"[Shooting in the Philippines] we went almost overnight from the scene where I get shot to my being in the Mexican whorehouse, crippled. It was like two different characters. Up to then, I'd had Ron there to talk with. I was just exhausted at that point . . . and one day, I was doing a scene that wasn't working. Sometimes I could play Ron so well that I didn't have to work on it anymore, so I'd start to second-guess it, *think* it, which was a problem. And that's what was happening with that scene. Oliver said, 'Look, Tom, forget everything and just *do* it. Show up now.'"[16]

At the end of filming, Kovic gave Cruise his Bronze Star combat medal. "We were at the Forum in L.A., shooting the final scenes," Kovic recalled. "Tom was in his dressing room being made up as me. He got up from his chair and hugged me. The film was ending and I wanted him to have something of me that I had been struggling to define and understand for twenty-one years. Just when he was getting back into his wheelchair, I gave him the medal. He said thank you and hugged me tightly and wouldn't let go. Then he went out to do the final scene of the movie. I finally found the person who deserved the medal."

The film was shot over sixty-five exhausting twelve-hour days. The next step was editing.[2]

Most directors have their film editors prepare a "rough cut," the dropped sequences known as outtakes. Instead, Stone had his editors choose "selects," camera takes for further consideration, in their sequential order in the script. For one scene, fourteen thousand feet of film might be printed, then five thousand feet of "selects" chosen, including two to five takes of that scene. When finished, this "first pass" of the film took eleven hours to screen. The directors and editors then discussed the material—camera setup, performances, reasons for preferences, directions the film would take. Typically, the director was more attached to his material, the editors fresh and detached about it.

As editing proceeded, this situation reversed. Stone admits he finds editing boring, and spent little time with it. Stone: "I like to come in as a blank slate. I purposely try to forget what we've talked out the day before. When you're doing production, there's always that sense of aggressiveness, of establishing a beachhead, like the marines. When you're editing, the question is how you get out of this thing gracefully. . . . Editing is the other side of the coin from writing. It's a chance to rewrite."

Stone and the editors chose the best of the takes, the others stored as "alternates" that could be accessed if Stone wanted to try them. An editor commented: "Oliver is very loose, very open to suggestions. Sometimes he knows what he wants, sometimes he doesn't."

Stone started by dropping sequences in the growing-up section: three wrestling scenes were reduced to one; a hint of Kovic hearing "angelic voices" was dropped, along with bulldozers wrecking the woods of his childhood.

Also dropped, a movie theater interlude in which young Ron is caught up in *The Sands of Iwo Jima* with John Wayne. Stone felt the recruiting marine officer Tom Berenger plays fulfilled the same dramatic function. In the end, the childhood section is cut down to a long credit sequence.

The very important scenes in which Kovic's platoon mistakenly destroys a village of women and children, thinking they're Vietcong, also was carefully edited. Stone told an editor he was unhappy with the first pass, second pass, and rough-cut edits: "Here's what's wrong with it. . . . Do something." Version one suffered from technical

24. *Born on the Fourth of July.* Tom Cruise as Ron Kovic, high school class-mates: "I don't see any commies in Massapequa—" *(Copyright 1989 Universal City Studios, Inc. Courtesy Museum of Modern Art Film Stills Archive.)*

25. *Born on the Fourth of July.* Tom Cruise as Ron Kovic: "The government is a bunch of corrupt thieves, rapists, and robbers!" *(Copyright 1989 Universal City Studios, Inc. Courtesy Museum of Modern Art Film Stills Archive.)*

mistakes and an excess of material, which made it tiring. Version two lacked emotional impact. The next version was done documentary style—swish pans, no reaction shots—as opposed to the traditional way, the marines getting hit, then immediately showing the attacking North Vietnamese Army. The new way has more suspense.

Stone also wanted to delay the death of Kovic's fellow soldier. An editor commented: "Oliver's original rationale was that these things really do happen too fast for you to think. But we're going to add more confusion to make it a little more hectic, chaotic. Sometimes I don't have a clear idea how to fix it; it's better to edit by accident. You switch the order of the shots and see what happens. In this case, it worked."

To sunshot images of a leafy woods; ten-year-olds with toy guns, spinning, confused, exultant, a boy's voice tells us: "It was a long time ago. Sometimes I can still hear their voices." He names his childhood friends as we see them playing war scouts.

A title: Massapequa, 1956.

Other boys leap from ambush: "You're dead and you know it!"

A high school band's version of "It's a Grand Old Flag." The July 4, 1957, parade in the Long Island, New York, town. Ten-year-old Ron Kovic watches from his father's shoulders, a big gentle aging man in glasses. Girls, floats, "Rock around the Clock," teens, clowns. Ron's nervous mom: "Was that a firecracker?" Veterans march past, then older vets in wheelchairs, another in a flannel shirt with a kind face but no arms.

A little girl runs up with a gift: "Happy Birthday, Ronny Kovic!" It's a New York Yankees cap. A cheerleader tosses her baton, we see a rippling U.S. flag, fireworks.

A Little League game. Ron gets a hit, runs home, parents cheering.

Ron's family watches Kennedy: "Let the word go forth. . . . We shall pay any price." Ron's mother tells him about a dream, Ron talking to a large crowd telling them important things. Kennedy: "Ask not what your country can do for you, ask what you can do for your country."

Ron struggles in gym class, the coach crying: "Climbing that rope is like life, you've got to suffer."

At home, his mom tells him: "Do your best! That's what matters to God." She finds *Playboy* in his room: "Filthy impure thoughts! Go to confession!"

Ron wrestles before a crowd, mother ecstatic, but he loses, and friends and family look betrayed.

Two marine recruiting officers address the high school kids, handsome and proud: "We want the best . . . we have never lost a war." Ron and his pals talk. "If we don't join up we'll miss Vietnam." "I want to do something with my life—a business BA." "Cuba's ninety miles away—the commies are moving in." "I don't see them in Massapequa—I'm looking out for number one."

Ron works for his dad in the supermarket. Shy, he goes up to teen Donna and friends, tells them he's joined the marines. She's going to Syracuse, he doesn't have time for the prom.

The prom: bored girls clinging to immature guys. Ron paces his room, his brother strumming "The Times They are A-changing." His father, concerned: "Thirteen thousand miles is a long way to fight a war . . . I hope they send you someplace safe."

But his mother adds fiercely, "Communism's got to be stopped. It's God's will you go!"

"I love my country, Dad!" Ron cries. "Ever since I've been a kid, I've wanted this. . . . I'll die there if I have to."

Ron prays for the answer. Crazy-faced, he runs through a rainstorm, to "Moon River," he dances with Donna, she smiling, his eyes closed, face agonized. The screen goes dark.

Burned orange images of soldiers. Explosions, birds, crackling radios.

Title: Near Cua Viet River, 1967.

Ron's a sergeant, platoon leader. A young Georgia kid enthuses to him about combat. Ron: "I've never seen a Georgia boy get hit yet."

Their lieutenant thinks he sees rifles. Over sand dunes they run toward the village, firing. Jerky images show women and children, horribly shot up, screaming—no guns: "We got beaucoup wounded!" "Motherfucker, we wasted them!"

In shock, the troopers run toward the dunes. Suddenly, there's shooting. Ron fires, and in slow motion, hits the leaping Georgia kid. He drops. Ron sees the medics working on him, chest a mass of torn-up tissue.

Ron tries to confess to an officer. "I don't want anyone coming to me with this shit! Carry on!"

A new patrol, through a broiling orange haze, a village before them. Heavy enemy fire! Kovic is hit in the foot, but keeps firing as the officer radios, a copter explodes.

With a terrible wet sound, Kovic is shot in the chest, goes down: "Corpsman, corpsman!"

A black soldier runs up, takes Kovic in a fireman's carry, world upside down.

A stunning sunset frames evac choppers, Kovic on a litter. A MASH unit: frantic orderlies, agonized cries, terrible wounds: "He's leaking like a sieve!" "I'm gonna jump-start you!" Casualty spasms to electroshock. A chaplain slides through the confusion, murmurs to Ron: "The docs are really busy. Try to stay alive. I've come to give you the last rites. I am the resurrection and the life."

Title: Bronx Veterans Hospital, 1965.

"My Girl" plays, a nurse enters, six black orderlies play cards, two men shoot up drugs in a closet. The ward is overcrowded, shabby, dirty. A rat appears. "Don't bother them and they won't bother you." A casualty feeds the rat. "That's what I'm doing!"

Kovic, wheelchaired, watches the enema room in action.

It's July 4. A TV shows protestors and cops in Chicago. Kovic tells them: "Love it or leave it, you bastards!"

Kovic talks with his doctors, one says: "Let me make one thing clear. The chances of you walking again are minimal. You will probably be in a wheelchair the rest of your life." He can't have children, and again, he'll never walk.

Defiant, Kovic works out furiously on the parallel bars.

An angry black orderly tells him: "Vietnam was a white man's war, a rich man's war."

At night, hookers come around, climb on the patients. Drugs come out. Kovic looks away.

Kovic, wearing elaborate braces and straps making his legs rigid, moves jerkily around on crutches: "It can be done, it can be done!" A radio plays: "This will be the day that I die!" Suddenly he falls, an orderly cuts away his trousers and is shocked.

Kovic lies in a circular framework bed. He seems to be in a wheelchair ward, getting up, walking out, into the light, smiling, ecstatic!

No, he's in the metal framework bed, covered with vomit, needs a bath. To the staffers: "I want to be treated like a human being! I want my leg! I fought for my country!"

A black orderly: "Vietnam don't mean anything to me or any of the others. You can take the Vietnam War and shove it up your ass!"

The pump on his leg dressing stops. A doctor: "It's the Vietnam War. The government just hasn't got the money to take care of you guys."

Kovic's face is frighted, he screams. The screen goes dark.

Title: Massapequa, 1969.

Their station wagon rolls into the Kovic driveway. His father helps with the wheelchair. Family and neighbors appear, expressions strained.

"Ronnie!" His mom, tormented. Ron and Dad go in: "It's really great to be back in my room!" The two embrace.

The pal that went to college has a hamburger place with bagel-shaped burgers. "My idea—saves about forty thousand dollars a year. Check out those chicks, I got them wearing those new mini-skirts. . . . I want you to come to work for me. You're a war hero. Not partner, you got to walk before you can run!" says the insensitive buddy.

Ron gets $1,700 a month.

"That's charity money! It's all BS, the government sold us a bill of goods and we bought it! You bought that communist bullshit lies! They were gonna take over the world? For what? BS lies."

Ron has dinner with his family: "No respect, nobody seems to care. I served my country, and I—"

His brother walks out. Ron starts raving: "You want to burn the flag? Love it or leave it. Where were they?"

His brother: "What did you get out of it? Look at you, man."

Title: Massapequa, July 4, 1969. Ron is in full-dress uniform, rides in the parade. But it's different: upraised fingers, shots, peaceniks, dubious-faced kids, marchers quarreling with the crowd. Ron has war flashbacks.

An American Legion man names the town's six Vietnam dead. Ron starts speaking: "We're gonna win that war, I have an unquench-able—" Somebody's baby cries, and Ron can't go on.

Agonized, he sees a man in marine khaki shirt, a schoolmate vet, "Let's get the hell out of here."

At home, the two talk, Ron relaxed for the first time. They don't have a friend left. The other, Timmy, has headaches. "Like I'm going crazy. . . . I do a lot of drugs."

"I failed Timmy, I killed someone, it's terrible, mistakes—. . . I'd give everything just to get my body back, to just be whole again, but I never will be."

Ron visits Donna at Syracuse. "I'm so sorry for what happened to you." But she's involved in the protests. Ron made a promise at the prom he'd love her forever. Abbie Hoffman and big black vets read off the schools closed, throw medals away, burn Nixon in effigy. The cops attack, club the kids, Ron dazed in his wheelchair in the center.

At a pool hall, strobes flashing as a rock band plays, Ron and Timmy drink. A tough World War II vet: "I was on Iwo. You served and you lost, you got to live with it." Drunk, Ron wheelchair-dances with a teen, flips over onto the floor.

Timmy takes him home. His mom: "We got a drunk for a son."

Inside, Ron rips down the cross: "I don't believe in Him. . . . I wish I were dead like Him. . . . They want to hide us, because everything they told us was a lie!"

His mother anxiously tells him he needs help. Ron: "You need help, with your god and your bullshit dreams about me. Fuck you! . . . We shot women and children! . . . They told us to go, thou shalt not kill. . . . Fucking communism won. . . . It's all for nothing. . . . There's no God . . . no country, just me in this wheelchair and this dead penis!"

"Don't say penis in this house!"

"Penis, penis, giant fucking erect penis. It's gone in some jungle over in Asia." Mother and son weep.

His father puts Ron to bed, hooking up his catheter. Maybe a trip down to Mexico is all you need. Ron: "I want to be a man again. Who's ever gonna love me?" He weeps.

Orange vistas, waves, beaches. Title: Villa Dolce, Mexico, 1970.

"Another limp dick!" Ron meets Charlie in the colony of disabled vets. Charlie: "Fuck the States!" He clutches at his Latina girlfriend, the vets chorus: "If you don't have it in the hips, buddy, you better have it in the lips." All wiggle tongue and lips.

In a whore bar, Ron goes with a good-looking girl. Upstairs she strips. She's beautiful: "We're gonna have a good time." He excites her, she throws her head around, cries out!

Ron buys her an expensive gift, but sees her just as affectionate with another. He tries to write the parents of the kid he shot.

On a taxi ride with Charlie, the two argue absurdly, like madmen, and are left in the road in their wheelchairs, cursing: Who was *really* in Vietnam, killed women and children? They end up sprawled in the dust and clay.

Ron: "Do you remember when things made sense, when there were things you could care about? Before we all got so lost. What're we gonna do?"

A bus lets Ron off in a U.S. farming town. A cab takes him to the grave of William Wilson, the infantryman. He studies the marker, gray, worn, and old.

The Wilson farm has yapping dogs, a stocky calm-voiced old father: "Any friend of Billy's is a friend of mine." Father, mother, widow, and child sit with Ron. Quietly: "We got a proud tradition in this town . . . and I reckon we're ready to do it again if we have to." The little boy plays with a toy gun as they speak.

Ron tells them how Wilson died: "The babies were killed by mistake. . . . I was the one that killed your son that night."

The father figure says: "What's done is done."

The widow says: "I can't forgive you, but maybe the Lord can."

"When Johnny Comes Marching Home" sounds, whistled, as Ron leaves, the camera panning to the sky. We see a rippling U.S. flag.

Now a great mass of protesting vets, some in wheelchairs, signs reading VETS AGAINST THE WAR, NOT ONE MORE DEAD, rolls up a ramp. It's the 1972 Republican Convention. On a TV monitor, Nixon: "I proudly again accept your nomination . . . four more years."

The vets roll in: "This war is a crime!"

Security men and officials try to stop them. Ron yells: "This war is a crime. You can't stop us from what we are here to say! This trickery is wrong. You tricked us into going thirteen thousand miles to fight a poor peasant people. I can't find the words to explain how this leadership sickens me! The government is a bunch of corrupt thieves, rapists, and robbers!"

Narrow cruel Republican faces in straw hats snarl at them.

The disabled vets battle the security men, are dragged out chanting: "Stop the war! Why are they gassing us? Because it is a lie. Because they have tricked a whole generation!" The security men try to block off the TV teams.

"We want them to hear the truth, you are killing our brothers in Vietnam!"

The security cops throw Kovic from his chair, try to handcuff him.

"Our steel is your Memorial Day on wheels! We are your Yankee Doodle come home!"

Nixon, on a TV monitor, smugly announces: "Let us give those who served their country the honor and respect they deserve!"

Dragged outside, more vets come to their rescue, battle the police and security teams in a nightmare counterpart of a night Vietnam firefight: choppers buzzing, shouts, shots, gas, and again a black saves Kovic in a fireman's carry. "It's a mess, they're attacking our people!"

Kovic: "We're gonna take the hall back! Fall out! Let's move!" They roll forward. The screen goes dark.

Title: Four years later, 1976, the Democratic National Convention.

Kovic, in tie and jacket, is being prepped: "You're the next speaker!"

A woman journalist tells him: "I love what you're doing." For a moment we hear his mother: "I had a dream that you were speaking to a large group of people, and that you were saying great things."

A voice is heard: "Our next speaker . . . a Viet vet who has something to say."

Ron rolls out. A newswoman: "Any plans for the future?"

"We'll see. It's been a long way for us, the vets, and just lately I've felt that I'm home, like maybe we're home."

Kovic rolls himself up a ramp, leaving us behind, into the amphitheater, meeting the lights and roar of the crowd. Once again we hear: "It's a Grand Old Flag," louder and prouder than ever.

The economic opposite of *Wall Street*'s tycoon-to-be protagonist, the main character of *Born on the Fourth of July* comes from a very ordinary working-class background—yet from the start is shown equally controlled and isolated from others and his own self. School, media, church, and especially family have filled his mind with abstractions and obligations—patriotism, competitiveness, family loyalty, and shame about his lower-class status. Afraid to ask a college-bound classmate to the prom, Ron Kovic can only speak of his coming Marine Corps tour in Vietnam. Like Stone's other heroes, he begins wrapped in veils of illusions, where neither parents, society, thoughts, nor feelings can help. In fact, he recalls the ex-student Vietnam GI in Wiseman's documentary *High School* who writes his classmates: "I'm just a body, doing a job."

Yet after the accidental killings and terrible wound, Kovic is equally cut off—to friends and family he becomes a source of guilt, shame, and embarrassment, to those against the war a symbol of the enemy government. His alienated status destroys any beliefs, past or present: "I'd give anything I believe in for a whole body." Like all Stone's isolates he goes as far as he can, abandoning home, family, and relations for the wild relationless never-neverland of the sexless vets. Unable to deal with its meaninglessness, he returns to the U.S. to beg forgiveness, and lead his "brother vets" against the government, "coming home," although in the end he seems as alone as ever.

The American society of *Born on the Fourth of July* has been praised for its depiction of home-front attitudes, even if we see so little of its social structure that the war seems to be a crazy conspiracy of the president, military, lower-class parents, and older townsfolk to torment the next generation, a conspiracy gradually seen through by college kids, minorities, and at last the vets themselves. The fact that we never see any of the social details and mechanisms, such as the craftily designed draft that stifled opposition by allowing the middle class easy escape, seems to me a major flaw, as well as leaving out how and why the government was "a bunch of corrupt thieves, rapists, and robbers" who tricked a whole generation. Like another social critic, George Orwell, who wrote, "England is like a family with the wrong members in control" and made totalitarianism real by portraying it as bullying cruel Big Brother, Stone has transformed the search for social justice into the search for familial forgiveness and love and dignity.

In general, the film got controlled praise from critics, along with criticism of Stone's excesses. Vincent Canby gave measured, noncommittal approval: "In effect, a bitter seething postscript to his Oscar-winning *Platoon*. It is a film of enormous visceral power, with, in the central role, a performance by Tom Cruise that defines everything that is best about the movie. He is both particular and emblematic. He is innocent and clean-cut at the start; at the end, angry and exhausted. . . .

"The screenplay is panoramic, sometimes too panoramic for its own good. . . . No other Vietnam movie has so evoked the casual, careless horrors of the paraplegic's therapy, or what it means to depend on catheters for urination, or the knowledge that sexual identity is hereforth virtually—theoretical.

"The film is stunning when it is most specific. . . . The film turns less persuasive as Ron acquires his new political consciousness . . . possibly because given everything that has gone before, the transformation is obligatory to the drama. . . . A far more complicated movie than *Platoon* . . . it connects the war of arms abroad to the war of conscience at home. As much as anything else, Ron Kovic's story is about the vanishing of one man's American frontier."[3]

Time's Richard Corliss commented carefully: "The movie is a jeremiad not just against the war but also against the cultural authorities who encouraged it from the pulpit, the blackboard, the dining room table, and the movie screen. This is an anti-Hollywood movie too. Everything that was terrific in, say, *Top Gun*—the war, the sex, the male bonding—is found to be toxic here. . . . The movie's uniqueness is in its tone. Stone plays director as if he were at a cathedral organ with all stops out. Each scene, whether it means to elegize or horrify, is unrelented, unmodulated, rabid with its own righteousness. And yet frequently the crazy machine works because of its voluptuous imagery."[5]

David Denby called the film "relentless but often powerful . . . a heartbreaking piece of work. . . . [Cruise's] Ron Kovic is not a natural winner like other Cruise characters but a clenched, patriotic working class boy who has to fight for every bit of patriotic and moral clarity he gets. . . . Stone and Kovic have consciously created an anti-myth. . . . Stone makes every line, every moment, part of Kovic's conditioning, as if the boy had no secret life, no *self*.

"Through most of the movie, Stone directs as if he were in as much pain as his impotent hero—as if he didn't have an obligation as an artist to shape his anger and then turn it loose. Mistaken, he tries to blow us away in every scene. Watching the movie is like being held in the grip of a brilliant monomaniac. . . . What Stone wants of course . . . is to bring us closer to the mess and suffering so we can't escape into consoling 'aesthetic' responses . . . but there's a problem in staying so close to Kovic's anger; his personal torments rather than any reasoned political arguments appear to be what turned him against the war. The movie seems out of balance. A young man's loss of potency is equated with the country's loss of honor."[8]

Christopher Sharett in *Cineaste* saw much of the film as a sharp social analysis, focusing on "the ideological character underlying not just American policy in Vietnam, but American society overall. . . . Kovic's Massapequa upbringing makes the repression of sexuality and its transformation into competition and violence central to the film's argument . . . Kovic's loss of a wrestling match is traumatic— the idea that America hates a loser is made into a graphic microcosm as the disappointment of his family and friends is evident as he lies distraught on the gym floor."[14]

(In passing, Variety's Daws sums up the idea more bluntly: "The forces shaping Kovic's values are about as gentle as a blast furnace forging steel."[7])

"Kovic's return home as a paraplegic eschews the romance of a returning warrior, as Kovic is depicted as annoying and virtually abandoned detritus. . . . Kovic's family clearly views him as an embarrassment. . . . There is a marvelous instant when Kovic's mother (Kyra Sedgwick) embraces her wheelchair-bound son; the camera catches her eye, registering discomfort and disaffection. The hometown folk treat Kovic with mild condescension and like his mother, constantly avert their gaze. The point is not merely the contempt for a loser, nor the disabled reminder of one's mortality, but the veteran as representation of the conflicts and contradictions of American beliefs.

"The narrative places the dominant ideology . . . squarely with the female. While men propel Kovic into all manner of guilt (including covering up the death of his comrade) it is a woman who is seen as the principal conditioning force. . . . There is not even an attempt to qualify this notion somewhat by suggesting that the mother, too, is a product of patriarchal culture."[7]

Finally, J. Hoberman thinks the film works, but wonders what it truly says. "A vast oozing wound of a movie . . . powerful and unflinching, crude but compelling . . . it's to Stone's credit that Born on the Fourth of July never forgets that the ultimate purpose of war is to inflict injury—to puncture, maim and destroy human body tissue. . . . Kovic's book, Stone's movie, and Cruise's performance are all intimately concerned with the failure of the body. This collapse extends to the dissolution of Ron's patriotic character armor. . . . Cruise's performance has the quality of a convulsive rebirth, moist and drooling, shooting pool and picking fights. . . . [These horrible and pathetic middle sequences] propel the events to an uncertain conclusion—Ron's moral regeneration as an antiwar activist. . . .

"Stone has a simple belief in catharsis and a maddening propensity to nudge the audience. The film is thick with unnecessary voiceovers and superfluous flashbacks [e.g., 'Soldier Boy' played at the prom, Mom's TV switch from demo to 'Laugh In,' 'Hard Rain,' and Abbie Hoffman at a college protest]. [Stone] wants to relive Vietnam

for all of us, for the national good. For all the muscle flex-
ing camera pyrotechnics, Stone is always ready to go slow and
tragic. . . . He's in touch with his grief over Vietnam—but what is
that grief exactly? . . . Despite (or maybe because of) a decade spent
strip-mining our resources, it's increasingly apparent that the Vietnamese conflagration marked the acme of American empire. *Born
on the Fourth of July* is like the jolt that failed. Stone's sincerity
is weirdly self-congratulatory. He denies his nostalgia even as he
indulges it."[10]

Critics who disliked the film saw it as either emotionally overwhelming and confusing or in truth not actually having much to say
at all. Pauline Kael[12] seemed to view it as an amalgam of *Carrie,
The Manchurian Candidate,* and *All Quiet on the Western Front.*
"It's inconceivable that Ron Kovic was as innocent as the movie and
the 1976 autobiography on which it is based make him out to be.
Was this kid kept in a bubble? At some level, everyone knows about
the ugliness of war. . . . [The film] appears to be a pacifist movie,
an indictment of all war. . . . You can't be sure, because there's never
a sequence where Ron figures out that war is wrong; we simply see
him go from personal bitterness to a new faith. . . . The movie is
carried along by Tom Cruise's Ronnie yelling that his penis will
never be hard again. The core of the movie is Ron's emotional need
to make people acknowledge what he has lost. There's a shrill demanding child inside the activist, a child whose claims we can't deny.

"We come out knowing nothing about him except his self-righteousness—his will to complain and make a ruckus—is rather glorious. I don't think I've ever seen another epic about a bad loser. (In
essence, *Born* is satire played straight.) The impotent Ron Kovic
holds the nation hostage. . . . [Stone] flatters the audience with the
myth that we believed in the war and then we woke up; we're turned
into generic Eagle Scouts. . . . You can't even enjoy [Stone's] un-
couthness, because it's put at the service of sanctimony."[12]

Michael Coving finds the film for the most part a clumsy heart-
breaker. "In a lot of ways it's a confusing, morally muddled story.
Suppose Kovic hadn't been shot? Would he then have turned so
strongly against the war? Or suppose he had been shot but during
World War II? Would he have accepted his paralyzed state more
easily because that was, as they say, a good war? (In one strong
scene, Kovic gets into an argument in a bar with a World War II vet
who calls Kovic a self-centered crybaby.) Or suppose the hospital

he had been sent to after the war had been better equipped, more accommodating. Would Kovic have acclimated more easily? Neither Stone nor Kovic really try to deal with these questions, and as a result a lot of Kovic's rage and sexual anger does seem to be self-serving, narcissistic. . . . Stone never really figures out how to deal with the mother beyond the image of the ogre; she becomes in the movie's eyes more objectionable and frightening than any machine gun toting Viet Cong. . . . [When Kovic visits the dead man's family] it's a terrible scene—Kovic relieves himself of all his guilt, but in the process makes the whole family feel horrible, like their boy died stupidly and in vain. . . . *Platoon* is a better larger movie . . . born of a grander, more tragic vision, while *Born on the Fourth of July*'s major note is a condemnatory one."6

Though Stone and Kovic insist the film is "realistic" and "the way it was" it should be noted that Kovic's service history is, at least statistically, very atypical. Christian Appy comments, "Most boys of that generation grew up liking John Wayne, trusting Kennedy, and loving their country. Yet fewer than half entered the military and only 12 percent went to Vietnam. . . . Most of the working class kids sent to Vietnam were drawn into the military not because they believed the military would bring social advancement and honor. They simply regarded it as an unavoidable duty."[1] The film also hides our shameful class/income-biased draft, and the fact that from the start the less educated were more often and more strongly for withdrawal.[18] Instead of Ms. Kovic, it would have been braver and more truthful to include Stone's upper-class stockbroker father telling the disabled vet what he smugly told his son: that the poor should be sacrificed to the interests of Wall Street (See chapter 1).

Robert Stone sees the film as just another commercial movie, a sort of *The Best Years of Our Lives*, updated. "It appears to derive the misfortunes of the Cold War from the inadequacies of life in Massapequa, New York. . . . The movie is all glib explanation: the paradoxes of populist democracy, the corruptions attendant on patriotism and world power, and the spiritual limitations of the American working class are reduced to stereotypes and subjected to a Hollywood treatment, banal in its obviousness and crass in its moralizing. . . . The shoddy machismo of a recruiting sergeant, the ghastly prudishness and petty bourgeois conformism of Kovic's parents are presented for judgment (disdain) at patriot displays and military posturing is exploited. . . . Are Massapequa's Fourth of Julys, so sunny and bright with their flags and their drums, no more than death traps through which ardent children are bent to the sinister wish of an evil government intent on war for its own sake? . . . The scenes showing the sufferings of the youth and his family are so gripping, their simpleminded blue collar Catholic unconsciousness so pathetic, that the subject of the picture seems to become the utter inability of Long Island's fetishes and idols—flags, uniforms, crucifixes—to protect its people from misfortune.

"Late in the picture Stone stages an American revolution for the kids to cheer for. Demonstrators, led by Tom Cruise in his wheelchair, are first brutalized by killer cops, then shown putting their delegates to flight, ruining their party, practically driving Nixon out of town. Cruise makes a speech, proclaiming his love of country, while denouncing the country's leadership as "robbers, rapists, and thieves." But fortunately . . . there's a new United States, symbolized by a Democratic convention. . . . Cruise/Kovic addresses his country at large. The Fourth of July presumably will never again be celebrated in Massapequa. . . . We end with radical theatrics, unconvincing liberal compromises, and cultural despair. In other words, commercial movies."[17]

The production team, however, appeared quite satisfied. Tom Pollack, head of Universal Pictures, the film's patron: "Tom Cruise is all America's all-American boy. The film's journey is more powerful when it is made by the maverick from *Top Gun*. It's not only Ron who goes through the wrenching story, it is Tom Cruise—our perception of Tom Cruise."[14]

Tom Cruise himself said at the end of filming, "It's a film that tells us we can't blindly trust the leaders of this country, that we ourselves must search and find out where we stand and what we believe in. It's not easy finding the truth about anything. . . . This is the truth of what happened over there. . . . When you get right down to it, Vietnam was basically economics."[14]

Ron Kovic, when asked if the film could set the record straight commented: "It has to. Great movies and great literature should protect. It should be so truthful that it keeps people alive. Movies should not merely entertain—movies have a responsibility. . . . Our acts of creativity—when we write, when we make films—should give direction, should be a map of the soul to betterment, a good map that gets people to their destination intact."[15]

After the film's first complete screening Stone said: "Ron's story is a coherent vision of the whole Vietnam experience, before, during, and after the war. The concept being, there was a second war when we came back. It was a real booby trap, we came back and got slammed in the back of the neck. We were out of step. People didn't care about Vietnam. Their attitude was: 'I'm sorry, that was a waste of your time.' It wasn't hostility. It was indifference. And so with Ron's story. I felt I could fit pieces of my own story and others."[13]

Responding to the film's critics, Stone said: "They say I'm unsubtle. But [Antonin Artaud said] 'We need above all a theater that wakes us up, mind and heart.' . . . I'm *in the face* all the time. Always in your face. . . . I hate the very concept of bullying any audience into anything. I put my passion out there, my honest feelings. That's all I do. Some people like that, and some people feel it's too strong" [noting the film's opening was the day of the U.S. invasion of Panama], it's a reflection of the same kind of thinking, that we can set other people's houses in order. It goes right to the point of my movie. . . .

"*Born on the Fourth of July* has more layers than *Platoon*. There have been no realistic Vietnam movies, and I felt it was important to remember the way it was, before we all get too old. I wanted to fix it in memory for those who were there, and to remind young people that it happened so they wouldn't let it happen again. . . . All the boys I knew who died—they'd have died for nothing if we hadn't remembered the war."[4]

Born on the Fourth of July did well commercially, and the Director's Guild of America named Stone Best Director of 1989 for it. It also was nominated for eight Academy Awards, and won four.

8
. . . . . .

THE DOORS

JIM MORRISON HAS a special significance for Oliver Stone. In interviews he said, "When he died in 1971, it was like the day JFK died for me. It was that shattering. I worshiped him."[16] Before starting to make *The Doors*, the writer-director said, "The other side of the coin to Ron [Kovic] in the sixties was Jim Morrison. . . . Ron was the good boy, and Jim Morrison was the bad boy. I can shed some light on that. There's a lot of the bad boy in me. There was a lot of the rebel: I really wanted to find the bottom of the barrel. . . . When I was [in Vietnam] I wanted to be at the lowest level, the guy who cut point. . . . I identified with Morrison. . . . He was a shaman. He was a god. For me, a Dionysian figure, a poet, a philosopher. I'd like to bring his life out into the light."[4]

Elsewhere, Jim Morrison had been called "the self-destructive-exhibitionist-poet-shaman-sweetheart-asshole who approached rock like a romantic crooner, a demented Sinatra singing the hit parade for a season in hell."[16] Another writer wrote: "He saw sex as the point of connection between pleasure and politics . . . was being eaten alive by his own erotic mystique."[9] A third claimed: "Morrison was either Michelangelo's David in black leather, the Samuel Beckett of Venice Beach, Oedipus on acid—or a boozy poseur with a pipeline to the zeitgeist."[1] Stone has said: "With Jim, I feel very warm, very comfortable. He's like my older brother."[3]

Interestingly, Stone's first screenplay, *Break* (1969), was in theme and imagery evoked by Doors music. In it the hero goes off to Vietnam, falls in with a jungle tribe, dies in the second act (shades of *Apocalypse Now!*), and goes to the Egyptian underworld, Doors music playing on the sound track. "I didn't know how to write that much, but it's really one of my favorite screenplays, because it's so

raw and surreal. It was all about passion, unbordered by technique."
It was found among Morrison's possessions after his death.

The journey of *The Doors* to the screen was a long and complex one, detailed elsewhere.[16] After he died in July 1971, Morrison's estate was tied up in court for eight years, the subject of claims by his common-law wife, the other three band members, Morrison's parents, and his wife's parents after her death. A Doors revival, starting in 1980, plus the book *No One Here Gets out Alive,* led to interest by Hollywood, but clearing all rights stayed a problem. John Travolta was interested, but the band didn't want to use an actor. In 1982 Brian De Palma prepared a script, William Friedkin said he wanted to make "the *Raging Bull* of rock movies," but all backed off in time. Only in 1984 did promoter Bill Graham secure all rights, Columbia Pictures buy the package, while poor scripts, staff changes, and Stone's on-again-off-again availability caused more delays. The band at one point rejected him as "too dark." In 1988 the two promoters of the project personally visited Stone at his home. "I wanted Val Kilmer," he recalled saying. "This is the guy." But *Evita* came first. By the end of 1988 the project's rights were locked, and it belonged to Carolco—where Stone had a two-picture deal. In August 1989 Stone agreed to shoot it after *Evita,* writing his own script, for three to four million dollars, plus gross points. Stone began conducting interviews and doing research, *Evita* disintegrated, and *The Doors* began preproduction. It had already run up two million dollars in development costs, and had seven producers, including line producer Clayton Thomas, and Stone's producer A. Kitman Ho.

Stone did extensive research and interviewing.[3] In the end he chose the route "where the central character confided in the camera and says what's on his mind. There is still a mystery, but the relationship to the camera is very frontal. He's not hiding. His innermost thoughts are coming out with the poems and songs."

As scripting proceeded, co-writer J. Randal Johnson's research turned up such new facts as that Morrison had suffered from impotence even before his stardom and drugdom, a problem, Johnson felt, that may have been the source of the singer's angst. A treatment he prepared showed a thoughtful mischievous Morrison, whose private fears of inadequacy fed his bravado in public. Johnson recalls the impotence script conference—Stone quizzical, promoter Graham choked up, producer Harari protesting. Johnson felt such nuances became obscured by the endless music and camera motions. Likewise, Morrison's two love interests were reduced to little more than "outward manifestations of drives. . . . Meg Ryan's Pamela Courson goes so far as to identify herself to a customs official as an 'ornament.'"[16]

Script problems were extensive. Pam Courson's parents had earlier gotten agreements that their daughter would not be shown taking drugs or involved in Morrison's death. They refused to let the film include Morrison's later poetry. Stone, who always felt Morrison's "mature poetry" redeemed his darker moments, searched for a compromise, but told *20/20 Magazine* reporters their attitude "pisses me off! I mean, those poems belong to the world, and even if the movie sucks, the words would speak out for themselves."

Morrison's parents finally agreed to let Stone use their late son's poetry, producer Sasha Harari seeing their view as: "Oliver takes very seriously the fact that Jim Morrison is a poet." But except for one scene, the parents were not to be depicted.

Stone also worked to include other real people. Former Doors manager Bill Siddons criticized a script that he felt focused virtually exclusively on the most sensational side of Jim's personality, and "not the man I knew—a bright warm human being who actually gave a shit about some people. . . . So much of it was inaccurate that I wanted to know if [Stone] had any interest in the facts or if it was just a fictional account. . . . He said it was fictional." Siddons in time allowed himself to be depicted.

After numerous drafts, Stone chose a structure that matched the emotional states of twenty-five Doors songs to the story's chronology. "I let the music basically dictate the mood of each movement. The first part of the movie is the more innocent songs, the second part is 'The End,' more towards the psychedelic. Then we go to the New York section, which I saw as darker and more twisted, 'Strange Days,' 'People Are Strange,' culminating in the decadence of 'Soft Parade.' Then coming back to 'Five to One' in defiance in Miami, and this coming to a whole softer thing in 'L. A. Woman' and framing the whole thing with 'American Prayer.' That was generally the movement of the film."[1]

After auditioning two hundred actors, Stone hired thirty-year-old Val Kilmer to play Jim Morrison—Kilmer's "audition" included dressing like the rock star, hiring a band, and shooting his own rock video. Stone reportedly liked his wide Slavic facial bones (very

26. *The Doors.* Val Kilmer as Jim Morrison: "They don't want me, they want my death—ripped to pieces—" *(Copyright 1991 Tri-Star Pictures, Inc. Courtesy Museum of Modern Art Film Stills Archive.)*

27. *The Doors.* Kevin Dillon as John Densmore, Kyle MacLachlan as Ray Manzarek, Frank Whaley as Robby Kreiger, Val Kilmer as Jim Morrison, Meg Ryan as Pamela Courson: "I'm just an ornament!" *(Copyright 1991 Tri-Star Pictures, Inc. Courtesy Museum of Modern Art Film Stills Archive.)*

American), implied arrogance, and antiheroic mold. Kilmer, a ringer for Morrison, had his hair dyed and permed to resemble Morrison's shaggy brown locks, and wore black contacts to simulate very dilated pupils. He also mastered the singer's stage moves. Kilmer, who had played Hamlet, saw parallels with Morrison: being a prince, resisting a leadership role, deciding something was wrong in the kingdom.

Meg Ryan was cast as Pam Courson, Morrison's longtime companion, who overdosed in 1974. Stone gave her a six-week cram reading course in the sixties: the beat poets, Huxley, Kerouac. Ms. Ryan concluded: "Pam was a totally defenseless girl. Her whole life was this guy, and she defined herself through his eyes. In many ways it's a very female situation. Love was her justification for everything, which is sweet and nice and wonderful but ultimately lethal."[2] Kilmer felt the two were locked in a dance of death, as depicted in one of several marathon fight scenes. "We were both picking glass out of our knees between takes. How we dealt with it was just with a lot of humor and sensitivity. We were very dependent on each other in that sensitive state which you have to live in when you're inside someone else's life."[13]

After eight years, *The Doors*, budgeted at $40 million with a three-month schedule, began shooting. The production included eighty locations and thirty thousand extras for the Miami concert over several days (though the rear rows of the Los Angeles Orpheum, doubling for the New Haven location, had cardboard hippies—these costing more than extras). Besides Los Angeles locations, filming was done in the Mojave Desert, San Francisco, New York, and Paris. The city of West Hollywood charged sixty thousand dollars for three nights of shooting on Sunset Boulevard. "It's definitely not the sixties anymore," said producer Ho. "It's the greedy eighties."

The concert filming involved several extra cameras and massive logistics. To make possible 360-degree camera moves, while the audience danced to the missing beat, a very low frequency tone "thumper track" was synchronized with the prerecorded music track, and piped in for the audience to sway to. In postproduction, the thumper was removed electronically.

To suggest the Doors music's anarchic energy and Morrison's poetry's surrealistic mood, cinematographer Bob Richardson extensively employed such sweeping camera work.

To replicate Morrison's vocals, the master tapes of the recordings were played in the studio minus the lead vocal track, so Val Kilmer could sing along. Besides listening to the words, the actor got a phonetic breakdown of Morrison's delivery. In the end, the filmmakers used a mixture of Morrison and Kilmer. The instrumentalists "played" in synch to Doors recordings, heard over tiny earphones. Their own instruments made no sound.

Describing work on the film, Ms. Ryan commented amusedly, "One thing Oliver does is provide the environment for you as an actor. . . . You just go to work, and all of a sudden it's 1969. You've got four thousand extras all dressed and all crazed, and you don't have to pretend you're strung from the tenth floor of a building on heroin. You actually are strung from the tenth floor, pretending you're on heroin."[2]

A journalist described the shooting this way: "Kilmer emerges from his stupor, and practically sweating on cue, sways in to full Jimness: taunting the audience, swinging his hips, opining insolently about the state of things in the U.S. of A. The crane rises above the screaming, shimmying extras, the smoke machine bellows, and the whole thing starts to feel kinetic and real . . . but it's not until several takes later, when the rumpled, distracted director takes the stage to thank the 'audience' that the people below become truly alive. Smiling young faces turn up towards him, eyes shining, beaming adoration. At this moment, he's succeeded in replicating exactly what he revered in Morrison, this eager mass of humanity is looking to him for an answer."[7]

Stone himself seemed to have enjoyed at least parts of the filming. He told one writer: "One time in San Francisco, we had all these extras on the street dressed in a hippie mode . . . and the people on the other side watching us were dressed in drab greys and greens. I looked at my cameraman and said: 'Let's pan the camera, right in the middle of the film, we'll see the eighties and go right back into the action of Haight Ashbury.'"[17]

A problem in the concert scenes was that Kilmer's voice began to deteriorate after two or three takes. A sequence filmed in the Sunset Strip's Whisky a Go Go was particularly taxing. "The air was heavy with smoke and sweat, sweltering from body heat and camera lights. For nearly three days, Kilmer had been raging back and forth on the crowded stage, unleashing the primal furies of 'The End,' Morrison's agonized call to generational incest and patricide. As

Stone finally called it a wrap, on what the actor figured was something like the twenty-fourth take, Kilmer slumped, enervated and exhausted: 'I felt like it *was* the end,' he said."[13]

After shooting was over, the editing team used George Lucas's Skywalker Sound Studio in Los Angeles, adding special effects inspired by Morrison's imagry. A critic noted: "The concerts appear on the screen in a kaleidoscope of fire and color, reds and blues and black, creating an operatic opulence. It is as though they had been staged in a Greek temple by a Fellini with a headful of Stregs."[2]

Morrison's political views were dropped, Stone commenting: "The only overt political statement Jim ever made . . . was in his 'Unknown Soldier' song, which was taken as a statement against the [Vietnam] war and banned by radio. . . . I had to cut that scene from the film for reasons of length. . . . To me, Jim represents a more basic, primeval form of rebellion that is very useful now. That in and of itself is a political statement. What more can you expect of a rocker?"[7]

Interviewed during the film's production about his theme, Stone said: "It's Jim Morrison's spiritual quest. The hero's journey through this landscape where he has to find something, and he doesn't know what it is. He's a man who sails from island to island looking for himself, looking for home. A man frustrated by limitations. He could never be happy, he always needed more, more, more. . . . It's more a mythic story that belongs to any era. . . . I'm trying to show how Jim Morrison represented the desire for Dionysus, which is something we all want in our fundamental soul. He lived the consciousness, he acted out every single wish. And he lived with death every day, he wanted death. . . . No matter what time you live in, you're always ready for Dionysus to come down from the mountain and lead you into the wild swinging orgy."[7]

Just before the film's release, Stone said making it had not changed his perception of Morrison. "I deepened the perception, questioned it, but what I found at the end of the tunnel was an endless fascination and mystery. It was like being in the belly of this peristaltic creature, this huge worm, stomach muscles moving, walking down through fifty ribs. I think this film wove its spell around me and Val [Kilmer] in the sense of being so sensuous and ravishing."[3]

Stone also thought it was worthwhile simply to film the sixties milieu: "The eros of that era shows—such an incredible sense of color and it's nice to remind people that such a time happened, that just for this brief moment of time, there would be a Camelot. That's a wonderful dream to hold on to and to look back on. You have to pass the torch."

On release, Stone braced himself for controversy: "No matter what, I'm going to get killed on this."

In a red-lit recording studio, an aging Jim Morrison, hair dirty, eyes haunted, yet youthfully handsome as a Greek god, reads his poetry. "The movie will begin in five moments. . . ."

Morrison cries: "Is everybody in? Is everybody in? The ceremony is about to begin."

Yellow-tinted desert vistas, a 1940s car and family on a dirt road. They pass a wreck; injured or stoically standing Indians, highway patrolmen, blood, silence. The child Jim exchanges looks with an ancient Indian. His mother tells the little boy it's only a dream.

In the desert, twenty-year-old Morrison hitchhikes west.

Title: Venice, California, 1965.

The boardwalk is crowded with hippies, freaks, beautiful girls. Music: "I'm Goin' Out West Where I Belong."

A beautiful redheaded girl walks her Labrador. Morrison follows.

She enters a home on Love Street. Music: "She has wisdom and knows what to do." Morrison watches until night, scales a tree to the roof where she's musing.

"Hi . . . you have a problem with doors?"

"Waste of time . . . I followed you . . . from the beach . . . 'cause . . . you're the one."

In a UCLA film course Morrison screens his creation. Flashes of a blond in black underwear, marching Nazis, Indian peyote ceremonies. Morrison's voice: "Listen, children, to the sound of the night. Have you ever seen God?"

Friend Ray: "It's great! It's nonlinear! It's poetry! It's everything good art stands for!"

The majority of the students mock him.

The instructor (played by Stone): "Pretty pretentious there, Jim."

"I quit!" Morrison walks out.

Morrison and Pam walk on the beach at night, she reads his poems on the rooftop, the notebooks full of arresting drawings of mythic figures.

Morrison says he's most alive confronting death. He's fascinated by Indian shamans—"The first one invented sex. He's the one that makes you crazy."

Morrison and Ray walk on the beach. Ray's trying to make movies, Jim's writing poems: "I've got a whole concert in my head."

Ray: "It's about to explode. . . . Sides are being chosen. . . . We got to make the myths."

Morrison wants their group to be "The Doors." . . . It comes from William Blake. . . . "When the doors of perception are cleansed . . . things will appear as they truly are."

The Band—Jim, Ray, John, and Robbie—work on their music: "Break on through."

Robbie sings a version of "Light My Fire," Jim hones it, they perfect it.

A club performance has crowds of young girls screaming.

Title: Sunset Strip, six months later. Blazing neon marquees, crowds of rowdy youths. Inside, Morrison leaping, crooning: "Light My Fire" making the mobs of women cry out.

A slick manager type tries to sign them up. "We'll have a band meeting on it."

"The musketeers—but loyalty doesn't pay the bills!" he mocks.

He gets Morrison alone: "The point is, drop those guys. Your looks, your voice, that's what sells records."

On drugs, they wade through crowds, traffic. They'll go to the desert.

Great golden picturesque sand dune fields. On drugs, the Doors and their women struggle through the sand, hug, dance. Morrison talks of seeing the serpent, seven miles long, the history of the world on its scales, digesting everything, a monster of energy.

The musicians confess their fears, their separateness, form a circle.

Jim: "I'll be with you to the end of time . . . ride the snake."

He runs off, appears in a canyon with the old Indian from childhood, in a sacred cavern with him and a mountain lion; sees the accident, cavern, a figure in a bathtub; the shaman and he exchange glances.

Title: Whiskey a Go-Go, 1966. The Doors perform "The End," women responding ecstatically, Morrison, stage frightened, turns his back, the band playing intensely. Singing "The End's" lyrics, Morrison goes wild: "Father, I want to kill you! Mother, I want to fuck you!"

Morrison screams and sways, the audience is shocked, a barrier crossed. The club manager throws them out. But a smooth music exec, Jac Holzman, from Electra Records, wants them. We see them record "Light My Fire."

Title: San Francisco, 1967: the Summer of Love's flower children, the Doors and their women among them, appear as home movies.

At the Filmore, enormous crowds respond to Morrison, swinging wildly on a great chandelier, finally swan diving into the crowd.

New York, 1967. Crowds of adoring women surround them, Ed Sullivan wants them. The network censors ask about "get much higher." The Doors offer; "Bite my wire." They sing it their way. "You shits, you'll never play Sullivan again!"

To "People Are Strange," Jim poses for a woman photographer: "They want to worship and adore you Jim Morrison . . . a god." Eerie isolating PR photos follow.

Morrison visits an Andy Warhol party full of druggy self-destructive sophisticates: "Does art imitate life, or does life imitate Andy?" The stunning blond Nico says hello, Ray tells Jim: "These people are vampires!" Andy, a frail effete man, gives Jim a golden phone: "They said I could talk to God with this telephone. Now you can talk to God." In an alley, they stagger about, Morrison going off. But when Pam buzzes for the hotel elevator, she finds the blonde Nico on her knees, face to his leathers.

At a press conference Jim says his songs are about: "Love death travel revolt. We're interested in madness, disorder. I believe in excess. . . . I live in the unconscious." He doesn't remember being born, and his parents died in a horrible car crash.

Jim and a beautiful journalist are in bed. Girl: "Don't worry about it. It happens to other guys."

Jim sees an ancient manuscript. She practices witchcraft. Ever try drinking blood? Where do you get the blood?

They cut themselves, dance naked in her loft to music, chasing, wrestling, yelling, fucking: "My rock god, fuck me, fuck me good!"

Jim and Pam in bed: "It happens to other guys too."

Jim: "Girls want my dick—not my words."

"Maybe you could put a little soul in your success?"

The two argue, fight, scream at each other, he hangs out the window: "I'm sorry baby, we're gonna fuck death away!"

New Haven, 1968. Backstage, Patricia the reporter/witch tells Jim his father isn't dead, but a U.S. admiral, she traced him through the colleges. Did he love you? Jim holds thumb and forefinger a little apart. His mother? A little more. "It doesn't matter. It's *you* they want now."

"They don't want me, they want my death—ripped to pieces."

A cop finds them. No one's allowed backstage. Morrison argues, the cop maces him, blinding him briefly. Morrison's entourage appears, guides him toward the performance, the stage, the armies of screaming young women.

Morrison onstage tells the mace story: "This little man in a little blue hat, little blue suit . . . he started pushin' me . . . because I was all alone with a girl, doin' somethin' he wanted to do—if he could get it up without a gun."

"You've gone too far!" The angry, hostile cops seize him, hustle him off. Flashback: Morrison recording as first seen: "Let's just say I was testing the bounds of reality. . . . I prefer to be hated. . . . In me they see what they want to see. . . . I think of myself as a sensitive intelligent human being but with the soul of a clown which always forces me to blow it at the most crucial moments."

In a bar, a drunken Jim insults and antagonizes the others, pisses on the floor.

Pam and Jim schlepp bags of groceries on a suburban street, seemingly comic rockers trying to be suburbanites. Where's the car? Oh, I destroyed it. You've got to change those stinky leathers. Ninety-five thousand dollars more to open a boutique.

Morrison looks stoned. "It's just some low-grade acid."

"You! I cooked. And some people are coming."

"It's cool. We'll trip and then we'll eat our feast. . . . Women are such noble creatures . . . women have basically a comic approach to life. . . . You carry on our names after we die . . . (but he refuses to discuss marriage). . . . I'm a spy in the house of love, I know your secret fear. Both grinning, he feeds her acid.

In their big tasteful home, the stoned pair greet the other Doors, their women, hippies, artists. Pam is introduced to the New York journalist/witch.

"You actually put your dick in this woman!"

"Well, sometimes, yeah."

Pam; defiant: "He's crazy but he's not that crazy. He loves me!"

The two fight hysterically, druggily. Jim pulling a knife: "Give me some death!" Jim attacks the roast-duck dinner instead. Pam: "You killed my dinner!" It's stomped into the rug. A Hell's Angel picks it up and eats it anyway.

The druggy couple embraces as a black guest comments: "This party is getting low rent."

San Francisco, 1968. An enormous red-lit concert hall, the Filmore West. A bellowing crowd responds to Morrison's: "Nothing left to do, but run, run, run."

Intercut with the concert, Jim comes home to find Pam and a guy in their bed using smack. The guy ducks out. Jim puts her in a closet, sets it afire, walks out.

The same mad red roaring concert.

At an eerie ceremony, Jim's made a warlock, the witch woman smiling. At the same thundering concert again, Morrison dances madly, the shaman seemingly appearing beside him. Morrison throws himself into the mass of people, is carried along on a sort of wave of uplifted hands, arms, bodies, flesh. Others strip as he cries out: "I am the lizard king! I can do anything!"

Alone, he wanders against a blue L.A. sunset.

In a recording studio, the singer looks bad, sounds bad, has a temper tantrum: "Why don't you suck a fart out of my asshole!"

Producer: "I miss Jim—and all the time he's sitting in front of me."

Morrison stops. On the studio TV, a car commercial uses "Light My Fire." The Doors made seventy-five thousand dollars on it.

Morrison: "You know what you're saying. . . . The Doors. . . . It was about using the music to break through. . . . We lost something!" He throws the TV through the recording studio window.

Jim sees Pam, tearful faced: "You don't have to torture me." They embrace.

Morrison records and there is another monster concert: Miami, 1969.

A rock group blasts out "Eve of Destruction."

A cynical young rock correspondent is recording a tape: "They've become an act. . . . The question is why are they here? . . . Morrison falls off the stage at least every other performance. . . . Are funerals entertainment?"

In a jet's first-class section, a bearded fat Morrison teases his manager: "You can get us some heroin man? . . . What's wrong with this flab?"

"Rock is cock man and yours is dying."

"You want to know what they really want? Something sacred. That's what they really want."

In a corridor, the group argues with the concert staff.

"Everybody thinks we're addicts."

"We took drugs to expand our minds, not to escape!"

Jim presses drugs on a band member: "You'll play like an orgasm!"

Blazing lights, soaring sound, the crowds see them and go crazy, throwing drugs onstage. The enormous hall thunders. A mad half-naked teen swan dives from the balcony.

Morrison sings "Five to One": "No one here gets out alive!" A special effect has them playing amid "bonfires." Naked women jump on the stage, the crowd is stripping off its clothes.

The shaman seems to be beside Jim, old face grim. The crowd screams, Jim screams back: "You're a bunch of fucking slaves! How long you think it's gonna last? How long you let 'em push you around? I'm gonna get my kicks before it goes down! You'd all eat shit, wouldn't you? Hitler is alive and well and living in Miami! . . . What're you gonna do about it?" Chaos, a free-form riot.

The band goes silent. Morrison rips off his shirt: "Come on up here and love my ass! Want to see it?" (Hands to hips) I'm gonna show it to ya! I want to see some action out there!" (Teasing again) "Go ahead! No laws, no limits!" The security people drag him off, amid the pandemonium, while "Break on through" roars.

In a courtroom, Morrison is charged with lewd behavior. The Doors sit there with him. Morrison, in his mid-twenties, is bearded, fat, aged, burned-out.

Pamela, pregnant by Jim, wants marriage.

"I don't want the responsibility."

"You're a coward."

"I was stoned, it seemed like a fun thing."

He's sentenced; the appeals begin. The Doors can't get a gig anywhere.

An exhausted Morrison watches TV: Martin Luther King shot, RFK shot, Nixon, napalm. Jim: "I think I'm having a nervous breakdown."

The Chateau Marmot Hotel, 1970. On the twentieth-floor window ledge, Morrison, drunk, staggers, bottle in hand. Below, streams of cars. Pam screams from a window, inches toward him: "I want to live with you!"

At Ray's house, there's a birthday party for one of his children. Jim, a fat bearded blinking wreck, arrives. He's leaving for Paris.

"We made music with Dionysus."

"We must get together again."

Flashback: in the studio from the start of the film, Jim records his poetry.

Paris, 1971. In their apartment, Pam, in a red robe, calls out: "Jim, Jim, is that you?"

In the bathroom, he's sitting in the French-style tub, face away, arms arcing around the curves of the rim.

"I've had it with you!" An unreal specter moves away through the shadows.

His face is now beardless, eyes shut, curiously youthful.

"Did you enjoy it when it came?"

We move through Père Lachaise Cemetery, past graves of Chopin, Bizet, Balzac, Proust, Molière, to intensely romantic classical music. Morrison's grave has a perfect Alexandrine bust of the beautiful youth, marked by flowers, ribbons, candles, the face made up, the image moving, even heartbreaking. There is an epitaph spoken on the sound track.

Once again, and again uniquely, Stone isolates the protagonist of his film, Jim Morrison. For Morrison is a young man whose artistic talents, early experiences, and special milieu allowed him independence and achievements of no previous Stone hero. Too cruel and strange to understand, he aspires to be an artist and more, a world shaker with a special vision and message. His view of himself as such is proposed but not validated by the film. Like Stone's other protagonists, he's cut free of his family, here in a profoundly shocking way, then continually challenges, rejects or transcends the limits of society. Conventional as well as modernistic figures representing culture, romance, law, and commerce he rejects, pointlessly provokes, or at best can barely tolerate. In this he is the most confrontational of all Stone's permanent isolate heroes. Yet he seems to be beating his head against the wall as much as breaking through. Indeed, Stone foreshadows failure, even comically in that the sweet valley girl and the witchy intellectual respond identically to his sexual limits ("It happens to other guys too"). Nor do lovers or concert audience's responses ever change from mindless timeless meaningless adulation.

The world Stone creates in his film is a special grim version of Morrison's vision. The masses of people, in particular women, are passive suggestible creatures, in a sense the slaves he accuses them of being (at least as portrayed). Above them, manipulating them, are the small class of performers and managers and communicators, illusionists who live by diverting and living off the mindless herd, a phantasmagorical extension of the society of *Talk Radio*. Finally, Morrison, artist, entertainer, shaman, would break through to somewhere else if he could, and if he could find a way to get anyone to follow—but such striving is not allowed, even should it prove possible.

Critical responses to *The Doors* were, in fact, surprisingly generous.

The *New York Time*'s new reviewer, Janet Maslin noted: "Unimaginable perhaps, but here it is anyway, *The Doors*, Oliver Stone's clamorous, reverential, much-larger-than-life portrait of the sixties most self-important rock band. Incendiary even by Mr. Stone's high standards, *The Doors* presents the group's career as a brave visionary rise, followed by a wretched slide into darkness, a slide implemented by drugs, alcohol, weirdness, world affairs and the demands of fame. This view is sure to arouse as strong a love-hate reaction as *The Doors* did themselves, but two things are certain: Mr. Stone retains his ability to grab an audience by the throat and not let go; and retain that hold for hours; and he's succeeded in raising the dead. . . .

"What ruined Jim Morrison? The film at times dares to make the outrageous suggestion that he died for his audience's sins, but it is possible to be haunted by *The Doors* without subscribing to that idea in the slightest. Mr. Stone is less successful in offering any final assessment of either the sixties or his hero than in bringing both back with strange and spectacular power. . . . *The Doors* concludes in Père Lachaise Cemetery . . . [explaining] with captivating intensity why Jim Morrison is the one who gets the visitors."[14]

David Denby, usually a Stone enthusiast, gave the film a supportive if very mixed evaluation. "Oliver Stone's movie *The Doors* is the only thing I can imagine that is more pretentious than the Doors themselves. . . . According to this movie, Morrison, who wrote high schoolish poetry and had a little (though not much) music in him, was an incarnated Dionysus. . . . Oliver Stone wants to make movies that are like bad dreams, and this one is an overpoweringly rich and assaultive mixture of drug visions, violence, and rock concert frenzy, with the usual cultural icons of the sixties—Blake, LSD, rituals, Nietzsche, rock journalists, the desert, peyote—thrown together in an endless flow of imagery. The images do burn, however, and despite the camera's rocking and swiveling back and forth, the film is surprisingly coherent. Stone can make controlled movies about uncontrollable passions, about people going over the top. He has considerable power, but I'm beginning to despair of him, because his strengths now seem to rule out the slightest trace of humor. . . .

"The Doors has some memorable moments (the concert scenes are especially good), and it captures one aspect of the sixties better than any movie before it; the dark narcissism that allowed a strutting poet-stud like Jim Morrison to feed off his audience. The infamous incident in Miami in which Morrison, drunk, supposedly flashed the crowd, plays here as a consummation of the sixties, a case of a star trying to tear down every last barrier between his inner and outer selves, and between himself and the audience.

"Mostly, though, the film wants to be an intimate portrait of Morrison. And that's where Stone's frenzied, one-thing-after-another approach takes its toll. As docudramas go, The Doors is more docu than drama. It simply presents Morrison's life and dissolution bottle by bottle, without really giving us a peak into his soul. Stone essentially buys into the star's myth about himself—that he was a pop culture shaman who lived to go over the edge. Then the movie undercuts the myth by showing us, in agonizing detail, what the booze did to him."[8]

Finally Robert Horton, in Film Comment, noted: "There's so little passion informing American movies that Stone's muscular, free swinging ways seem all the more vital. It is possible, also useful, to note the excesses of Stone's films, but one at least comes away from . . . The Doors . . . well, having had some kind of experience."[12]

Those who attacked the film did so largely for its lack of irony, lack of content, exploitation, and excess. J. Hoberman in his essay "The Lizard King's New Clothes," wrote: The Doors isn't exactly The Glenn Miller Story, except that in a certain sense that's exactly what it is—the putative saga of a generation, awash with the music of its martyred protagonist. . . . Here, as with Tom Cruise . . . Stone gets a strong turn by putting his star under make or break duress. Against all odds, the stage performances are actually the movie's most compelling scenes. . . .

"Enjoyably bombastic as this movie can be, it bellows in a mono-tone. There's no dialectic or order and disorder—it's all chaos. . . . For *The Doors*, [Stone] puts on a party hat and won't take it off. He's determined to out-Dionysus Dionysus when the material itself begs for something a little more, uh, Apollonian. (Morrison's own tastes in movies, the script makes clear, ran towards austere black and white.) Perhaps there's a moral after all. If nothing else, Stone successfully disproves the Blake maxim that has been affixed like a mezuzah to the Doors: "The road of excess leads to the palace of wisdom."[10]

Time magazine's Richard Corliss agrees with the recent Paris cemetery graffiti: "Val Kilmer n'est pas Jim." Since Kilmer lacks Morrison's looks, intellectual seductiveness, and sexual powers, and the Doors were not political pathfinders and musically negligible, Corliss sees Stone having few aesthetic options. "So Stone turned *The Doors* into a display of pop culture's wretched excess. Perhaps Stone wanted to show that Morrison was the victim of sensuality—death's hunkiest groupie—rather than its agent. But the film really proves only that Jim was a bad drunk and a worse friend, and that in no way was his life exemplary."[5]

Terrence Rafferty, *New Yorker* reviewer, in an essay "Stoned Again," commented: "You don't have to have been a big Jim Morrison fan to find this treatment of his life offensive. *The Doors* is pure exploitation; Stone gobbles up Morrison and rock and roll and the sixties as if they were drugs. . . . *The Doors* offers no perspective on those strange days. It's an extended self-important freakout, an exercise in disorientation. . . . In *The Doors*, Oliver Stone reduces the richly contradictory experience of the sixties to the myth of Morrison, and in the process, reduces Morrison and the Doors as well. . . . Stone portrays the crowds at the band's concerts as if he were a unanimous constituency—gatherings of the devout, all dying to be whipped into Dionysiac ecstasies.

"It's all done tongue in cheek. [Morrison] once said: 'I don't really take it that seriously.' That's supposed to be ironic. Stone doesn't provide even a glimpse of a Morrison who could say something like that, or any suggestion that there was humor in the sixties aesthetic of deliberate, outrageous provocation—that virtually all the popular art of the era was conceived in the spirit of the put on."[15]

Finally Jerry Hopkins, a professional rock journalist and author of two books on Morrison, wrote, "The film was, in fact, a one-man tour de force. . . . Unfortunately, the script did not give Val Kilmer the dimension that Jim deserved, and that his story demanded. Oh, Jim was portrayed accurately enough, but only up to a point. Oliver's 'take' on Jim showed him to be a mean self-indulgent self-destructive drunk. All true of course. But he also was charming, witty, intelligent, articulate, and he had a sense of humor about himself. . . . Oliver's movie gives a narrow, ugly picture. . . . As I left the theater after one viewing, I heard somebody say, 'I couldn't wait for that sonofabitch to die.' I went home feeling as if Oliver had betrayed Jim. I don't think Jim should be held up as a role model for future generations. But when you trash a man as thoroughly as Oliver Stone trashed Jim Morrison in *The Doors*, the good stuff that Jim had to say gets trashed as well."[11]

Val Kilmer commented, "Ultimately, the movie isn't about the sixties, it isn't even about Jim Morrison. It's about fame . . . in my feeble way, I've been trying not to suffer those pains."[13] Elsewhere, he calls director Stone's take on Morrison "tits and acid."[11] Meg Ryan apparently came away from *The Doors* happy she had missed the sixties: "I kept saying to Oliver, 'This is a cautionary tale, isn't it?'"

After release of the film, Stone was interviewed by a number of writers on his final view of the subject. To one, he said, "I think he was a Dionysian figure. Remember, Dionysus was a god who came to earth to play and tease, to seduce and drive the women mad. Many of Morrison's performances resemble the bacchanals . . . so I would associate Jim more with a pagan spirit. I think he had a problem with the Christian God concept. I think he knew god. He read and adored Nietzsche. But he combined his philosophy with an Indian spirit, a sense of a pre-Christian god, riding the snake, animist . . . like, do you know he married a Celtic witch in New York? We re-created that. . . .

"I believe in Morrison's incantations. Break on through. Kill the pigs. Destroy. Loot. Fuck your mother. All that shit. Anything goes. Anything."[9]

Asked what he thought a sixteen-year-old would get from *The Doors*, Stone told a second writer, "I hope he'll come out and impregnate his girl friend. . . . You never know. You just put your film out there and hope. Very probably, they'll miss the point. . . . There probably will be people who will object to the drug taking in this film. I tried to show that drugs back in those days were meant to expand minds, you know. And we shouldn't deny that.

"As to young people, I hope they'll remember that there was a time, a little bit of time, when a sun shone in and kids questioned everything. They were rebelling. They questioned their parents, and they questioned authority—legal authority and military authority. . . . There was a little Camelot of time when alternate ways of thinking and behaving were allowed and were examined by people like Jim and Janis [Joplin]—to give people an alternate view of history."[1]

9

JFK

WHILE WORKING ON *Born on the Fourth of July* in 1988, Oliver Stone read Jim Garrison's book, *On the Trail of the Assassins* (1988), optioned it for a reported $250,000, and began to research the subject. He soon optioned Jim Marrs's book *Crossfire*. The writer-director found the story line "more of a 'whydunit' than a 'whodunit,' with a small-town district attorney, Jim Garrison, following a small microscopic trail in New Orleans. . . . That little crime, that report of a pistol-whipping [on the assassination night] leads Garrison to the realization that the crime has global consequences."[13]

Even before the release of *JFK*, a Gallup poll said 77 percent, three out of four Americans, were convinced that the Warren Commission was wrong, and there was a conspiracy. Stone said he made his film because "it was a hell of a thriller . . . [and] Kennedy . . . was like the godfather of my generation. He was a very important figure, a leader, and a prince, in a sense."[13]

After Garrison's book, Stone read everything that was credible on the subject.[6] He thought the Marrs book a good overall compendium, praised Sylvia Meaghers's *Accessories after the Fact*, and read about two dozen books after that.

Stone's research coordinator, Jane Rusconi, was hired straight out of Yale University, and read one or two hundred books, also becoming an expert with the subject files. An interview suggests the enormous research efforts made for *JFK*, not simply the recorded words and movements of those involved, but such matters as clothing worn, hairdos, detailed appearances of all locations at the times of events (e.g., for the Book Depository scenes, three thousand exact replica boxes, with stamps and outside printing); pictures and/or films of all characters to help the actors prepare as well as their counterparts or equivalent experts (e.g., sharpshooters, medical examiners) to coach the actors and answer questions.

The research team not only had to locate all sorts of information and character helpers, it also had to track down experts on facets of the assassination (e.g., ballistics), as well as historians and individuals with relevant knowledge. Such resources as the capital's Assassination Archive and the Center for Defense Information proved invaluable. A major, somewhat comical problem was that enthusiasts, some money-hungry, increasingly offered all sorts of assassination goodies, from the "real" death rifle to a letter of congratulation from the president to the "actual" killer.[3] Findings were not simply accumulated, but designed to meet needs of the prop people, art director, costume designers, and others, not the least the scriptwriters.

The annotated script clarifies how much of the research was incorporated into *JFK*.[17] For example, the gay Willie O'Keefe character did not really exist, but was a composite creation drawn from four of Garrison's actual witnesses (p. 65). Garrison also never met a top spy like Mr. X until several years after the trial (p. 105), so apparently just had his own guesses about "the big picture." Reading this script makes one aware of the enormous amounts of reshaping, consolidating, dramatizing, and other transformations the real events underwent. Though Stone does use black-and-white footage to tag flashbacks, and the narration usually notes if we are seeing historical re-creations, Garrison's "speculations," or real period material, more could have perhaps been done to differentiate among them. A sequence attacking a *Life* magazine cover of Oswald with his rifle, it has been noted, is in color, implying Stone's version is the truth, not a speculation.

Stone has said: "Everything we say of a factual nature is correct . . . about the Oswald story. We take the Warren Commission material and we show where the Warren Commission contradicts itself. We're pretty solid on that. We do make some speculations, but those are openly speculations."[13] In other words, caveat emptor.

Stone initially described his concept of the film to Warner Brothers' president Terry Semel as three stories: Garrison's, Oswald's, and How Vietnam Began.[3] His concept of "the whydunit as opposed to the whodunit" resembled Kurosawa's *Rashomon*, a kaleidoscope of possible realities, with the audience finally choosing the truth: "You will leave the theater ready to think about things, and I hope, rethink them, and begin to wonder about some of the sacred cows, some of the official story."[3]

In his first call to cowriter Zachary Sklar (Garrison's book editor) his vision was still open-ended, kaleidoscopic. "I see the models as *Z* and *Rashomon*. I see the event in Dealey Plaza in the first reel, and again in the eighth reel (seventy minutes later), and again later, and each time we're going to see it differently, and with more illumination."[7] Sklar looked at the films, seeing "basically people telling stories, with flashbacks weaving in and out to show what, and we ended up doing a lot of that."

Stone and Sklar worked apart (Stone's usual method). He asked Sklar to prepare an overall treatment, to "flesh out" the book, putting in more scenes than could possibly fit in a film. Sklar spent a year, researching and writing 550 triple-space pages (three times as long as a normal screenplay).

But Stone apparently had his own structure in mind from the get-go—and so did his own first draft, which Sklar found a surprise. Stone: "We would first see the assassination from a conventional point of view, and then throughout the movie, we would see it again and again and again, like peeling an onion skin, until we got to the final moment, when the motorcade makes that turn, and this time you would really see it for the first time, and you would get it. . . . I wanted people to really feel that sense of dread."[6]

Sklar: "He rewrote it from top to bottom and got it closer to the size of a normal screenplay. The basic story line was from Garrison's book, but he also wanted to incorporate information that had been subsequently gathered by citizen researchers."

The script went through at least five substantial drafts, Stone's rewrites were sent to Sklar for suggestions for cuts, alternate scenes, and language changes—editing, Sklar felt. The two met in L.A., but mostly worked separately. Sklar opined: "We really didn't differ on a lot of issues, so there wasn't a great deal of give and take. Basically, I made suggestions in the text and attached explanatory memos. But Oliver made the final decisions, the final rewrites.

Sklar wanted the facts on solid ground because they touch on so many nerves, are in dispute, are not known. Some things had to be speculations, but nothing that allowed critics to say: "Oh, look, they put this in, so we can discredit the entire film."

Sklar noted: "At the same time, Oliver's a real stickler for trying to enrich the dialogue, to tighten the structure, and to condense an enormous amount of material in the film. A lot of our effort was to eliminate the extraneous, to get to the essentials, and there are so many directions you can go. . . . The final script is much longer than the actual film. Oliver cut a quarter of it after it was shot and assembled, which required some revision as well."

At least one writer[3] felt there were a number of serious disagreements between Stone and Sklar, including the treatment of women characters and the portrayal of the Shaw character's gay activities. He also wrote that Stone distorted key facts, e.g., the Ferrie character's natural death from cerebral hemorrhage (according to the coroner's report) became thugs shoving a lethal drug overdose down his throat.

At the same time, the published script does not suggest a *Rashomon*-type kaleidoscope design, but a very focused, if a tad overwritten, story line:

RICH MAN: The son of a bitch is gonna get reelected. He's gotta go, Lou, the election's gotta be stopped [Freudian slip and inside joke— Louis Stone, the director's late father, worked on Wall Street]. (p. 18)

Ms. CONNALLY: Mr. President, you can't say Dallas doesn't love you. . . . (sound of gunshots). (p. 9)

HIGH OFFICIAL VOICE: Thanks for taking care of us down in Dallas. Lady Bird and I will always be grateful. . . . We got to show 'em we got this thing under control, Captain. You got your man, the investigation's over, that's what people want to hear. (p. 177) ·

Even as he was working on *The Doors*, Stone had approached Warner Brothers, who supposedly wanted him to do a film about Howard Hughes. Instead, Stone told Warner's president Terry Semel: "If you're really serious about doing something about corruption, the biggest corruption of all is the Kennedy murder." He described the politically neutral kaleidoscope version to Semel, and in the end got $40 million for the project. Semel's response: "Wow! What a powerful and great idea for a movie!"[3]

An anonymous "top Hollywood producer," commenting on the *JFK* "green light," noted that "as has often been heard in the industry, political and ethical questions about a film are dwarfed by money considerations. All these guys sit in a room, look at Oliver's talent and track record, look at the fact that they'll get Costner and they

28. *JFK*. Kennedy Assassination: "When Kennedy gets in the kill zone, it's a turkey shoot—three teams, professional riflemen, serious people." *(Copyright 1991 Warner Brothers. Courtesy Museum of Modern Art Film Stills Archive.)*

29. *JFK*. Kevin Costner as Jim Garrison: "The magic bullet theory—" *(Copyright 1991 Warner Brothers. Courtesy Museum of Modern Art Film Stills Archive.)*

say: 'This is a good roll of the dice for us.' All the rest really doesn't count."[18] (Stone included this quote in his book on JFK, the film).[17]

At one point Warners apparently became worried about the script, which had become extremely complex, with 212 speaking parts, 1,000 camera setups, 95 scenes, 15 film stocks, and an enormous number of intercuts and flashbacks, surpassing four hours in length. They were encouraged by a Gallup poll they conducted, indicating a 70 percent interest by respondents from eighteen to fifty-four in an Oliver Stone film on the assassination.[3]

In casting his film, Stone felt he was dealing with very dense material. To keep the audience interested, he wanted familiar faces. (He compared *JFK* to *The Longest Day* in this regard.) Stone: "In Kevin [Costner], I found someone who had a sort of fundamental decency to him, and integrity, and I associate that with Jim Garrison. . . . Jimmy Stewart comes to mind, I kept thinking of Gary Cooper." Costner was paid a reported $7 million.

Stone's other casting included Sissy Spacek as Garrison's wife ("gave importance to the domestic side of Jim's life and the toll that took on him, that made him a man, not just a symbol"); Jack Lemmon, Walter Matthau, and Donald Sutherland ("an older generation . . . saying that they agree with my script and these speculations"); Gary Oldman, Tommy Lee Jones, and Kevin Bacon ("fit the characters perfectly. Gary [as Oswald] has got a quality of an anonymous everyman, within a crowd, with a sense of danger. . . . Jones . . . looks like [Shaw] with . . . strong facial bone structure. . . . Bacon's a [composite of several hustlers]; Joe Pesci ("perfect for me as David Ferrie. Volatile, difficult to pin down . . . he says strange things . . . he's inconsistent as a character, on purpose. . . .").

Principal photography began April 15 in Dallas, the first ten days in Dealey Plaza, refurbished to look as it did in 1963, complete to the School Book Depository. Because the sixth floor was a museum, the seventh was used for the assassination sequence and Garrison's visit. Other Dallas locations include the police headquarters where Oswald's press conference was held, and where he was later killed; the Texas Theatre where Oswald was arrested; Oswald's boarding-house, and the actual neighborhood where police officer Tippett was killed.

The weeks in the New Orleans site included filming in the criminal courts building, where Shaw was tried. Washington, DC, locations were filmed last.

Stone paid forty thousand dollars for use of the Zapruder film, owned by the family now. Considerable time and money was spent re-creating other period amateur and news footage.

Filming the assassination, Stone placed various gunmen in various positions, heard the gunfire, saw the bullet trajectories. The writer-director realized: "How difficult it is to kill the president from the sixth floor of the depository through that tree in that time frame of six seconds."[13] Filming revealed that Dealey Plaza had the acoustics of a western canyon—the gunshot echoes becoming inaudible in various pockets, assuming that they came from different locations. This would explain why different eyewitnesses would recall different versions of what happened.

This was in fact the first restaging, revealing, Stone felt, the places from which the head shot and throat shots must have been made. Stone realized how easy it was for three gunners to kill JFK in Dealey Plaza; "which is really structured like a perfect L-shaped ambush, which we used in Vietnam. Actually there's no doubt in my mind that [it] was a military-style ambush."

Though demanding, filming had its lighter moments. The last of the seventy-nine-day shoot was in Washington near the Vietnam Veterans Memorial. Stone's directing of Sutherland and Costner apparently involved going through everything again and again, so each dialogue fragment and facial tic was just so.[3]

Meanwhile, the crew and actors waited for the cast party. "What's Ed Asner playing?" somebody asked. His double replied: "The Texas School Book Depository." Stone made his final retake, the Garrison character learning why JFK had to die. A moment later, two pig-tailed black girls commenced dancing over the Washington knoll. And Stone, happily, leaped up and joined them, smiling.

Stone said that the editing was partly preconceived, partly necessitated by the interweaving of so many simultaneous events. Stone: "I wanted to do the film on two or three levels—sound and picture would take us back, and we'd go from one flashback to another, and then that flashback would go inside another flashback, like the Lee Bowers thing. We'd go to Lee Bowers at the Warren Commission, and then Lee Bowers at the railroad yard, all seen from Jim's point of view in his study. I wanted multiple layers because reading the Warren Commission report is like drowning. The levels and consciousness of reality created through sound—the work done by Wylie Statemand and Michael Minkler is incredible—was also in the script. But Warner Brothers was confused by the script—you can imagine 158 pages filled with flashbacks like that, and I think there are some 2,800 shots in the movie—so I took out all the flashbacks and gave them a simpler script, which they liked. Then I and the editors—Joe Hutshing, Pietro Scalia, and Hank Corwin—ended up putting all the flashbacks back in the editing room, and adding quite a few new ones in a sort of prismatic structure."[6]

Art Simon pointed out some of the subtleties implicit in the use of real archival and restaged historical images. "Integration of old and new footage suggests the dual time frames . . . the way in which historical revision is locked into the present while working with fragments from the past . . . mixing historical footage with Stone's own. . . . *JFK* is able to suggest that Oswald's identity is more difficult to document with certainty . . . underscoring the way in which theories about doubles and stand-ins have complicated the evidence . . . scenes depicting events which may or may not have taken place . . . demand of spectators a critical stance . . . which resists associating that which is seen with that which is true."[14]

Simon's remarks suggest the basic historian's problem of dealing with probabilities, guesses, lies, mistakes, and unanswerable questions. The fact is despite Stone's visual "multiple choices," we only hear Garrison, a detective tracking down the truth, a Hollywood convention. Is there another possibility? During World War I, one radio newsman read *all* battle reports—French, German, British, American—in different accents but the same self-serving tones. Imagine adding the hypothetical comments of Earl Warren, Lee Harvey Oswald, and Lyndon Johnson to *JFK*'s narration track, and trying to draw any conclusions! Like Stone's assassins, the writer-director needed a patsy.

In any case, a kaleidoscope design for *JFK* was dropped early, and a single detective story structure was used. Indeed, alternate culprits (Castro, the mob) are acknowledged, then cleverly "discredited" (e.g., the FBI turns a Garrison man by slyly telling him that they know Castro is guilty, so Garrison must be stopped to prevent atomic war—no real discrediting of anybody is done). Of course, dropping all alternatives but one avoids story problems (could a Hollywood blockbuster end with Garrison crying out, to appropriate images: "Khrushchev! Castro! Don Corleone! LBJ! Richard Helms! *Some* permutation of you will pay for this some day!"

The first cut of *JFK* was about 4½ hours long. For Stone, the worst part was cutting scenes he liked: witnesses linking Shaw, Ferrie, and Oswald; more Shaw material. Ultimately he sees JFK as four movies—compared to the three he originally saw (see above, p. 184): Garrison in New Orleans against Shaw; Oswald's background story; the assassination; and the deep background in Washington, DC.

Before release, Stone described *JFK* as "an alternate myth to the Warren Commission, to kind of explore the true meaning of the shooting in Dealey Plaza, what the murder of John Kennedy meant to his country, why he was killed. The movie unfolds as a mystery, where you unravel layer after layer and you come out at the end with a very strong speculation as to what might have happened. We don't say this is exactly what happened and this is who did it. I wouldn't be that presumptuous, nor do I know. . . .

"I just think a lot of the press has had an agenda to go after this film. . . . They're protecting something, they're protecting an old crime. . . . [The assassination] deeply scared my generation and our culture. I think a lot of our problems—distrust of government started in 1963. I don't think we believed our leaders after that. . . . And I think the American people have become increasingly cynical. They don't vote. The young people don't vote. The country has had race wars as a result. . . . . The country has had a civil war, essentially. A very subtle civil war, but one nevertheless.

"I think in the Warren Commission, [the audience] smelled a rat. I think they're going to like the movie, and I hope to God it will come to be seen by the young as an alternative explanation to JFK's death."[13]

JFK was released nationally in December 1991. What follows is a summary of the director's cut, what Stone calls the "extended version":

Title: To sin by silence when others doth protest makes cowards out of men.

Newsreel flashes and narration: a 1950s cliché family, jet bombers, Eisenhower, JFK taking his oath, Castro, bananas, CIA bosses, Cuban exiles, a JFK speech. Narration: Ike's warning of dangerous military-industrial power complex, Bay of Pigs disaster, lying CIA, brink of atom war, rumored JFK weaknesses: communism, Khrushchev deal, possible Vietnam and Laos pullouts. A JFK speech: "We all inhabit this small planet . . . and we are all mortal."

A hooker dumped on a country road. JFK lands in Dallas. In a hospital, she implores: "They're gonna kill Kennedy."

JFK and Jackie, to drums: motorcade, gawkers, confetti, grim music, the cars, turning a corner, JFK waves, black screen, shots, a flock of birds rises.

The CBS TV newsman: "Three shots were fired . . . seriously wounded."

In New Orleans, an aide walks into the office of District Attorney Jim Garrison, a slender, thoughtful, determined forty-three-year-old.

"Boss, the president's been shot."

In Napoleon's restaurant, locals watch the TV. Newsman: "Blood transfusions . . . priest has administered last rites."

Garrison and his investigator watch. A young Cronkite announces JFK's death. The customers are shocked, numb, a black woman saying he did so much. An anonymous ugly oldster applauds. Garrison: "God, I'm ashamed to be an American."

Eyewitnesses give conflicting stories. Bannister, a Cuban sympathizer, black hater, and private eye, announces: "Camelot in smithereens!"

On TV Oswald is shown, awkward but unafraid: "I emphatically deny these charges."

Bannister enters his office with Martin, his bar pal. Seeing a file ajar, he pistol-whips him.

Garrison, at home with wife Liz and five kids, sees Oswald say, "I'm just a patsy. . . . Nobody has told me anything." A brief superficial bio: Marxist, bad marriage, New Orleans resident. Garrison calls his staff.

Anonymous informers hint David Ferrie, a gay pilot, was the getaway man. Meanwhile, on TV, Oswald is asked if he has anything to say. A moment later Jack Ruby kills him.

On TV we see the JFK funeral, LBJ pledging to continue Vietnam. Ferrie, a jittery weirdo, denies everything. Later, the FBI releases him.

Garrison: "So let's get on with our lives."

The TV announces appointment of the Warren Commission.

Title: Three years later.

Airborne, Garrison talks with Senator Russell Long. He doesn't believe the Warren report, or in a lone killer. Three FBI experts

couldn't do it: "I think Oswald was a good old-fashioned decoy."
Meanwhile, the U.S. is going to hell.

At home, Garrison reads the Warren report: Oswald had a twelve-
hour interrogation, no lawyer, no record. Testimony ignored, leads
not followed up, sloppiness, all broken down, spread around,
points lost.

His wife isn't interested. Garrison reads, flashbacks to testimony
and events, awakes. "Oswald was a trained secret agent. . . . I've
been sleeping for three years!"

Downtown, with his team, Garrison shows Bannister's office, Oswald's pro-Castro group (different street entrances, address, but
same building!). On TV, Oswald claimed to be a Marxist-Leninist.
Garrison: a U.S. double agent! We see flashbacks of both, also Clay
Shaw, an arrogant aristocrat. All this amidst the city's U.S. spy
agency headquarters offices.

Garrison is going to open the JFK case again—starting with pilot Ferrie.

They talk to Jack Martin, dead Bannister's flunkie. After the pistol-
whipping he called the DA's office. The attack was over Operation
Mongoose—training Cuban exiles for a new invasion. Bannister &
Co. helped stockpile guns and explosives—pilots, black operations,
soldiers. Flashbacks: training at a hidden camp. Bannister, ex-FBI,
ran it, Ferrie helped. JFK shut it down. But the FBI let their old
pal off. Oswald was involved, and a top man (We see aristocrat Shaw).
All hated JFK. Suddenly Martin's scared: "What's the *problem?*
You're so *naive!*"

Garrison talks with Andrews, who told Warren a Clay Bertrand
asked him to be Oswald's lawyer. He denies all. Flashback: Andrews
and Bertrand talk. But he won't help: "It's bon voyage, Deano—a
bullet in my head."

In prison, Willie O'Keefe, a handsome pederast, is interviewed
by Garrison, based on his crimes. Flashback: a gay party—Ferrie, O'Keefe, Clay Bertrand, armed Cubans, Oswald with a rifle.
O'Keefe has no reason to lie: "I'm already in jail!" Then rages he
hates JFK for stopping Mongoose, would kill him and blame Castro,
three rifle men at three locations—and one more man sacrificed.
Defiantly: "You don't know anything, Mr. Garrison, because you've
never been fucked in the ass!" He's telling them because JFK stole
the election, fascism is coming back, his death was a great day for

the U.S., killed because he was a communist! O'Keefe: "You're not a bad-looking man, Mr. Garrison—we could have some fun."

Meeting with his staff, Garrison says hoboes spotted that day were let go, the railroad man that spotted them is dead. The hooker who shouted a warning dead in a hit-and-run. If they see Ruby, publicity will kill them. Oswald's taxes are secret. A new Oswald bio with visuals: lonely kid, renouncing U.S. citizenship, sojourn in Russia, a marriage, revealing of radar secrets, causing the U-2 shootdown, ending peace talks, new passport, easy return to U.S. In U.S. joins Dallas émigré community, works for defense contractor, praises JFK, has a "CIA handler." Later his widow calls him violent and psychotic.

Garrison sums up: "He was not a real defector . . . he was an intelligence agent on some kind of a mission. . . . Maybe Oswald didn't even pull the trigger."

Someone asks why he bought a gun via a PO box, when he could just use a fake name and buy one for cash that could never be traced.

Garrison: "We've got to think on a different level, like the CIA. We're through the looking glass, white is black, and black is white."

Interviews with eyewitnesses suggest there were shots from behind a picket fence and behind a hedge, one cop found lots of footprints in mud there; a woman saw a pickup truck with a rifleman, reported it to the FBI—nothing. Flashbacks: riflemen, firing, four to six shots, an angry-faced interrogator telling a witness: "You heard echoes! Echoes! You're not to talk about this to anybody!"

Another witness recalls visiting Jack Ruby's nightclub. While beautiful strippers disrobe, Ruby introduces her to friends Oswald and another man (Shaw). But: "If they can kill the president, do you think they'll think two seconds about a two-bit showgirl like me?"

Flashback: In jail, a sick Jack Ruby tells Earl Warren: "There are people here who do not want me to tell the truth. . . . My life is in danger! Can you take me with you? . . . If I am eliminated there won't be any way of knowing. A whole new form of government will take over." Warren does nothing.

In the Book Depository, Garrison and an aide try to duplicate the shooting. "Three shots in five point six seconds—time me!" They can't, and neither could anyone else who tried. "The essence of the case! The guy couldn't *do* the shooting."

Garrison's investigator states the obvious. The commonsense approach was a frontal shot coming up the other street. If it misses, shoot again. But shooting on the other street allows a triangulated crossfire, the second shot a flat low trajectory from the fence, a third shot from a low floor on the opposite building. "When Kennedy gets in the kill zone, it's a turkey shoot . . . three teams, professional riflemen, serious people. Hunters."

The parade route was changed to make it possible, so they'd have to slow for the turn. And the mayor's brother was a CIA deputy director who called Kennedy a traitor.

New findings show (via flashbacks): A "false Oswald" buying a car, at target practice, bad-mouthing JFK, always drawing attention. There are also phony pix of an "Oswald" in Cuba, to blame Castro. The team reviews a *Life* magazine cover photo: Oswald and rifle. But the shadows on Oswald's face don't match the rest of the picture. Still other records show Oswald buying vehicles when he was abroad. "Oswald was moved around like a dummy corporation in the Bahamas!"

In the present, TV news shows the endless war, LBJ looking sanctimonious.

Garrison has an appointment with aristocrat Shaw/Bertrand. His wife emotionally tells him he's missing a special family day (Easter Sunday), but at last he encounters Shaw, a tall, sophisticated exec type. Garrison narrates a gay encounter between Shaw and O'Keefe, meetings with Oswald, espionage for the CIA. Furious: "You're the first person I ever met who considered it an act of patriotism to kill his own president!" Later he tells his team: "A man may smile and smile and be a villain. Goddam it, we got one of them!"

Next morning, presumably alerted by Shaw, the media swarm in. Garrison gives his team a chance to pull out. Meanwhile Ferrie, hysterical, makes contact. He can't get past the press to his home: "There's a death contract out on me! The agency plays for keeps! . . . Shaw is 'untouchable,' highest clearance, no mafia link, CIA, more to this than you dream!"

Who killed the president? "It's a mystery wrapped in a riddle inside an enigma! Even the shooters didn't fuckin' know! . . . All I wanted to be was a Catholic priest! But I had this one weakness."

At Garrison's office, there's a call: Ferrie's dead. His naked grotesque body is covered by a sheet in his shabby apartment. There are two suicide notes, empty medicine bottles. A flashback: the medicine forced on Ferrie.

Garrison says Ferrie alone expressed remorse over JFK. It got him killed.

His supposed CIA handler was found tortured and shot. So's the case.

At this point, an anonymous FBI man approaches a Garrison aide: The truth is Castro killed JFK. Help us stop Garrison, or (by implication) there will be a war.

Meanwhile, in Washington, Garrison meets a military man who asks to be called X. Everything he'll be saying is classified top secret. X claims to be from World War II in "black ops"—assassinations, coups d'etat, rigging elections, propaganda. Kennedy's not invading Cuba again angered many such people. X worked on the Vietnam pullout plan, but was sent to the South Pole during the assassination. Coming back, he read New Zealand newspapers that had full details too soon, as if ready in advance. As black ops boss, he checked— JFK's Dallas military guard was stood down, the limo's speed cut, all Oswald files destroyed, the limo route unacceptable, Washington's phones failed that day. . . . "He could not be allowed to escape alive." Afterwards Allen Dulles was appointed to help investigate the JFK death—the man JFK dismissed.

"The real question is 'Why?' . . . Who benefitted? Who had the power to cover it up? X's answer is Action Memos 55, 56, 57—JFK's ending the reign of the CIA, the Cuban operation, fifty-three U.S. and twenty-one overseas bases cut. "The organizing principle of any society is war. . . . Kennedy wanted to end the cold war, call off the moon race, was set to withdraw from Vietnam. . . . But that all ended in November 1963.

"Money was at stake, big money, a hundred billion dollars—the big defense contractors, the big oil bankers. One day a call was made: this fall, in the South. It's as old as the crucifixion. The key is there are no compromising connections, except at the most secret point. What's paramount is it must succeed. The perpetrators must be on the winning side—that is a coup d'etat. Does it really matter who shot from what rooftop?"

A (reenacted) flashback: LBJ in the Oval Office: "Gentlemen, I want you to know I'm not gonna let Vietnam go the way China did. You get me elected, I'll give you your damn war!"

Garrison: I can't believe it. They killed him because he wanted to change things.

X is adamant. Politics is just power. He won't testify or help. Garrison threatens the national security structure, they'll try to destroy his credibility. He has to reach critical mass. . . . Fundamentally, people are suckers for the truth . . . and the truth is on your side. I just hope you get a break.

Clay Shaw is arrested, booked. Garrison tells a press conference that notes he's not even in the Warren report: "Let justice be done, though the heavens fall."

On a TV news special the smiling host lists charges against Garrison: intimidation, bribes, drugged witnesses, exploiting the nation's grief. Meanwhile a strange man starts to talk to Garrison's daughter on the phone, so his wife becomes furious.

Garrison's team reports on the trial preparations: the attorney general won't serve his subpoenas on the CIA and FBI, so they can't show a Shaw connection. Hate mail, fan mail. New findings: A possible Oswald-Shaw link, an Oswald warning to the FBI—or an assassination warning? A Telex assassination warning by Oswald was removed as an embarrassment. Bill, turned by the FBI, denies their complicity, argues such a big plot wouldn't work. They can't win. Maybe it's a Mafia plot that the feds avoided probing because of old feds-Mafia links. Garrison argues the Mafia's in, but hasn't guts or power to do what they've uncovered. . . . A coup d'etat with LBJ waiting in the wings.

An investigator walks out.

A glib talk-show host introduces Garrison. Host: "We've heard Cuban exiles killed the president, then the mob, then the CIA, FBI, Pentagon, and White House."

Garrison: "Let's just say I've stopped beating my wife." Audience cheering.

"Reports that you've gone beyond legal means."

Garrison tries to bring out photographs of suspects, but such pictures can't be shown, he's informed. They hustle him off.

In an airport, Bill tells him of a death threat, to which he replies recalling his order not to pass on rumors. Garrison slips into the men's room, then out ahead of what looks like a gay frame-up and police squad working over.

Arriving home, he's witness to RFK's murder, and a report that a staffer's turned, given everything to the feds. Garrison tells them it's like the book *The Old Man and the Sea*. A great fish is caught, but all that's left is the skeleton. In the court of public opinion, they're going to strike the first blow.

Garrison tells his wife about RFK. In the bedroom, they embrace passionately.

The trial begins. Garrison's witnesses to Shaw's meetings with Oswald, and Ferrie are ridiculed. Shaw's alias leads to evidence being rejected. Shaw denies all.

Garrison argues: proving conspiracy means proving more than one man. He subpoenas the Zapruder amateur film of the assassination. A head shot and seven wounds to Kennedy and Connally mean there was a second rifle and a conspiracy. Flashbacks show the body, the forced shifting of the autopsy. Garrison: "The departure of Air Force One from Love Field was not so much a takeoff as a getaway—" He points out the inexperience of the military doctors, their subservience to the big brass. Flashbacks show the autopsy, or its re-creation. Garrison uses diagrams to show the "magic bullet theory," the impossible key shot following a snakelike path back and forth and back and forth through the two bodies to produce all the wounds. The bloody bullet-torn limo, with all its evidence, had been cleaned and rebuilt. The president's brain had disappeared from the National Archives—and with it, the concept of justice.

Garrison asks: what really happened? A diversionary epileptic attack. Meanwhile, Team A to the book depository, Team B in the opposite building, Team C behind the picket fence. Flashbacks: the teams on-site. Garrison: "Three teams, three shooters, a triangulation of fire . . . a turkey shoot."

On the screen, we see a carefully, elaborately edited expanded Zapruder film, intercut with staged re-creations. Garrison: "The first shot rings out. . . . Sounding like a backfire it misses completely. Kennedy stops waving as he hears something . . . Connally turns his head . . . the second shot hits Kennedy in the throat from the front . . . the third shot, the president has been hit, driving him downward and forward . . . Connally shows no signs of being hit . . . the fourth misses Kennedy and takes Connally in the back. The fifth shot misses completely. . . . The sixth shot is the key shot. Back and to his left . . . inconsistent with the shot from the depository . . . back and to the left . . . back and to the left . . . back and to the left." On the screen Jackie's blurred, horrified face seems to rush toward JFK.

Birds rise, crowds scream, the shooters disassemble their weapons and flee, false Secret Service men and hoboes vanish.

Garrison now follows the movements of Oswald. Not terrified flight, but shown as strolling out, realizing he was the patsy, a moviehouse arrest. The media convincing the country, then Oswald disposed of, a neat official legend. The deaths of RKF and King are linked to this one, men whose commitments to peace and change made them dangerous to men committed to war, also killed by "lonely crazed men" who remove our guilt . . . the machinery of legal action scarcely trembles."

Garrison notes the Zapruder film, autopsy pictures, and hundreds of documents locked away for "national security. . . . It's fascism!" November 22, 1963, was a coup d'etat. Its most direct and tragic result was a reversal of President Kennedy's commitment to withdrawal from Vietnam. War is the biggest business in America, worth eighty billion dollars a year. The president's murder was planned by those at the highest levels of U.S. government, and carried out by fanatical and disciplined cold warriors . . . among them Clay Shaw . . . including J. Edgar Hoover and Lyndon B. Johnson, whom I consider accomplices after the fact."

Garrison says the presidency has been reduced to a transitory office. He speaks out for peace, but he acts as the business agent for military hardware manufacturers. He asks the government to release the secret background documents on the assassination, instead of waiting seventy-five years. "Because the government considers you children who might be too disturbed to face this reality. . . . Individual human beings have to create justice and this is not easy because truth often presents a threat to power and we have to fight power at great risk to ourselves." Garrison tells the jury it's up to them.

Shaw is found not guilty, but Garrison tells the press: "It just shows that U.S. intelligence operations are beyond the law. . . . If it takes me thirty years to nail every one of the assassins, then I will continue for thirty years."

He walks out alone with his family, while the press swarm around the smug Shaw.

End titles state the CIA's Helms admitted a conspiracy, Shaw's death, Garrison's reelection, Vietnam costs and casualties. Congress concluded in 1979 that there was probably a conspiracy, and in 1992, as a result of the film, a committee was set up in Congress to determine which documents would be made available to the public.

Title: Dedicated to the young, in whose spirit the search for truth marches on. . . .

JFK's protagonist, Jim Garrison, is an interesting variation of Stone's archetypal isolate hero. Local DA, combat vet, National

Guard officer, good family man, his obsession with the assassination gradually ends or empties of meaning all these for him. Nevertheless, he retains his position and power, staff and funding to follow his compulsion with total excess (pursuing the ultimate government corruption, he increasingly inadvertently resembles trapped politicos comically trying to justify a fixation on unnecessary globetrotting, the ponies, or Las Vegas cuties). His other big difference from Stone's usual raunchy, or career-minded heroes is his old-fashioned honest patriotic citizen quality, a Jimmy Stewart impersonation complete to catch in his throat. Though the real Garrison had many faults, and his Shaw prosecution remains unreasonable, Stone's view of the real man, and certainly the film's ambitions, led to a straight-arrow characterization. In fact the forty-five-minute trial, suggesting the end of *Mr. Smith Goes to Washington,* aside from visuals, is often more curious than convincing. Plainly the Warren report has its faults, and the mechanics of Stone's three teams are plausible. But Garrison's efforts to build sympathy for JFK don't work—he remains in the film a distant, dubious daddy figure as he is for many in the nineties. Likewise, the pleas for Oswald as a tormented outsider are odd, as he's shown to be a low-rent James Bond who lied and betrayed and surely knew what being a spy really entails. Garrison's patriotic rhetoric is Jimmy Stewart sentimentality on supersteroids—if the whole government and U.S. business are money-crazy maniacs, what can Garrison hope to accomplish? In the film, after the trial he promises to carry on for thirty more years, but apparently never did again, just wrote his book, the way the real protagonist in *Salvador* wrote a screenplay.

The world of *JFK* is notable as Oliver Stone's first large-scale treatment of U.S. history and government. Although he does a good job of showing an alternate assassination theory, and blunders if not deceit at high levels, other aspects of his film world can be faulted. The treatment of the New Orleans connection, for example, reveals a viper's nest of violent America-hating gays, so exaggerated gayness itself seems to be the source of right-wing behavior. His treatment of his assassination theory, while thorough ("three guns" seems repeated thirty times), leaves out all governmental, military, and corporate leadership, (no doubt touchy to depict[!]) and instead auspiciously appeals to horror-movie conventions and clichés. The killers mysteriously appear, shoot, and vanish, like hypnotized zombies or aliens. In truth *JFK* recalls Stone's horror films *Seizure* and

The Hand in many ways—evil characters at heart mysterious if not incomprehensible, and filmed as black-and-white possibilities in a sort of Twilight Zone; Mr. X telling Garrison: "If they really saw us as a threat, they'd kill us or put us in an insane asylum!"; even LBJ's evil intimation is borrowed from *Citizen Kane's* monster publisher. ("You get me elected . . . and I'll give you your damn war" versus "You provide the photographs . . . I'll provide the [Spanish-American] war.") It's as if Stone really sought to drag the audience into his oldest nightmare. All this "movie magic" makes the project more suspect.

In addition, Stone made special claims for *JFK* as a cultural myth[15]: "Myths have always expressed the true inner meanings of human events. Myths are dynamic. They interpret history in order to create lasting universal truths. . . . Our film's mythology . . . hopefully . . . will replace the Warren Report, as *Gone with the Wind* replaced *Uncle Tom's Cabin*, and was in turn replaced by *Roots* and *The Civil War*."

Considered as a myth, however, *JFK* leaves much to be desired. The original Greek myths, the made-up characters and conflicts of their humanistic gods, were a way to explain the world and give people hope and faith. More recently, the term has been applied to artworks that reinterpret central modern beliefs, as the various Civil War epics Stone mentions. But a true myth doesn't just give a new version of events, it renews our hopes and increases our understanding. Consider Stanley Kubrick's *Dr. Strangelove*, loosely speaking, a sort of countermyth to our faith in America's cold-war "balance of power." Kubrick shows how accidental war might happen, based on real possibilities. But more importantly, he fearlessly dramatizes the human limits, blindspots, and obsessions of our revered military, political, and scientific leaders (humanized gods indeed!)—providing the real rewards of a myth—new understanding, renewal of hope, perhaps liberation from feelings of helplessness and doom.

JFK, by comparison, leaves us in the dark, facing a corrupt, evil, frightening mystery. If it's a movie myth, it's closer to one like *Close Encounters of the Third Kind* (the *truth* about UFOs). All three include a mysterious conspiracy of the powerful, struggling everymen heroes, a climax of near hopeless defeat, followed by stunning special effects that support a "happy" resolution. But don't count on any declassified assassination paperwork turning up a real giant government/corporate conspiracy, any more than real giant UFOs landing on the White House lawn and a reconstituted living JFK strolling out.

Despite much hostility to *JFK*, perhaps due in part, as Stone suggests, to its implied critique of the U.S. press, there were numerous positive reviews. In any case, its initial January 1992 two-week gross was $30.8 million.

Perhaps *JFK*'s most distinguished enthusiast was Norman Mailer, who saw it as primarily a way to stir up the public.

"Oliver Stone, like many a movie man before him, has mislabeled the product. He has not made a cinematic history, and indeed, to hell with that! He has dared something more dangerous, he has entered the echoing halls of the largest paranoid myth of our time—the undeclared national belief that JFK was killed by the concentrated malign power in the land. . . .

"The question to ask is whether the attempt to capture greatness has become the most unacceptable aesthetic endeavor of them all. In that case, *JFK*, the crudest of the great movies, but a great movie, will have to rest in peace."

"If on the other hand, *JFK* proves successful, then there is no way in which the point will not be raised . . . that [JFK] is a monstrous act, for it is going to be accepted as fact by a new generation of moviegoers. One can only shrug. Several generations have already grown up with the mind-stultifying myth of the lone assassin. Let cinematic hyperbole war with the establishment's skewed reality. At times, bullshit can only be countered by superior bullshit. Stone's version has, at least, the virtue of its thoroughgoing metaphor."[11]

Critic Roger Ebert supports *JFK* as worthwhile, extraordinary moviemaking. "People go to the movies to be told a story. If it is a good story, they will believe it for as long as the movie lasts. If it is a very good story it may linger in their memory somewhat longer. In the case of *JFK*, which I think is a terrific example of storytelling, what they will remember is not the countless facts and conjectures that the movie's hero spins in his lonely campaign to solve the assassination. What they will remember (or if they are young enough, they will learn) is how we all felt on November 22, 1963, and why for all the years afterward a lie seemed to lodge in the national throat—the lie that we know the truth about who murdered Kennedy. . . .

"What he has achieved is among other things one of the most complicated films I have ever seen. By that, I do not mean it is hard to follow, the main thought is always there, and the audience always knows what it needs to know. But Stone's screenplay uses countless sound and image bites, it jumps around freely in time, it shows the same events in different ways from different points of view, and even in Garrison's long summation to the jury, the movie jumps back and forth from testimony to flashbacks to conjecture to possibility. At the end Stone deliberately makes it impossible for us to know exactly what he thinks happened on November 22, 1963. The movie is more urgently about what he believes did *not* happen."[10]

Like Ebert, critic David Denby praised *JFK* as amazing valuable filmmaking. "The movie is appalling and fascinating—unreliable, no doubt, but an amazing visual and structural experience nonetheless, an experience of dread in the flux of life. . . . The movie is an amalgam of facts and speculations, but at its core . . . Stone re-creates, from many points of view, what might have happened in Dealey Plaza in Dallas on November 22, 1963. . . .

"*JFK* is a monomaniac's treasure trove. In its ceaseless piling up of detail, it will give the untiring 'conspiracy community'—American nuts of the highest salt!—enough to argue over for years. But saying that *JFK* isn't always convincing is hardly to dismiss it, as many overly liberal types, blind to the powers of film, have already done. Stone has established a dense web of contingency, 'coincidence,' and design. He has made, if you insist, a fiction of the assassination, a counter-myth, though I hasten to add that his version, at least as an account of the events of Dealey Plaza is a lot more convincing in its physical detail than the Warren Commission's. There was, I believe, *some* sort of conspiracy to kill the president. . . .

"As the new version of the assassination came together at the end, I felt a sickening thrill of dismay and fear, an intimation of mortal design in the flux, malignity revealed. Even God would be frightened."[9]

Finally, *Newsweek's* David Ansen viewed the film politically with measured approval. "My advice is don't trust anyone who claims the movie is hogwash. And don't trust Stone either. Movies are almost by definition a demogogic art form; they can persuade you of almost anything. . . . It is, quite deliberately, a *Mr. Smith Goes to Washington*, complete with climactic courtroom peroration that is a ninety-proof Capraesque barn raiser, down to the Jimmy Stewart catch in Costner's voice. . . .

"But is possible to remain skeptical of *JFK's* Edenic notions of its heroes and still find the movie a remarkable necessary provocation. Real political discourse has all but vanished from Hollywood filmmaking; above and beyond whether Stone's take on the assassination is right his film is a powerful radical vision of America's drift toward covert government. What other filmmaker is even thinking about the uses and abuses of power? . . .

"What *JFK* tells us may be more than many people can or want to swallow. No one should take *JFK* at face value; it's a compellingly argued case, but not to be compared with proof. But my hat is off to the filmmaker—and Warner Brothers—for the reckless chutzpah of the attempt. Make no mistake, this is one very incendiary Hollywood entertainment. Two cheers for Mr. Stone. A troublemaker for our times."[2]

While praised, there was also much harsh criticism of *JFK*, both as fact and film. The *New York Times* reviewed it twice, Vincent Canby taking the first shot.

"*JFK*, for all its sweeping innuendoes and splintery music video editing, winds up breathlessly but running in place. . . . [*JFK*] shortchanged the audience and at the end plays like a bait-and-switch scam. . . .

"What the film does so effectively is to present the case for the idea there actually was a conspiracy, rather than the lone gunman, Lee Harvey Oswald. Beyond that *JFK* cannot go with any assurance. This is no 'All the President's Men.' The only payoff is the sight of Mr. Costner with tears in his eyes. . . .

"By the time *JFK* reaches the Clay Shaw trial, most uninformed members of the movie audience will be exhausted and bored. The movie, which is simultaneously arrogant and timorous, has been unable to separate the important material from the merely colorful. After a certain point, audience interest tunes out. It's a jumble."[4]

A week later, Janet Maslin argued *JFK* was designed on purpose so it could only be accepted totally and blindly. "Images fly by breathlessly and without identification. Composite characters are intermingled with actual ones. Real material and simulated scenes are intercut in a deliberately bewildering fashion. The camera races across bewilderingly supposedly 'top secret' documents and the various charts and models being used to explain forensic evidence. Major matters and petty ones are given equal weight. Without a knowledge of conspiracy trivia to match the director's, and without any ability to assess the film's erratic assortment of facts and fictions, the viewer is at the filmmaker's mercy."[12]

Though I'm concerned with *JFK* as a film, there's been much criticism of its underlying historical idea that JFK really wanted to end the cold war, pull out of Vietnam, and so forth. One writer, Michael Albert, in Z magazine, argues "Why take the risk before trying other means to stay Kennedy's hand? . . . He did not have the country behind him. There were no mass movements seeking radical ends or any progressive change at all. So if you're the head of Lockheed or the CIA, or whatever else, why not just use threats of capital flight, media manipulation, and other time-honored mechanisms available for restraining unwanted government initiatives to so limit Kennedy's capacity to cause trouble that his time in office could be ridden out peacefully? If we want to claim that the Pentagon, CIA, and corporate America assassinated Kennedy, at a minimum we need to show they had already tried to coerce him via the safer, system maintaining mechanisms they ordinarily use to get their way. . . . There is no such evidence."[1]

Noam Chomsky's *Rethinking Camelot: JFK, the Vietnam War, and U.S. Political Culture* (Boston: South End Press, 1993) is mostly devoted to showing that there is no on-the-record evidence whatsoever for *JFK*'s thesis, and an enormous amount for the opposite view. Journalist William Pfaff also comments on *JFK*: "Running away from the serious question, which is why the American policy elite, and American political class and press, all of them acting with good intentions, should have gone so wrong and done so much evil."

Finally, Alexander Cockburn sees *JFK* as a dangerous, contradictory false myth that, (true or not) discourages and cripples effective political action. "Stone tries to have things both ways. He maintains that *JFK* is all true until someone demonstrates forcibly that it isn't. Then he tilts the other way and claims he is trying to construct an alternative myth. . . . The wizardry of the film lab, which can produce a grainy news film of LBJ making deals with the masterminds of JFK's assassination—part of Stone's mythic truth—can also produce Arafat urging Sirhan to kill RFK. Every artist deals in myth, but anyone arguing for Stone's manipulation of history should be aware of the morally tricky terrain and the downside of mythmaking. . . ."[5]

The movie industry had its own responses to *JFK*. Warner Brothers advertising and publicity president Robert G. Friend issued a statement that "controversial films raise a lot of questions and stimulate a lot of debate. . . . We endorse and continue to endorse the right of responsible filmmakers to make their ideas heard and are proud to be a part of such an outstanding motion picture."

Reportedly, Warners helped pay for mailing thirteen thousand copies of a *JFK* study guide to high schools and college history departments. The text, approved by Warners, was accompanied by a film poster and a two-page exercise sheet. Promotion of film attendance was presumably also achieved.

Other industry figures had other opinions. One studio chief, who chose to remain anonymous, stated: "In this case they're not presenting it as Oliver Stone's version of the truth, as one man daring to tell his version, or something like that. They're saying, this movie is the truth. It's not irresponsible to make the movie, it's irresponsible to say [that it] is the truth."[18]

Thomas Baer, a film producer and Kennedy appointee, pointed out the film's sweeping allegations: "In this particular instance, since a living family's nightmare and a nation's torment are perceived by one person's skewed imagination, I would have hoped more control would have been exercised."

The harshest words were from Jack Valenti, head of the Motion Picture Association of America: "In scene after scene, Mr. Stone plasters together the half truth and the totally false and from that he manufactures the plausible. . . . In much the same way, your German boys and girls in 1941 were mesmerized by Riefenstahl's *Triumph of the Will* in which Hitler was depicted as a newborn god. . . . Mr. Stone and Leni Riefenstahl have another genetic linkage, neither of them carried a disclaimer on their film that its contents was mostly pure fiction."[19]

Subsequent to its release, Oliver Stone addressed the National Press Club, including the following remarks: "Thomas Jefferson urged on us the notion that when truth can compete in a free marketplace of ideas, it will prevail. There is as yet no marketplace of history for the years of the Kennedy assassination and immediately afterward. Let us begin to create one. What I have tried to do with this movie is to open a stall in that marketplace of ideas and offer a version of what might have happened, as against the competing versions of what we know did not happen and some other possible versions as well. I am happy to say, based not only on the nine million people who have already seen the movie, that our new stall in that marketplace of ideas is doing a very brisk business and we expect by the time this film is played out in videocassettes, etc., that another fifty or so million Americans will have a little more information on their history."[16]

JFK was nominated for eight Academy Awards, including Best Picture and Best Director, and won for editing and sound. Stone got the Golden Globe Best Director Award of 1991.

10

HEAVEN AND EARTH

THE BOOKS *When Heaven and Earth Changed Places*, by Le Ly Hayslip and Jay Wurts, and *Child of War, Woman of Peace*, by Le Ly Hayslip with James Hayslip, told the story of a Vietnamese woman's life during and after that conflict in Vietnam and the U.S. Stone explained how he was drawn to them for several reasons: "Buddhist spirituality, reverence for ancestors, and respect for the land were three of the strongest elements of Le Ly's story that attracted my interest. . . . I was eager to explore them dramatically and visually.

"I also wanted *Heaven and Earth* to respond to, in part, the blind militarism and mindless revisionism of the Vietnam War as typified by a certain odious brand of thinking that has snaked its way into our culture over the past decade or so, in which the conflict is refought in comic book style with a brand-new ending . . . we win! Within the moronic context of these ideas, hundreds of nameless, faceless Vietnamese are casually shot, stabbed, and blown to smithereens, utterly without the benefit of human consideration. Entire villages are triumphantly laid to waste, with not one microsecond of thought or care given to those inside the little bamboo hamlets. Who were they?

"There were names and faces and histories attached to those bodies littering one end of Vietnam to the other between 1963 and 1975. *Heaven and Earth* is the story of just one family."[10]

Stone apparently worked on the script for over a year, condensing and broadening the story in several ways. Le Ly's husband, for example, Sergeant Steve Butler, is a composite character of four American men who impacted on her life in Vietnam and the U.S.

In an interview he said he saw and presented his protagonist's life as a series of transformations, her identity remade by each encounter with a critical new person in her life, a spiritual odyssey. Stone: "It reminds me of those old inspirational movies, or *St. Joan*. It's *The Sound of Music*."[9]

Stone visualizes the film completely at the writing stage: "I have an image in my head—the size, the feel, the look"—all visualized on paper. He tries to have a definite shot list as well, a fixed shot sequence, and tries to abide by it during filming: "That's very important, how you attack a scene, what's your first shot."

The director in fact sees the camera from the start as an actor, a participant—not a recording device. "The director must deal with the camera, have an attitude towards it—or it's just TV!" In fact, there are a number of shots in which the camera makes the viewer very aware of it—for instance, as it comes hurtling, bomblike, over the calm rice paddies toward the ancient untouched village.

Stone wrote in very few POV shots, however. He felt that since the entire movie was one character's life, they didn't make much difference.

Stone also had from the beginning a stylistic overview. "That Vietnam should go from one extreme to the other, that it should be very beautiful and then very polluted and ugly, which it became . . . but at the end . . . [the film] deliberately repeated several opening shots: to suggest a cycle—life is a turning wheel. I would relate her experience to a rotating wheel—she went through every phase. Nothing changes in Asia, especially in these areas. . . .

"We felt the same way about America . . . from beautiful to ugly would be the motif for both acts. Originally it was scripted as Vietnam intercut with the U.S. It didn't work [laughs]."

A version of the script with that pattern exists,[11] including most of the events in the final film, as well as many others. It reorganizes the final chronological version as follows: (1) opening, V.C. and U.S. abuses, V.C. rape and death threat; (4) U.S. arrival, U.S. problems, dream of Saigon lover; (2)Saigon arrival, Saigon troubles, exile from Saigon; (5) taking job in U.S., more problems, U.S. husband's grim revelations and death threats; Saigon-Danang move, street troubles, U.S. man marriage, V.C. attack and separation, reunion; (6) U.S. divorce, husband's suicide, Viet family reconciliation. The script version's advantages are abstracting her life, and setting up a pattern of conflicts and happiness, a Buddhist view perhaps, as well as an equivocation of Vietnam and U.S. stresses and abuses.

In any case Stone went back to the "classic narrative backbone"— straight chronological order.

Casting got under way in September 1991, Stone deliberately using many nonactor Vietnamese as both characters and extras.

Hiep Thi Le, a young Asian-American beauty, who'd never acted before, was chosen for the central role. Stone: "There's a light around Hiep and a purity of character that's astonishing. She is exactly what she appears to be, a totally spontaneous person." The role called for her to age thirty years, and perform every day of the sixty-four day shoot in Thailand and the U.S., plus L.A. rehearsals and Vietnam field research.

Tommy Lee Jones was cast as Sergeant Steve Butler, the war-haunted marine she marries. (He appears in *JFK*.) He prepared for his role with extensive reading about the marines in Vietnam, "as if" these were his own experiences.

Joan Chen, cast as her mother, starred in *The Last Emperor*.

Dr. Haing S. Ngor, Academy Award winner in *The Killing Fields*, was her father.

Debbie Reynolds played Eugenia, Butler's all-American mom.

In search of a location resembling the real Ky La Village, Stone's team chose Phang-Nga, in the south of Thailand. Its shimmering green landscape and towering rock formations were very similar to those of the Vietnamese hamlet.

The thirty-four stone and concrete hardback houses of the village (soft bamboo and thatch ones as well) resembled those of nineteenth-century European farming villages. The art directors also created the surrounding rice paddies that were the source of the village's beauty. Thousands of plants, flowers, shrubs, and palms were brought in from nurseries elsewhere. The buildings actually served as equipment-storage facilities, between takes actors' shelters, and one air-conditioned structure as the makeup unit. The Buddhist temple became a real place of worship.

Before shooting, a special field trip was made to the Ky La village to allow Stone to renew his knowledge of the milieu, and his two main women characters to go through a sort of "paddy-farm boot camp."

Meanwhile, Stone's director of photography, Robert Richardson, spent two weeks traveling through the countryside getting establishing shots of landscapes, cityscapes, and people.

Filming commenced October 19, 1992. As usual, Stone's produc-

30. *Heaven and Earth.* Steve Polk as USGI, Hiep Thi Le as Le Ly: "No deal, Big Mike, Le Ly not that kind of girl." *(Copyright 1993 Warner Brothers. Courtesy Museum of Modern Art Film Stills Archive.)*

31. *Heaven and Earth.* Hiep Thi Le as Le Ly, Debbie Reynolds as Eugenia, Tommy Lee Jones as Sergeant Steve Butler: "If we didn't sell arms to these people, the goddamn communists would!" *(Copyright 1993 Warner Brothers. Courtesy Museum of Modern Art Film Stills Archive.)*

tion had a unique pace. "There was at least three times as much activity at any given moment than other film sets. *Heaven and Earth* was often an astonishing six-ring circus of thunderous movement and forward momentum. While Stone would be shooting an important scene featuring much dialogue and acting about half a mile away—in the rice paddies at the foothills of the limestone peaks overhanging Ky La—retired marine captain Dale Dye, the film's military advisor, might be using his . . . talents to whip a bunch of extras into shape as a platoon of American GIs.

"A mile or two beyond, Mike Stokey—another military advisor . . . might be applying his knowledge of fighting the Viet Cong to creating a core group of VC for the movie from [candidates] that included Chinese and Vietnamese youths, from Hong Kong and Thailand. . . .

"Meanwhile, the Thai Army might be rolling tanks and armored vehicles—each repainted with the markings of the U.S. army—down the one road that connected Ky La with the main Phuket/ Phang-na highway."[7]

Late in the production, the village was destroyed while the cameras rolled. All that remained were husks of bent rice, the temple ruins, and the shells of the buildings.

Though "close up and personal," the film had a budget of $33 million. The Qui Nihon Highway scenes, jammed with fleeing refugees, required coordination of more than a hundred people, and hundreds of vehicles and animals.

Thailand settings were used for the period locations in Da Nang and Saigon, employing sites in Phuket Town and Bangkok, the subtly French architecture recalling Vietnam. A magnificent 1915 Chinese businessman's mansion was used as the Ahn residence, including period European furniture and a library of flown-in Vietnamese books.

Bangkok's Chinatown, with its ancient alleyways and storefronts, provided suitable urban backgrounds. One sequence, involving numerous military vehicles and extras in uniforms, led to rumors of a government coup.

Throughout the filming, Le Ly was beside Stone every day, as a creative and technical consultant, and "spiritual collaborator." She provided in fact a "tear meter"—the expression on her face an indication of whether a scene was accurate.

Shooting ended with four weeks filming in Los Angeles.

In terms of editing, Stone said of the story development and design: "The pacing is classical, I think: Asiatic, stately, slow. You have to establish a kinship with land, sky, and ancestry, because that's what she keeps returning to."[9]

Though later versions of the script resemble the released film, Stone has said the original cut started with a black-and-white story, part of which is used in the dream sequence at the Ahn's house— Le Ly in a white dress wandering through a ruined landscape. "It was inspired by *Yojimbo*—the tumbleweed in the streets in the wind; that was the opening."

Before release, Oliver Stone said of his film: "We are headed towards a new era in the twenty-first century, I hope, of total consciousness. People of all colors will be sharing this planet. It's necessary for us to get out of our skins and cross this spiritual and devisive gulf that people have formed. . . ."

Heaven and Earth is the story of one Vietnamese and her family that's played out again and again whenever strife replaces love. Therefore it's a universal story, accessible to everyone, everywhere. Hopefully, a Vietnamese woman will matter to an African in the Sudan or an Indian in Bombay or an American in Tuscaloosa. There are no borders between human experience. Suffering occurs everywhere . . . and thank God, so can enlightenment."[10]

Title: The film is based on a true life story.

The young Vietnamese girl Le Ly walks across a lovely farming village landscape, windswept paddies, coconut palms, a curving river.

Her voice tells how a young woman went to fight in wars, love madly, had children, returned to her village, the most beautiful place on earth.

Glimpses of village life, charming postcards: paddies, happy faces, kids and ducks, a maker of paper lanterns, orange-robed Buddhist priest, the girl.

Her earliest memories: working in the rice fields beside her stern-faced mom; playfully asking where babies come from: your belly button! We see the quiet joyful village life: family dinners, Buddhist ceremonies, kids playing.

The French military conquerors arrive, burn the lovely huts. Her father weeps, but the village is rebuilt, just as beautiful. The eternal way of life returns.

In 1965, she narrates, the way of life changed forever. Viet Cong fighters slog in, remind the villagers of foreign invasions, insist Vietnam must choose its own government—a family needs *one* father! We are your family.

Her two brothers, whom she loves, join the V.C.

Le Ly speaks with her kindly faced dad. He explains her brothers may not return. When China ruled them, many died, as with Japan later. Her parents worked like slaves for the Japanese: "Freedom is never a gift, it must be won and won again."

They embrace. Her voice tells us her father taught her to love God and her ancestors, but his words would be twisted by events.

Powerful winds, crackling radio noise. U.S. and Republic copters and troop carriers occupy the village. They remake the village, she tells us; signs, barbed wire, a school. They must turn in the VC for money rewards. By day, she adds, it was a government village, but at night, playing war games, "there was no shortage of Viet Cong." One night the V.C. return, kill the teacher, put up the V.C. flag.

Her family quarrels. Mother calls her a "little princess with blinking eyes" and would send her to the V.C. Her father refuses: "Are you in such a hurry to get rid of your family?"

In BW (black-and-white) flashes, she dreams of a U.S. copter, her brothers interrogated, thrown out, finally herself. She wakes up screaming.

Le Ly explains that in the V.C. you didn't move up, only inward: "The ant is the moral model." She and other youths in the V.C. cadre dig bunkers.

Troops rush into the bunkers—a suicide grenade kills villagers and Republic soldiers.

They come for Le Ly, hold her in a grim room. A Republic interrogator works on her, as a U.S. officer watches: kicking, electric shocks. "Where is the V.C. base!" "I'm just a girl." "Liar! How would your baby like you with no nipples?"

Le Ly and others are tied to a pole, feet doused with U.S. aid honey, ants set loose. A Republic man drops snakes down their dress fronts. The girls scream, the soldiers laugh. Le Ly has a BW vision: her brothers blindfolded, executed, Buddha's face.

The girl is released to her mom, who used her dowery as a bribe. But the village is suspicious. On a rainy night, V.C. soldiers take her to the cemetery and have her kneel before an empty grave, rifle to her head. "My life is in your hands." They don't kill her, but rape her in the mud: "You talk about this, we'll kill you for real."

Village life over, girl and Mom go to Saigon, streets jammed with cars, bikes, rickshaws, Asians, soldiers. Local girls made up as hookers sashay to a crooning "Can't Take My Eyes off You."

The women find domestic work with a kindly rich man, Mr. Ahn, and his svelte wife, cleaning and caring for children. Serving, Le Ly has BW image thoughts: wandering in her bombed-out village. Alone with Ahn, he caresses her, soft music plays, they sleep together. Made pregnant, her mother cries. "You stupid girl!" She's exiled to Da Nang, with a promise of money, not fulfilled.

Le Ly, grown-up, pregnant and streetwise, works the streets cheerily selling bootleg whiskey, cigarettes, and joints to infantrymen. Da Nang is a wartime boomtown, jammed with troops, peasants, whores, shops. She makes sales, denies being a hooker, but is shaken down of her profits by the MPs.

She now lives with her sister Kim, a bar girl in cheap U.S. finery— Le Ly keeps to Asian black trousers and a flowered top and no makeup. Their apartment's a trashy club for GIs. When their dad visits, shy and earnest, Le Ly hides, and a GI tells him to get out: "Old asshole!"

The GI embraces Kim: "Six weeks in the fuckin' bush—I need some pussy bad!"

Her father sits, shamed. Dad came to see Le Ly, but Kim claims she's out. Father: "She has brought shame on us. An unwed mother. But she is not the only one who has brought shame." He says to tell her he misses her, she shouldn't worry. "Life finds a way to balance itself."

The old man leaves. Le Ly tearfully: "Your boyfriend treated Papa so bad, this is not the way Papa taught us to be."

"Do you think I like doing this? Somebody has to make a living!" The two struggle. "No more charity for you! You're spoiled!" She throws her out.

Le Ly narrates how she survived. She picked at the U.S. garbage dump, seeing the remains of poor prostitutes that had been murdered by men.

But she joyfully has her baby, though the doctors advise her to give it away.

She's offered a job on the U.S. base. The officer tells her: "Providing you play along." He unzips, she throws a chair through a glass door. "This man tried to rape me."

Le Ly speaks of the decay of the city: prostitutes, pimps, everything has its price. She's working the streets again. A sergeant pal approaches, gestures at two shy GIs: "They want a real souvenir, they want to boom boom you." It's four hundred dollars, enough for her family for a year, no work, you just lie there, they do the work, do it for world peace! She has a vision of her crying infant, walks slowly toward the two shy men.

Her father dying, Le Ly returns to her village—now a dusty, smoky, brown and gray burned-over fortified U.S. camp, noisy with copters and tanks, no green anywhere.

The villagers she sees have lost legs, arms, feelings—they stare as she passes. Her exhausted mother tells, to BW images, how soldiers forced her father to enter a booby-trapped bunker—he came out, but two who went in after him set off the charges. The soldiers beat him, put him in prison.

Her father sits under a dead tree, gray, bearded, burned-out. He says her mother is also changed. To BW images: the V.C. visited the village, killed suspected women, screamed she was a traitor, too, put a gun to her head, but listened when her uncle pleaded: "How could a mother who sent two sons to die betray the V.C.?" "Tell her to keep her mouth shut!"

Le Ly says she never should have left, but stayed to fight them all. Now she's just a tramp, begging in the streets.

Her father consoles her: you did the best you could. You were born to be a wonderful wife and mother. Don't ask who is right and wrong—dangerous questions! Love is all that counts! Go back to your child. That is the victory that you must win!

They embrace. He dies soon after. She buys her father the best funeral he could have, and they mourn him for one hundred days.

A year passes. Le Ly narrates. She works at the Korean embassy, a tall smiling grown-up lady in a purple Asian gown, riding her purring Honda. In the street a friend introduces Sergeant Steve Butler, a tough but charming fortyish infantryman. The woman took money for her five kids, now they should run. But Butler follows Le Ly to her one-room home. He just wants to talk, will wait until she comes back from work. That night, he's still there. "Me no want boyfriend!" He charms her, admires a photo of her son, sleeps on the floor because it's raining.

Later, lightning makes Le Ly recall in BW the torture interrogation. On the floor Butler also groans; with bad memories, pulls his
knife: "Oh God I'm sorry!"

The two are in bed together, making love.

In the morning Steve leaves, then comes back with Christmas
presents: toys, a fuzzy bear—and an engagement ring. Steve: "I just
want to be with you—and give you another piece of happiness."

"I have bad karma."

"How could bad things happen. . . . It's time for me to settle
down. I'm going home . . . I want you to be there with me. You'll
be safe, you'll be free, your boy will have an education. My first wife
taught me a real lesson . . . I need a good Oriental woman. I want
you to be my wife."

A year passes, Le Ly says. Steve and his new family are posted to
the central highlands, with a home on the base. They have a new
son. Soon they all will visit Disneyland!

Her mother visits. Her father did not want her to leave the land.
But Le Ly loves Butler, he loves her.

Her mother tells her Americans have no beginnings and no ends,
they don't care about their ancestors, so they're free to do anything!
And your father's spirit will not rest.

The base is attacked. Le Ly runs, the kids in her arms. Explosions, soldiers fighting. A chopper drops from the sky, Steve hops
off, gives Le Ly a note identifying her, then screams to the pilot.
Up they go! Without him.

By a country road jammed with overloaded vehicles and fleeing
masses of refugees, the chopper lets her and the kids off: "End of
the line!"

"Fuck you!" The little family joins the fleeing hordes. Le Ly:
"My family was blown to the four winds. My whole country was
collapsing."

V.C. troops stop a bus they're on. Le Ly slyly pretends to be sick.
The V.C. pull fresh teenage girls off, dump used bruised ones from
their vehicles.

In Saigon, all is chaos, U.S. relations swarm the embassy gates. A
soldier hears names, checking: MIA, sorry, MIA, sorry!"

Like a miracle, Steve comes out of the crowds, picks his whole
family up in his arms.

Jet roars, pounding rock, U.S. suburbs. An ecstatic Le Ly: "It
was everything I dreamed of—America. Big Slices and giant people

crushing me in their arms! Best of all, Marine Sergeant Steve Butler!"

From a ranch-style home comes Steve's mom and sis, stocky ladies in perms and harlequin glasses: "A little China doll! I just want to hug her to pieces!" "I'm so happy to meet ya!"

After Nam the ranch house has rooms like airplane hangers, with ugly rugs, eight grotesque mini-Lassie dogs. They show off the kitchen, with a colossal double-door refrigerator that seems as big as the Grand Canyon, and jammed with chilled edibles. To "Sugar," dinner is made, sizzling steak, immense potatoes, canned goods opened, all in close-up like a documentary about a steel foundry.

The Americans gobble and swill, shamelessly chatting of Vietnam drug use and Steve's pay. He drinks so heavily he mispronounces her name.

Alone, Steve tells her he has plans, three more years in the marines, then a big-bucks civilian job at sixty-five thousand. He won't say more.

They visit a supermarket, another gigantic temple bursting with foods and fat Americans. Le Ly want to stock up, but stores here stay full and open. There are hostile stares at the biracial couple: "We'll lick them together!"

Thanksgiving, another mighty repast. His relatives insist she eat, remember the starving. Angrily, Butler tells them of villages where the old folks cried: "Please sir, don't kill me!" Amputees in hospitals waved to GIs because they were happy to be alive! "So don't expect Le Ly to do handstands over your goddamned turkey!"

In bed, however, Steve wants his kids out.

"They more loving when they stay with parents." And Le Ly wants to work to make money—in a factory, a restaurant.

Butler doesn't like it. He tells her about the big job: "Arms! Selling arms!"

"You joking."

"What do you think a military advisor does? I go into countries the U.S. is helping and teach them to use the weapons our corporations make."

"You sell guns to governments so they can blow up women and children?"

"If we didn't sell arms to these people, the goddam communists would."

"Guns, communism! Is that all you Americans ever think about?"

Le Ly tells Butler they don't know anything about each other. You lied to me in Vietnam.

"It was a white lie, a good lie."

Le Ly tells how she gets a job in a circuit-board factory, borrows money to start a business. She realizes Steve wants to control her, but Vietnamese women have their own money. They fight, have more fights. She starts to behave like an American: talking back, scowling.

Steve: "Buddha doesn't know shit!"

Le Ly: "Why did you use four hundred dollars on two more guns?"

"These guns are worth something. Some day they be the only thing between you and death! I want to teach my sons to hunt and shoot."

"I've seen too many guns in my lifetime."

"Fuck you!" Steve tells her he saw the letter from her dink lover.

"Ahn just asked for pictures of his son. Steve—I think one time I love you—but now I see we are too different inside to be soul mates."

Furious, drunk, Steve jams a shotgun against the back of her head. A napalm image, BW images of the V.C. about to execute her. Le Ly says it's a payback for past lives.

Steve collapses, sobbing. He can't live without her. The Marine Corps has him so tied up. He won't get the civilian job. They'll kick him out.

"I'm a killer, baby, I killed so many. . . . Black Ops, three or four a night, all kinds, rice farmers, it was a mind fuck, Psych Ops, knives—rip a man's guts out . . . take a bite out of his liver so he can't get into Buddha heaven . . . drugs, running guns, slavery . . . killed a gook girl I was shacking up with because we weren't sup-posed to fraternize . . . slashed her throat from eat to ear. I was in hell, maybe I went dinky-daw. . . . The more I killed the more they gave me to kill."

BW flashbacks: knifings, shootings, killing helpless Asians. Like being eaten alive by a bellyful of sharks . . . then I met you, and it all changed. But nothing ever changes—so fuck me!"

He sticks the shotgun barrel in his mouth, but she stops him.

Le Ly: "I lie, steal, hate . . . now I pay . . . long time no man love me. . . . No respect . . . we can't give up . . . we must try."

They embrace.

But the fights go on. Le Ly saw a lawyer, thought of going home. On rainy day, Steve moves out. He comes back to take the kids to mass. Le Ly, distrustful, jumps in the van. At the church, the priest is glad to see them. But Steve runs out with the kids, takes off.

He calls her, voice cold and distant. If she wants to see the boys again, tell her lawyer to change all the papers, put it all in his name. Le Ly begs him not to hurt them.

She sees a Buddhist priest, insulted in the insolence of men. Priest: "We may cry for the dead, but not deny the wheel of incarnations. . . . Throw him away, you reject your own redemption . . . the future, the past are the same . . . the path to nirvana is tricky and steep."

In BW images, she imagines herself with her father again.

Her sister, who married a GI, calls. Steve's there, he's taking the kids to Canada. She pleads with him. He weeps, rigid faced. She races over.

In the rain, in the driveway, the van's front door is open, Steve is naked against the wheel, a suicide. She screams.

Le Ly sees a Buddhist priest. Her husband forgives her. The priest tells her the home's front and back doors line up, so money, men, happiness pass through—he's right!

After thirteen years, Le Ly returns to Viet Nam. She's middle class, in real estate, a partner in a restaurant, on a jetliner with the boys.

Mr. Ahn is a humble laundryman now, but happy to see her and his boy.

Her village is green again, but the legless still sit there. Violins play softly. She walks through, looking good, the locals trailing.

Her mother is burned-out and gray. "I'm a ghost, I don't see you." but she's happy to meet her grandsons. Le Ly's surviving brother is there too.

The reunited family dines together; her sister with them.

Her brother, agonized, speaks: "I cannot accept her gifts. . . . You have no idea of the suffering the Americans caused. . . . All we had to hold on to was the future . . . we kept dying . . . then more war, the Cambodians, the Chinese. . . . We had to give up the land . . . just two old ladies, scavaging to stay alive."

Her mother adds: "Heaven and earth changed places. . . . War produces cemeteries . . . and in cemeteries there are no enemies." Her mom cries: she sent her son to war to die, would've kept Le Ly home, so *her* sons died.

Le Ly tells her she's come back, completed the circle, poor to rich, sad to happy, that's what matters.

Her mother will die soon. She looks forward to meeting Papa. Le Ly dreams of her and her father—for the last time.

Le Ly walks in the rice fields, which are green and lovely again. She concludes: "I had come home . . . but home had changed and I would always be in between. . . . It is my fate to be in between. When we accept our fate, we are at peace. In your heart you can hear the voice singing since your moment of birth . . . lasting victories are won in the heart, not in this land or that!"

A title: For My Mother.

In Le Ly Oliver Stone has chosen for the first time a woman protagonist, and a Vietnamese at that. But as such her differences from his previous heroes are more apparent than real. Once again she endures ever-growing isolation—from alien invaders, cruel government, vicious "liberators"—but also, ever increasingly, from a weak father, unsympathetic mother, spiteful sister. Her romantic feelings for Mr. Ahn lead to more exile, and her first adult successes are given up for a bad marriage, her supportive husband becoming a treacherous madman. Only when she takes command of her life alone, becoming a keen businesswoman, does she seem at peace. In the end she remains far from her family. Significantly, Stone excludes her charities, seeing them perhaps as irrelevant. She's left with a few feelings, and an abstract faith.

Stone likewise seems to be shaping a new worldview, where for the first time family feelings and personal loyalties are what matter. As several critics note, the film tries to show the U.S., nationalists, and V.C. as equally tormenting at the personal level, just as the U.S. and Vietnam societies are "equally" harsh and unfeeling toward people "in trouble."

Films have been made on this theme, notably the 1994 surprise hit *Forrest Gump*, whose subnormal hero is unaware of politics, but thrives by simple decency and kindness (a sort of Occidental Le Ly). In fact the two movies have similar episodic, circular designs. *Forrest Gump*, however, is careful to sustain its repressed, decent tone. Stone's film includes brutal rapes in the mud, government torture, gun-to-the-head executions, and a homicidal-suicidal psychopath, all depicted with a sensual if hysterical fascination that undermines his "family values" thesis, and probably revolts or confuses *Gump*ish viewers. The equivocation of U.S. and V.C. harm is also clumsily done, the V.C. shown as teenage rapist/killers suggesting Asian versions of Vic Morrow's JD in *Blackboard Jungle*, while U.S. troops are sweet sex-hungry innocents or insensitive slobs willing to pay for cheap "boom-boom," X-rated characters from *No Time for Sergeants*. Le Ly's husband is a special case, a symbolic loving mature daddy who turns out to be a government payroll serial killer (Interestingly, such a Black Ops government mass murderer was an automatically trusted *hero* in *JFK*). The fact is, fifty-eight thousand Americans died and two million Asians died, we paid $220 billion (two months of the U.S. budget) and they paid with a nation and people in ruins, and most of all we did it to them, horrors impossible to equivocate or mollify.

Heaven and Earth seemed to get few reviews. But some, however, were approving. Jay Carr, in the *Boston Globe*, sees *Heaven and Earth* succeeding almost in spite of itself. "The movie could only have been made with the passage of time and the purging of the anger in *Platoon* and *Born on the Fourth of July*. It's made with obvious regard for Le Ly Hayslip, the woman who endures harrowing atrocities almost from the day her peaceful village is whipped into a froth when noisy, imperious, disruptive helicopters announce: "Your village will be happy and peaceful"; and of course it never is again.

No fictional screenplay would dare to put its heroine through so much. . . . Perversely, though, Stone's jolting style has the effect of distancing us from the material, not drawing us into it. . . . It seems to indicate a lack of trust in the material's intrinsic ability to jolt us without being punched up. *Heaven and Earth* is never less than involving, but you're conscious that it would have deepened its impact if Stone moved back a step and let it seem to tell its own story.

"*Heaven and Earth* is at its best . . . when he allows some bit of convincing behavior to grab us—such as Le Ly's guilt at neglecting her duties as a mother because she's been trying to make it in the U.S. . . . Nothing said by Haing S. Ngor as her father or Joan Chen as her mother conveys their suffering as beautifully as their facial expressions, nothing conveys the chaos of the Vietnam War as powerfully as the densely textured crush of people filling the screen in teeming desperation. Even the tall grass bent flat by deafening chopper blades registers more strongly than Stone's underlinings exacerbated by his cattle prod score. *Heaven and Earth* succeeds

. . . but it would have been a better film if Stone had eased up on the throttle."[1]

Gavin Smith, a Stone enthusiast claims remarkable strength and sensitivity for the film, claims made nowhere else. *"Heaven and Earth* stands outside Stone's body of work. . . . It is more reflective than narrative, more authentically lyrical, and more introspective and spiritualized than might be expected. . . . Stone's best films contain moments of profoundly moving pathos and compassion, and *Heaven and Earth,* which is one of them, gives itself over to this almost entirely. . . .

"When Stone makes a film he *means* it. . . . A penchant for un-fashionable moralism and a tilt towards the schematic are redeemed time and time again by the pleasure principle contained in moments of cinematic brilliance and spontaneity. . . . Stone never did a half-hearted setup, camera move, or cut in his life."[9]

Pat Dowell, a fan and political writer, in *Cineaste* gave the film a shrewd evaluation and very limited praise. "Its visions of torment are all carefully funneled into emotional channels familiar to anyone who has ever seen a soap opera or *Gone with the Wind.* . . . The voiceover creates a stifling emotional mold for the images, and serves to Americanize the story by taming its more uncertain ideological moments. 'The ant became our moral model' we hear when the village begins to work happily with the Viet Cong who have come to organize them. Visually, the film's heaven, the village of Ly La, is full of golden vistas, saffron robes in a green landscape, and the flares of war."[2]

Stone carefully picks his way across the political minefield of a Hollywood Vietnamese movie by showing the peasants caught be-tween two ruthless forces. . . . A pox on both your houses is the methodology Stone employs, demonstrating Le Ly's dilemma with parallel scenes that comprise one of the film's few effective uses of narration [viz., U.S. torture vs. V.C. rape; Asian big-city humili-ations vs. a U.S. Viet vet madman]. . . . It becomes clear that *Heaven and Earth* presents the Oliver Stone version of family val-ues, and that it isn't going to rise above the liberal cliché of imputing ethnic characters with a warmth and humanity that whites have lost.

Many of the reviews of *Heaven and Earth* criticized it harshly. Robert Stone's critique also acknowledges Stone's paralleling design, but sees it as a fault. "The story of *Heaven and Earth* is not one that lends itself to the kind of big screen action scenes Oliver Stone stages most effectively. . . . This is preeminently a story of suffering, loss and exile. . . . The mood is somber and almost ceremonial, and perhaps for that reason the many emotional scenes fail to move us. . . . The viewer expects the worst and waits for a change of tone which is not forthcoming—not necessarily a fault of Stone's.

"Stone has predictable fun with the reaction of a Vietnamese peasant girl to the gross abundance of American supermarkets and her encounter with a blue collar world . . . but every once in a while Stone departs from her narrative, for reasons that seem to suggest his impatience with subtlety and his passion for emphasis [e.g., the naked suicide]. Maybe he wanted to echo the Book of Common Prayer. In the book, when Hayslip is tortured . . . there's no mention of Americans being present. . . . *Heaven and Earth* shows what plainly appears to be a U.S. advisor on the scene, standing by indifferently at parade rest.

"The best filmmakers seem to have resisted the pull of simplification. . . . Stone wants to be a vet and a protester, to be for the GIs and the Viet Cong, an American and a Vietnamese. The funny thing is that—in life—it's no trick . . . but it's different in art, ever so much harder. You can do it sometimes, but you have to be an artist, not a Hollywood pro."[12]

Other critics were more straightforward in their displeasure. James Vermiere of the Boston Herald[13] saw the film as fragmented and incoherent. "*Heaven and Earth* addresses the issue of spiritual healing. . . . [It] looks at Vietnam through the eyes of a Vietnamese woman . . . although the view is often compelling and entirely unique to Stone's films, it is finally too splintered and crazed. . . .

"Stone presents the dilemma of Le Ly and Steve as a microcosm for the one facing America and Vietnam. How do these two people, living reminders of the horrors each has suffered, find peace and learn to embrace their intertwining destinies? It's a question Stone can't answer, nor can the Buddhist monk who counsels Le Ly about her 'man hate' and actually refers to her as 'my little orange blossom.'[1]

"Like Steven Spielberg, a filmmaker he resembles in many ways, Stone works in a kind of visual high volume, an effective style but easily abused. . . . Stone may call for reconciliation, and argue that neither nation can purge itself of its bad karma, without the help of the other. But . . . some viewers may think he's just on a wacky, liberal guilt trip. Stone may be arguing for healing, but his film has multiple fractures."[13]

Todd McCarthy, in *Rolling Stone*, feels: "Stone and his audience have been here before, and the point of diminishing returns has definitely been reached. . . . (The film is) "an attempt to show the war and its aftermath from a Vietnamese point of view, but the sledgehammer approach to storytelling merely results in audience numbness and distance from the potentially moving material. . . .

"Stone presents nearly forty years in the life of Le Ly as a succession of events with a melodrama quotient that might have challenged even Joan Crawford or Lana Turner. . . . There are numerous other problems as well. Lecturing tone is set from the beginning . . . characters speaking a sort of pidgin English that makes them seem more simple and less natural than they should. . . . Worst of all is the score . . . which thunderously announces and then underlines the film's every occurrence. . . .

"Stone has taken no overt political position, and consequently adds very little to the general discussion of Vietnam or his own. . . . [The] story doesn't provide him with a forum to say much new or interesting. Nor . . . does he make it feel personal or impassioned."[5]

Le Ly said of the completed movie: "When you see this film, you will feel a bond with the people who made it, and through the wonder of this connection, feel new compassion for those people whose lives it depicts. . . .

"Soul, I believe, are what Oliver's movies are all about. . . . Oliver has given us many strong 'sons' this way. I am pleased and honored that, with *Heaven and Earth*, he has now also raised a daughter worthy of his warrior's heart.

"The film . . . is like a great warm blanket or a splash in the icy sea. In a darkened theater, it surrounds us and dominates our senses. In the space of minutes we laugh and cry and feel pulse-pounding excitement and emotions come to the surface—breathtaking beauty and absolute horror all mixed. . . . Because of this I ask people who see *Heaven and Earth* to take a few minutes afterwards, at a quiet time and place, to think about what they saw and felt."

Stone told a film journal interviewer: "There's always resistance to difficult subject matter and whatever people say, I think they're sometimes looking to see it fail. That's a difficult position to be in. Certainly, *Heaven and Earth* is risky because we don't have any stars and we have an Asian woman as the protagonist. I think the movie is good, but it will be difficult to market."[3]

In August 1994 the critic for the *New Yorker* wrote: "*Heaven and Earth* wasn't just a flop, it was a resounding, scary flop (It cost 33 million dollars, and grossed only 6 million dollars in the U.S.)."[6] In an interview in *USA Today* for August 26, 1994, Stone blames bad timing, among other things, for the film's failure. "Immigration is a problem right now and Vietnam is not exactly popular." The lack of a female star for the lead role also hurt: "I think *Heaven and Earth* would have done much better if Julia Roberts were in the movie. But I think the critics would have been even harder. The picture . . . was a tremendous journey."

11

NATURAL BORN KILLERS

STONE BEGAN WORKING on *Natural Born Killers* shortly
after finishing *Heaven and Earth*. Of his intentions, he said: "I
wanted to have fun. I really wanted to do a combination of a road
movie, like *Bonnie and Clyde*, and a prison film, like *The Great
Escape* and *Papillon*."[15]
The film originated as an original script by Quentin Tarantino.
Notably, the 1991 script has most of the elements of the final film:
main characters, dialogue, plot turns, including the opening massacre, reign of terror, escape via TV exploitation show (whose anchor
screams threats to sue), and final reversal execution.[13] Dropped were
such ideas as aspects of an exploitation movie about the couple, a
trial at which a demonic Mickey defends himself and murders a
witness on the stand, and a "sentimental" view of the killer couple:

PSYCHIATRIST: In a world where most people can't make the simplest of
relationships work, and the slightest emotional commitment is considered devastating, Mickey and Mallory have a romance of Shakespear-
ian magnitude.

According to Stone, however, the original script excited almost no
one. "Quentin Tarantino's script was brilliant and wacky and certainly hinted at different formats. . . . I found after I paid a lot of
money for the script that everybody had read it and passed on it,
including B and C directors. It was embarrassing (laughs)."
In April 1991 Tarantino met producers Don Murphy and Jane
Hamsher of J. D. Productions—at the time having no money and
working out of their living room, they *had* to make *NBK*, though it
was turned down by companies all over Hollywood. After the usual

"myriad setbacks and false starts," Stone met with the couple, promising to do *NBK* as a quick, inexpensive project similar to *Talk Radio* ($10 or 12 million). Stone commented: "I never wanted to shoot the Tarantino script. There was a structure and I liked the ideas and there were some very funny scenes, but it was not a movie I wanted to do. I never had any doubt about that—I always knew there was another level I wanted to try for. That may be good or bad, and people may revile me by saying: 'It should have been a B-film, and that's it.'"[17]

Hamsher commented: "The problem with matching up the [original] script with Oliver Stone was character based. . . . It was not right for a $20 million dollar plus movie. What Oliver wanted done entailed fleshing out the relationship between Mickey and Mallory."

For this, screenwriter Dave Veloz was called in. "Quentin's script had an absolute in-your-face quality, great dialogue, great surprises . . . and a great love for white trash culture . . . but Oliver wanted to temper the *Badlands* element with a more romantic angle."

Working with Stone, Veloz started by adding primarily the things that lovers do: "A motel scene where Mallory washes Mickey's hair. At one point he realizes she's not wearing her wedding ring and explodes. There's this creepy couple having this really domestic scene, but then the camera pans over and we see they have a hostage tied up in the corner that they're going to torture and murder later on. So it's *Ozzie and Harriet* with this sadistic bent . . . something like the bond between wolves. They would never betray each other, never lie and never let one another rot in prison, but in a moment of rage or jealousy they could kill each other."

Stone apparently felt that by making the couple's love such a primeval force, whatever they did for it was justified—making the film an "emotionally grounded fantasy"—the kind of love most people long for and dream about, at least at some point in their lives, transcending the original action thriller story line.

The main change amounted to a new first act. Stone: "[It's] about the road and what the Mickey and Mallory characters are really like. There are a lot of moral choices on the road. What are these characters about? They're not just victims, there's something going on there. Through flashbacks, we see where they're from. Its clear they're different."

Veloz adds: "[There's] a kind of twisted flashback where Mickey has a dream showing how he and Mallory met. We tried to build into his character that he was fascinated with people's fascination with him . . . almost like voyeurism twice removed. (He also watches a lot of TV.) The only way Mickey could conceive of himself in a fantasy situation would be as the star of a TV show, 'I Love Mallory.'"

Asked why this character killed, Stone said: "Mickey is a total predator. He understands the universe only from a predatory stand-point, and he justifies what he does that way. Mallory is a different question because she comes from a different space, and we clarify their different motives. But within our satire, we're surrounding Mickey and Mallory with such scumbags that predation seems like the natural, Darwinian thing for them to do in that world."

Cowriter Veloz adds romantically: "They're almost healthy in what they do, their murder spree. Instead of being sick, they're just plain evil. In another time, they might have become heroes worthy of attention, but in the mediocrity of our times, they just become serial killers."

Richard Rutowski, the third revisionist: "One aspect I contributed to was the demon concept . . . that Mickey and Mallory are not simply driven by things we can understand, but ones we can't, and that they are just as real—just as physical." Supposedly the film *shows* us these evil selves and sinister outside forces: bloody demons, smoking dragons, shaping the future, flashing on the screen, as one critic suggests, to remind the audience that evil exists and always seeks to master us.

Interestingly, at least one critic felt the original Tarantino script with its layered structure, was superior before being "flattened to a linear, and humdrum, if endlessly frenzied narrative . . . as if Stone had said: 'This kid's supposed to be so cool, I'll take his script and show 'em who's still the coolest of all.'"[3]

In casting the film, Stone chose Woody Harrelson for the male serial killer, who described his role as "a journey into the heart of darkness. I was much in the headspace of the character, surrounded . . . with books and videos about serial killers, interviews with Man-sons. . . . I went into my own shadow, my own rage . . . it was like opening a wound."[2]

Of Juliette Lewis's role, Stone said: "Mallory's a killer. She's an *animale*, a cunning creature. Of course, Juliette is slight in stature, but she's very convincing."[16] Lewis: "I just met with Oliver and I sold him on the idea that only I could play somebody who could tear your throat out with her bare hands." In fact, Lewis's questioning of the girl's background was the source of the "I Love Mallory" sequence.

Robert Downey, Jr., chosen for Wayne Gale, the "I Am the Story" host of the show "American Maniacs," hung out with "Current Affair" reporter Steve Dunleavy to research his role, and adopted his Australian accent and manner.

Stone saw the cop character, Jack Scagnetti, played by Tom Sizemore, as a counter to Mickey Knox because "he's also in love with the heroine, Mallory Knox, and tries to abduct her. . . . [He] wants to live Mickey's life, but wants to live it on the side of the law."

The film's prison warden, played by Tommy Lee Jones, likewise abuses his authority. Jones saw his character as obsessed and putting on manners, like his stupid little pencil-thin toothbrush mustache ("an elegant man, in his own mind").

To prepare his actors for the film, Stone sent them into the desert to fire guns, and played deafening rock music between takes. During the prison sequences, he had them mingle with real convicts.

In terms of pure cinema, Stone's director of photography, Robert Richardson, stated that *NBK* was totally unlike his thematically based projects—*JFK* or *Born on the Fourth of July*—where it was clear from the start (e.g., *JFK*'s Zapruder film and assassination) how it would be shot, the colors, how far the boundaries of reality are to be broken.[1] Richardson: "But *Killers* is more based on a fantastic approach to the lives of serial killers, involving things like love, brutal exercises in violence, and the impact of the media. And all those areas came with different visual approaches. So we used video for the media pieces, as well as other formats. . . . It was . . . a case of developing the look as we went. And that's also true of the way we lit every scene. Much happened on the spur of the moment, like abstract painting."

Personally, Richardson experienced tremendous levels of angst. "The subject matter was difficult for me to deal with. It's extremely violent, and the randomness of the material forced us into a similarly random approach. There's no rhyme or reason to the way it was shot, except for the moment you're shooting it. . . . All we're really trying to do, I think, is form a new vocabulary of texture . . . whether its B&W, color, video, or super 8. (We sometimes decided upon a film format with a coin toss.)"

The idea of using many formats and unusual lighting setups began with the shooting of the title landscapes—from snow to deserts, to

32. *Natural Born Killers*. Juliette Lewis as Mallory Knox, Woody Harrelson as Mickey Knox: "By the power vested in me as god of my world—" *(Copyright 1994 Warner Brothers. Courtesy Museum of Modern Art Film Stills Archive.)*

33. *Natural Born Killers*. Robert Downey, Jr., as tabloid TV star Wayne Gale, Woody Harrelson as Mickey Knox: "Was an instant of purity worth a lifetime of your lies?" *(Copyright 1994 Warner Brothers. Courtesy Museum of Modern Art Film Stills Archive.)*

be used in expressionistic rear projections, the couple sitting in the car. Richardson shot black and white (B&W), then tinted it, then color, then tinted that—producing very interesting effects. Later, when they shot the scenes with Woody and Juliet driving on a stage, the color kinematics (changes over time) were altered by lighting the characters with kino flos (special lights) matching the road footage. Stone said: "This is pretty interesting. I love it."

One theme of the film is demons, so lead-character demons were shot—literal devils, or the normal characters dressed in certain costumes taken through lighting changes (hard top lights, simple side backs, different color zones) and this material altered or strobed and used for "demon moments."

Extreme visual approaches were used throughout the film. The brutal filling station seduction/murder is lit with green gels on fluorescents, anticipating a later scene in a giant warehouse pharmacy, lit only with fluorescents (kino flo green), when the couple search for rattlesnake poison antidote. Other road sequences involve an enormous lighting rig around the rolling car, in order to match the onstage color changes, one resembling a traveling rock-and-roll stage show.

Stone's set is largely closed to outsiders, and Stone keeps his shot list, the daily work schedule, a secret from everyone except his cameraman. Scripts are numbered, so that if one is leaked to an outsider, it can be traced (head producer Clayton Townsend: "Then it's time to behead someone"). Stone actually directs from inside a sort of tent or "cocoon"—three tall cloth-lined walls housing a twenty-inch TV monitor and director's chair—supposedly designed to provide privacy while Stone considers each take, and forestall unwanted advice from amateur auteurs.

Actor Robert Downey felt Stone: "created an environment that was like purgatory on a per diem. What's bearable to Oliver is excruciating to most. Like being somewhere where it was very hot, and we could have had more fans but he opted not to. I mean it was like psychological warfare—loud music, these very hot sets, and certain phrases from Oliver like: 'What are you doing? You're going to ruin my movie!' And a Saturday night with Oliver after a long week is basically pagan Rome 26 A.D. We went down the tubes a thousand ways from Sunday."[12]

At one point, Stone wanted a point-of-view shot that had the Mallory character run up to the observation window of her cell and smash her head against it. Cameraman Richardson did it several times, stopping eight inches from the door. But that was insufficient. Finally he slammed into the wall, fell back, hit the floor, and broke a finger. After that Stone used the second-unit photographer, who finally ran into the wall and needed four stitches in his eye. But Stone got his shot.

According to Richardson[1] the prison sequences, shot over two weeks in Joliet and Stateville, Illinois, were the most difficult for all. Half the inmates were murderers, many others guilty of armed robbery and similar crimes—making the cast and crew understandably nervous. One day a storm caused a power failure, leaving Stone's people alone in the dark with two hundred convicts. Richardson: "I felt hands all over me, because they'll steal anything they can get." A few minutes later, the backup generator kicked in.

The riot scenes were also frightening. The prisoners were playing themselves in a staged, full-scale prison riot. Richardson: "At that point, the line between acting and reality disappeared. Of course Oliver loved that, but he was the only one."

The filming at Stateville, Illinois, prison involved payments to the institution, as well as to individuals (twenty-five dollars a day), prisoner-extras and prisoner-production assistants. Rubber guns were allowed only if no inmates were in a scene, and were always chained to the user, with a real guard always present who held them between takes.

Throughout the film, Stone was undecided and finally shot two endings: they live; they die. Stone: "In one, they are killed, it's a surprise. There's a psycho who turns the guns on them and kills them. A bizarre scene, fitting that after killing so randomly, they would be randomly killed. In the other, they live. . . . I feel I used the accurate, correct ending. It had more juice."[2]

Natural Born Killers was shot in fifty-three days.

It took eleven months to edit. Coeditor Harry Corwin: "We wanted an impressionistic feeling, but there was no randomness. Every two-frame flash was thought out. This style can work on anything. It could be one of the futures of filmmaking."

The film-editing pass included dropping several extremely violent sequences. Some involved parts of the "American Maniacs" TV show chronicling Mickey and Mallory's career. One sequence involved the pair cutting the legs off two brothers who are actually great fans, and who later say it gave them "an extra challenge." (The section was put in to give roles to two potential backers who insisted they appear in the film.) Another dropped sequence had a victim broiled alive in an oven and Mickey acting as lawyer at their trial.

One hundred fifty separate scenes were eventually removed to get *NBK*'s Motion Picture Association rating changed from NC-17 to R (including five separate screenings for the rating board). These included rioting prisoners putting their warden's head on a spike, and an image through the bullet hole Mallory shoots in the TV reporter's hand (as with *JFK*, they are restored in a 1995 director's cut extended version).

What really distinguishes the film's editing, however, is its special style. Critic Stephen Schiff: "[Stone has concentrated on] how much dislocation, cross-referencing, near subliminal imagery, and ironic counterpoint he can pack into every moment of screen time. Within fractions of a second, Stone whiplashes among camera angles, lenses, and film stocks—35mm, 16mm, super 8, videotape, color, black-and-white, still photographs, bits of animation—to create an unstable, lurching spectacle that resembles nothing so much as an evening of crazed channel-surfing. . . . Empty and repugnant as Mickey and Mallory themselves may be, their odyssey is a rich thing to watch: you feel as though you were seeing their conscious and their unconscious lives, and the forces that formed them, all at once."[12]

Stone added: "You have to re-create the climate of madness in the culture and you do that by these free associations that occur throughout the movie. The world is violent and we're swamped in it in this century. So I mirror that—I'm a distorting mirror, like in the circus. I'm making the point that the killers have been so idealized and so glorified by the media that the media become worse than the killers. I'm making the point that we have reached a proportion that's almost insane." In other words, we've come a long way since that judge said nobody was ever seduced by a book.

In any case, the final cost of *Natural Born Killers* was $34 million.

In some ways, Stone's most recent film refers back to his very first one, *Seizure*, turned upside down, with the man-and-wife loving-couple protagonists demon-driven, and willing to destroy the ruling forces of their "reality." In this regard, Stone's prerelease comments on the film are especially interesting:

Stone: "The psychology of [*Natural Born Killers*] is Jungian—with a little Nietzsche. It's really about the idea of a superman and the need to control all life and attain true wisdom. At the same time, though, while Mickey and Mallory are pursuing this, they are cursed by a demon from the very beginning and they inherit the demon at the end. . . . It has to be an unconscious meditation on violence; it can't be conscious or *explained* violence, but so deeply engraved in the psyche that the Jungian is the best approach to the material. Pointing to the mother and father isn't enough—you have to point to the cultural factors too. So what we're trying to do in the movie is reflect many of the things that happened in the twentieth century: the Nazi death camps, Stalin, the concept of violence in America, which is so random. . . . TV and the movies only reflect the violence that's in the air. . . .

"I'm approaching this film from the direction of satire and humor, and I'm pushing into areas I haven't been to before . . . but I suppose I don't take all of it, violence included, that seriously. . . . What characterizes the film is a complete lack of consistency to the point of being deliberately, totally illogical—which is fun. Don't ask me to explain it but it's a style that comes out of making a lot of films—coming down to deciding what formats to shoot, when and how, and changing perspectives. There's nothing fixed about the film's universe. It's a sort of wacky place, like this world is now. . . . [The protagonists] rediscover their behavior as they go. They're totally spontaneous animals, reinvented human existence on a murder-by-murder basis (laughs)."[16]

Elsewhere Stone offered another take on his movie: "Mickey defends killing. His justification for it is that 'murder is pure.' It's in his mouth, it was written by us. We put it out as his belief system. We take him seriously . . . but I don't think you can say that is glorification. That is satire."[2]

Stone is satirizing our society, the "most violent in history. . . . [Those characters] who represent the establishment are by contrast wholly perverted and our establishment is perverted and corrupt."

Note: this summary barely suggests the film's extraordinary editing and imagery, apparently putting us inside characters' heads as well as suggesting our surreal media culture, parading fantastic images of lust, hate, and violence.

A craggy western landscape, a diesel freight train, a diner.

On a TV screen: "Leave It to Beaver," Nixon's farewell, a monster/demon.

A sexy dangerous-looking eighteen-year-old in hip huggers and a halter top dances to jukebox rock.

A pleasant young man in tinted shades and jeans, a bit like John Lennon, at the diner counter orders key lime pie, reads a paper. Headline: Mickey and Mallory Kill Six Teens at a Slumber Party.

A pickup truck pulls in, three overalled rednecks come inside.

The young woman dances along, one truckman joins her. "Are you flirting with me?"

Suddenly the temptress lashes out, punches him, smashes his head on a table, kicks him in the groin, knifes him, half in BW images: "How sexy am I now!"

Her man Mickey slashes the face and chest of another redneck, cuts off a finger. When the cook waves a meat cleaver, Mickey shoots him. Drumbeats, power chords, and throbbing rhythms cue punches, gunshots, slashes—a comic massacre. The third man tries to flee, but Mickey's knife flies after him, camera following it like Robin Hood's arrow, spinning, into its target.

A bullet chases another man, hesitates, penetrates.

Two live. Mallory: "Eenie, meenie, miney, moe." Now only a pop-eyed cook remains. The woman, as if to a child: "Say it, Mickey and Mallory Knox did it."

The couple twirl to "La vie En Rose," the diner dark, stars on the ceiling, fireworks exploding softly.

The couple drive madly through a maelstrom of sound; through a tunnel, paralleling a racing train, knocking down "road closed" signs, past immense dandelions, past a dragon—kissing, kissing, kissing through clouds of flames.

Quiet, darkness. Mallory dances along against the dark sky. They've stopped in the desert, Mickey pisses on the sand.

Mallory, softly: "I see angels, Mickey, they're comin' down for us . . . you ridin' a big red horse . . . the future, there's no death, because you and I are angels."

"I loved you, Mal, since the day we met."

A heart-shaped "I Love Lucy" graphic. Title: I LOVE MALLORY.

Grainy, color images follow. A terrible lower-class home, fat repulsive mom and pop, goofy kid brother, and Mallory as a baby-faced teen in nylons and a dress barely to her thighs.

Pop: "You ain't goin' out, you stupid bitch. . . . Take a shower, I'll come up after and see how *clean* you are--she won't see my face for half an hour!"

Mickey, dressed as a butcher boy, arrives with fifty pounds of meat in a slovenly bundle. Boy and girl spot each other: "I'm Mallory." "You ought to change your name to Beautiful . . . you believe in fate, Mallory?" To soft music, the two slip away.

Pop: "He stole my car! Call the cops!" TV credits race up the screen.

Title: Apprehended for Grand Theft Auto: Mallory visits him in jail, in grainy BW images, to a sickly sung "You Belong to Me." "Even though I'm in here, I'm with you every night." "My daddy's moving. . . . If you ever show up, he'll kill you."

Prisoner work detail on a ranch. The tall eerie column of a tornado in the distance. In the chaos, Mickey throws himself on a horse, makes a break. When a guard tries to follow, his horse is terrified by a rattler.

At Mallory's home, Mickey fights her bloated pop with a tire iron. Dad ends up head in the fish tank, eyes peering at the guppies, dead to "Mate, Spawn and Die." Mallory dances with glee. Mom's tied and gagged in her bed, lighter fluid sprinkled and lit. Mallory: "You never did nothin'!" Flames jump up. Kid brother is told: "You're free, Kevin!"

To fireworks, the lovers peel out, Mallory in man's underwear turned sideways, legs wiggling around Mickey's neck: "You make every day feel like kindergarten. I'm a new woman!"

The two stand on a bridge high, high over a great gorge and river. Mickey: "It's time to grow up. We've got the road to hell in front of us. Will you marry me?"

Mickey says this is their church, slices their palms (Mallory: "Fuck! That's not what I had in mind!"), mixes their blood. In animation, blood drops with their faces dive riverward ("We'll be living in all the oceans now!"). They put on twin rattler wedding rings.

A truckload of yelling Mexes zips past, but: "I won't murder anybody on our wedding day . . . by the power vested in me as god of my world." Her long white veil drifts into the wide windy gorge, eerily.

A ridiculous bearded Aussie newsman, Wayne Gale, in a pseudo-masculine voice: "After that there was no stopping Mickey and Mallory!" TV show titles announce "American Maniacs," his name on all credits. A reenactment shows the couple asking a cop for directions, then blasting him. Chased, they comically shoot down a harmless marathon bicyclist, head down as he pumps away.

In the show's video-editing suite, the host browbeats his team: "Repetition, repetition, this is junkfood for the brain!" The monitor flashes a smug unshaven lecherous mug. Scagnetti, a serial killer hound.

Sound bites show idiotic youth worldwide. Blond-dyed Japanese girl teens cheer Mickey and Mallory. U.S. kids: "The best thing to happen to mass murder since Manson!" Newsmag cover stories. A "serious" kid: "I'm not saying I believe in mass murder, but if I were one, I'd want to be Mickey and Mallory!" Paris teens: "Soup-peer-cool!"

The couple drive, to "Back in Baby's Arms." "Do you think I'm still sexy?" "We may have to find us a motel—so I can put my lovin' bride on the bed and tie her up."

Night. A motel. The two embrace. The window frames this century's history: lions having sex, then Stalin, war, H-bombs, insect sex, buzz-saw murder, Belson, Hitler, killers from Stone's movies.

Mickey gets frantic, Mallory took off her ring! The two make out, as a pretty near naked captive, tied and gagged, watches terrified. "Let's throw her into the mix!" "Fuck her!" "Maybe I just will."

Mallory storms out, drives away. At a gas station, jailbait in a miniskirt, she comes on to the teen attendant, making it on a Corvette hood. "Tell me I'm beautiful." The kid, idiotically: "You're Mallory Knox!" She shoots him.

Next day, fat locals and serial expert Scagnetti look over the murder scene. The fat sheriff holds up her panties, thumbs apart. "That's a perfect ass!" Scagnetti sniffs them, reconstructs the crime from drops on the hood, envisions the ghost of the seductive killer woman.

The couple drive through the desert: "I'd go down on a lawman for a gallon of gas."

They quarrel: "Just relax, I'm not some demon, not a father!"

They find an Indian hogan, knock: "Got any gas we can buy?"

A smiling oldish Indian in T-shirt and trousers asks them in, though there's a rattler on the floor. He's Mick-ee, I'm Mal-or-ee."

The old man and a boy speak in Amerind: "She has sad sickness. Lost in a world of ghosts." Glowing letters appear on the couple, visions: DEMON and TOO MUCH TV. He sends the boy off, tells him to be a man, talks to other snakes as people. The two doze, he tries to use his medicine to help them. Images flash on the hogan's wall: monsters, Mickey as a child, his cruel parents. Indian music whines.

Frightened, Mickey kills the medicine man.

For the first time, Mallory is upset: this is bad bad bad!

They cover the body: this was an accident! Outside, many rattlers appear, attack them, as they scream.

Sick, desperate, the couple drive. Phantom movie Indians gallop beside the car, then their dead victims. But bad asses don't die!

In a motel Scagnetti's in bed with a very young whore. They kid around, he begins strangling her, as a freight train rumbles past, images mixing.

An eerie poisonously green-lit drugstore that night—"Drugzone." Mickey and Mallory, bitten, stagger down evilly glowing green aisles, pain expressed as cartoon demons. But the anti–snake venom is sold out.

Behind bulletproof plastic, a fat clerk sees a TV story on M&M. Mickey appears, he hits the alarm but Mickey sees the red blinker, blasts in, starts grabbing bottles, kills the clerk.

Mallory, dazed, runs outside, where the police and a Japanese TV van have arrived. She is seized by Scagnetti, knife out: "I'll cut her tits off!"

Mickey shoots back, reloads, runs, fires. The Asian girl anchor: "Mickey is quite virile. . . . He has a very large gun!" Mallory, sick, helpless, madly sings numbly: "These Boots Are Made for Walkin'."

Mickey comes out, the cops charge him, firing high-voltage tasers, then start beating and kicking. Japanese: "He's now rendered impotent!" Religious organ music.

A title: One Year Later. Batongaville Prison, a long high white wall. Interior shots of quiet cons.

The cop Scagnetti and Warden McClusky, both smug, unshaven, crude, middle-aged cynics, trot down a prison corridor. "Welcome to Hell!" the warden tells him, grinning revealingly. In the past year, Mickey and Mallory have caused the deaths of three inmates, five guards, and one shrink. Two guards, small-time sadists by their manner, trot behind them. Striding along, bloody brutalized prisoners they see are ignored, others, furious-faced, unacknowledged.

Scagnetti was drawn to serial-killer work when Charles Whitman killed his mom as a child. Her chest exploded, her forehead flew off.

The warden agrees with his attitude. "We got an army of shrinks in here, but that's all bullshit!"

The prison is tremendously overcrowded, at 200 percent of capacity, he says. It's not a prison any more, but a time bomb. In the cafeteria, to stop a fight, he uses special nose pliers on a con. Scagnetti: You could go on "American Gladiators"!

Scagnetti was chosen to deliver the couple to Nystrom State Hospital for the Criminally Insane. With vicious pleasure, the warden says nobody will cry if something happens to them.

In solitary, Mallory sings: "I guess I was born, naturally born, born bad!"

The two arrive. She runs up, smashes her head on the door (happens all the time!).

They've got Mickey in the deepest darkest cell in the dungeon. But he's got a very special visitor, Wayne Gale. . . . You don't say no to the media, Jack.

The newsman talks with Mickey. Gale: "We're doing a series on serial killers—" Mickey corrects him, "Technically, mass murderers." He asks about ratings, and learns he's tops except for Manson. "Well, it's hard to beat the King."

Gale pitches. "You and Mallory killed, but you're not insane. They want to put you into a hospital and turn you into a vegetable. Today they kill your mind, tomorrow they kill my mind." He wants to put him on TV.

From outside the warden and Scagnetti watch. Scagnetti asks why the warden's allowing the TV interview. If he doesn't, he'll be excoriated by the press. If he does, even if the case is appealed, the two will be toast before it ever happens. Nobody gives a fuck about two dead losers!

Inside, the newsman asks what's the answer. Mickey: "I say go for it."

Mickey writes Mallory: "Dearest Mallory . . . I've got more feelings now than I ever had before. . . . I did yoga, but the guy pissed me off. (We see him kill him.) . . . I think of kissing you for hours, I remember every single time you laughed."

Wayne Gale slaps his show together, even as he rants on the phone with wife, mistress, network. In the editing suite, the psychiatrist's face is on the monitor, a vaguely sickly smiling dazed expression. He says of Mickey and Mallory: Insane, no. Psychotic, yes. They know the difference between right and wrong, they just don't give a damn. What about Mallory's being abused as a child? I never really believe what women say to me.

Footage of their trial is limited to shots of a hysterical crowd outside the courthouse: a righteous cop speaks of men killed in the line of duty; teens wearing I LOVE MICKEY AND MALLORY T-shirts scream wildly, and prisoner Mickey grins at the cameras: "You ain't seen nothing yet!"

Super Bowl Sunday. The warden and Scagnetti grin maniacally at each other.

Alone, Mickey totally shaves his head.

Wayne Gale, coming in with his team, asks an ancient moping black con what he's in for. Murder. "Yeah, that's a rough one, man I'm with you," he tells the convict, giving him an oafish shameless buddy hug.

On TV, a special "American Maniacs" is announced. One on one with the most dangerous man in America.

Mickey in blue prison coveralls is brought into the special big cell being used for the TV interview. Standing around the walls are half a dozen guards with shotguns, the TV team, the smug warden and righteous-looking Wayne Gale: "Mickey Knox, we've got a few questions for you. What were your first thoughts about murder?"

When he was born out of a flaming pit of scum. His father and his father's father were evil. Flash images of the boy in a field, his father, the gun shot. "I didn't kill my father!"

Wayne asks him about innocence.

Mickey discourses very calmly. "It's just murder. All creatures and species do it. I know a lot of people who deserve to die. . . . That's where I come in, fate's messenger. A wolf doesn't know it's a wolf."

Gale comes in, obnoxiously glib. "The world is predatory, life is a hunt? I don't think so, but maybe you're right. [Flashes: clear-cutting, polluting smokestacks.] Yes, I saw how it all came down— in Grenada! [The stage-show battle is emphasized like World War II!] But fifty dead? In three weeks?"

Mickey's expression shifts, his face changes for an instant into alien clay: he cares about the last one, the Indian. He saw the Demon. We've all got demons. The ordinary world is just illusion. Murder is a moment of realization.

Mickey tells Gale: "I have a certain purity. I don't think I'm any scarier than you are. That's your shadow on the wall. You can't get rid of your shadow, can you, Wayne?

"You know the only thing that kills a demon—love. That's how I know that Mallory is my salvation."

Scagnetti and two guards are at Mallory's cell: Rise and shine, turn around, face the wall.

Alone with her, Scagnetti asks: "Remember the last time you got fucked? That's never gonna happen again. After electroshock, he's not gonna be worth shit."

Gale asks: "But was it worth it?"

Mickey: "Was an instant of purity worth a lifetime of your lies? You and me are not even the same species. I used to be like you, then I evolved. You're not even an ape, you're a media person. Media's like weather, only it's man-made weather. Murder is pure. You're buying and selling fear. You say why, I say why bother. When you hold a shotgun in your hands, it all becomes clear. I realized my true calling—I'm a natural born killer."

A group of cons are watching him on TV in the cafeteria. Someone shouts: "Right, Mickey!" Someone else hurls a mop and bucket, shattering the screen. Riot!

In the TV interview cell, Gale hugs Mickey: "Every fuckin' moron in the world just saw that!"

The phone sounds. A voice tells the warden: "We got a riot!"

The warden demands they close the cameras down. Gale argues. Warden: "Don't try to tell me what to do in my jail. You stay here and shut up!" He rushes away.

The riot spreads: Rampaging cons beating guards with sticks, setting fires, clanging garbage-cans lids against bars.

In the interview cell, the guards stand around as Mickey acts out an elaborate dirty joke, moving around, all grinning. At the punch line he grabs a shotgun, blasts guards and TV men, disarms the rest, and forces the stunned survivors, with a working video camera and Gale, to march toward Mallory's cell.

The corridors are full of fury. Mickey forces them along, immediately shotgunning anybody who looks like trouble.

In her cell, Mallory tells Scagnetti, "I'm actually a very nice person."

Scagnetti, turned on: "I've done some pretty bad things. I actually killed someone."

Mallory, passionately: "You know what I think about? Sex, fuckin', hands on my tits, flesh.

In an instant, she jumps Scagnetti, is a violent cartoon, breaking his nose. Then the guards rush in, and he maces her.

At the TV station, an anchorwoman reports the riot. Distorted images arrive from the prison camera. Gale: "The final chapters of Mickey and Mallory!"

Mickey fights down the corridor, bursts into Mallory's cell, kills the guards. There's a Mexican standoff between him and Scagnetti . . . until Mallory comes from behind and cuts the cop. The outlaw couple embrace in a moment of romantic music. Mallory to Scagnetti: "You still like me now?" She blows his brains out.

The warden in the guard post scans the TV monitors: riots, fires, corpses. Warden McClusky: "We're on live TV!" But instead of handling the riot, he's going after Mickey and Mallory.

Mickey leads Mallory, Gale, TV cameramen, and guards through the riot.

Gale: "I can't believe this is happening to me!"

Squads of new lawmen in lemon yellow coveralls enter the prison—the special tactical unit.

A strange calm man calls: "C'mon Mickey, this way." He leads them into some empty tunnels: "It's where I come to think when things get hectic."

Wayne Gale, newsman, shoots back at the guards, ecstatically shouting, "I'm alive for the first time in my life." Mickey takes the gun, gives him the TV camera.

Warden and guards face off down a stairwell with the Knoxes and their hostages. Mallory shoots a big hole in Gale's hand to show they're not kidding.

Mickey and the rest retreat to a shower room, bloodstains down the wall tiles and a couple of lynched figures hanging from shower heads.

Mickey to Mallory: "No matter what, I love you."

Wayne Gale: "I'm alive! For the first time in my life!"

He uses his cellular phone. To his wife: "I don't love you. I love me!"

Mallory: "To hell with goin' back to our cells! Let's go out in a hail of bullets. Then we'll be free."

Wayne Gale to his mistress: "I love you, Mai!"

Mickey slings guns on Gale and a terrified guard, so the muzzles point up at their jaws.

They rush the warden's forces, headed for the front entrance, camera live, Wayne Gale screaming: "I am a respected journalist. If I'm stopped, I'll report on conditions in our prisons. I am a personal friend of President Clinton."

Meanwhile, from behind, a great mob of mad cons overwhelms the warden's forces. He climbs the bars, turns Mace on them, but they drag him down, even as they continue to howl and storm, furious fists upraised.

In a quiet forest, three survive. Wayne Gale broadcasts: They made their getaway, there were no helicopters, so without further ado—

Mickey and Mallory just want to be alone together. It was fate. They'll sleep for two days. Then—Mallory's been thinkin' about motherhood.

The newsman wants a wrap-up.

Mickey: "We'll be blowing your brains all over that tree back there. You're scum, Wayne. . . . You don't give a shit about anybody except yourself. . . . You did it for ratings. . . . I kind of like you, you egomaniac. . . . Killing you and what you represent is a statement, I'm not exactly sure about what it's saying'—"

"All right, I'm a parasite. But don't you always leave somebody alive?"

"We are—the camera." The two use their shotguns. "C'mon, missy."

The TV station, without images, goes back to its usual programming: Tonya Harding, Waco, O. J. Simpson, the Menendez Brothers, Wayne Bobitt, then endless monsters, demons, faces streaming blood, and roaring flames. . . . On the sound track, Leonard Cohen sings: "I have seen the future, and it's murder."

The final credits roll, over images of—Mickey and Mallory in a camper van, two kids, Mallory pregnant with a third, cruising down the highway.

In *Natural Born Killers*, Stone's isolate hero has fissioned for company, yet is ever more alone in disturbing new ways. No longer trapped in illusions, their driving demons and devils are visible onscreen—as several writers point out, we live inside the protagonists' heads, seeing their emotional surges as lively cartoon imagery. Likewise, where in previous films Stone's protagonists rejected, denounced, or fled their families, here they simply have them wiped out—so much for the Stone critics' "search for dad" motif! Society is likewise volatilized: Stone's protagonists are totally detached from the start, and anyway the characters standing roughly for society's law, community, and understanding are all Swiftian nightmare figures. Love makes the heroes into an alien species heartless toward humanity; reason is seeing through society as a total fraud and craftily playing on others' self-delusions about that. Mickey and Mallory use excess against social corruption so total it is arguably almost pure evil. Of course, if lying is so monstrous, the biggest liars should be the targets, but that would mean a comedy advocating. . . .

The universe of *Natural Born Killers* also extends and exaggerates the ones Stone has recently created. In *The Doors, JFK,* and *Heaven and Earth* minor characters are passive, helpless, manipulated—fans, bystanders, peasant victims—here they're reduced to targets and prisoners of bullets and/or the media. Likewise, our "leaders"—wardens, cops, showbiz stars—are corrupt and contemptible—their schemes so thin and obvious a butcher's delivery boy can take one look, and turn into a Susan Sontag of social criticism (and has to, for his own survival). Stone doesn't much care if we like his mass murderers, but does suggest their strong feelings and self-awareness count (their cartoon demons, likable or not) against the ever-increasing lying that's the basis of conning and controlling the public, lying so overwhelming we lose track of what we are and believe (viz., "I Love Mallory," a corrective to "I Love Lucy" or "Leave It to Beaver," and "American Maniacs," indistinguishable from "Hard Copy" or "A Current Affair"). Stone's satire is extremely bitter, but perhaps needed in a media-saturated society, where TV imagery, ideas, and characters determine so much of so many lives, yet are as suitable for that role as eating the brightly colored cardboard used as food containers is in place of actual food.

In passing, Stone and numerous critics have linked *Natural Born Killers* to Kubrick's *A Clockwork Orange,* suggesting a comparison might lead to insights about the films. Much simplified, Kubrick's movie is the story of Alex, a charming teen thug who robs, rapes, accidentally murders, is jailed, and is scientifically conditioned against violence. Freed, he's helpless before any enemies, who mug, torment, and by accident decondition him. Hospitalized, he dreams of doing more violence. Kubrick saw his film as a satire on psychology, and a comic view of the myth we're better off, rather than crippled, due to society.[7] In a way Kubrick's film seems a pencil sketch for Stone's nightmare painting. His protagonist, for example, is a conscienceless criminal but not a mass murderer. Likewise, Kubrick tries to defuse his violence by making it a dance, while much of Stone's is nakedly, savagely real. Both films' protagonists have mad fantasies that are visualized. Both films stack the plot to make conservatives *and* liberal humanists corrupt and self-serving (Mother Teresa would be a cackling secret sadist, savoring her patients' agonies). Both heroes delight in bondage sex. Alex hurts people because he enjoys it (Freudian), the Knoxes murder because people are bad, spirits want it, and it's the last pure thing (Jungian and Nietzschean). Last, hood Alex is a secret aesthete (viz., his Beethoven passion) while Mickey is potentially a masses-inspiring radical leader (viz., triggering a prison-wide riot). Ah, the secret vanities of these Hollywood genius-millionaire rebels!

As always, Stone had his attackers and defenders among the critics. The review the director quotes most often is that of Richard Corliss in *Time:* "Stone Crazy." "*Natural Born Killers* plunders every visual trick of avant-garde and mainstream cinema . . . and for two delirious hours, pushes them in your face like a Cagney grapefruit. The actors go hyper hyper, the camera is ever on the bias, the garish colors converge and collide, and you're caught in this Excedrin vision of America in heat. The ride is fun, too, daredevil fun of the sort that only Stone seems willing to provide in this timid film era. *Natural Born Killers* is the most excessive, most exasperating, most . . . let's just say it's the most movie in quite some time. . . .

"It's . . . on the surreal side, and not just in the carnage that almost earned the picture an NC-17. *NBK* is also a blanket indictment of the American family (breeders of abuse), the justice system (sadistically incompetent), and the avid media that find in tabloid crime the no-brain modern equivalent of Greek tragedy. And intentionally or not, *NBK* romanticizes its hero and heroine, because they are smarter and sexier than their pursuers. As the kid in the movie's fake news footage says, 'If I was a mass murderer, I'd be Mickey and Mallory.'"[4]

A review for the industry, Todd McCarthy's "Stone's Killers, a Bloody Good Show," gave the film *Variety*'s thoughtful approval. "*Natural Born Killers* is a heavy-duty acid trip, quite possibly the most hallucinatory and anarchic picture made at a major Hollywood studio in at least twenty years. As a scabrous look at a society that promotes murderers, as well as a scathing indictment of a mass media establishment that caters to and profits from such starmaking, the film has a contemporary relevance that no one can miss. It also happens to be Oliver Stone's most exciting work to date strictly from a filmmaking point of view.

"The glorification of Bonnie and Clyde that Arthur Penn's film made note of twenty-seven years ago is shown here to have magnified into a virtual definition of a vulgar culture and seems quite appropriate to an age dominated by such figures as Amy Fisher, the Menendez brothers, Tonya Harding, and yes, O. J. Simpson. Stylistic and thematic motifs are established at once, as some stunningly off-kilter floating shots intercut with black-and-white alternatives and inserts of animals living and dead, lead up to . . . shooting up a roadside café. They kill for the sake of great love for each other, they say, and the film's psychological ambitions never get much bigger than that. But the wild stylistics will be a turn-on for viewers ready for a visceral ride with the feel of an elaborate souped up sixties exploitation road picture."[9]

J. Hoberman, in "True Romance," gives the film his academic's approval. "In theory, the movie sounded like a belated postcript to the serial killer craze. In practice, it's fresher than fresh. . . . Clearly *Natural Born Killers* is meant to be a comedy—although Stone never fences with a rapier when he can wrap his mitts around a Louisville Slugger, presenting, for example, Mallory's life as a sitcom complete with laugh track and Rodney Dangerfield as her abusive lecher of a father. As in *Badlands*, Terrence Malick's more subdued treatment of similar material, the delinquent couple begin their spree by disposing of the girl's parents—here, however, they bludgeon dad and drown him in a fish tank, then torch mom in her sleep, telegraphing Stone's strategy to obliterate David Lynch and beat Tarantino's premise to a hallucinatory pulp. . . .

"Unlike Tarantino, Stone is obsessed with generating significance. Mickey and Mallory alternately reflect their society, representing an endless cycle of abuse and enact timeless Jungian archetypes. Hence, the self-canceling aspect of Stone's mania. The body count rises but nothing can quite project the couple's absolute evil. The scenes in which she murders the hapless gas jockey she's seduced into going down on her or he shoots a happy snake-handling Indian shaman (Russell Means) are meant to show Mickey and Mallory's worst, most secret transgressions. But (for all their killing) they only achieve notoriety. . . ."[6]

Finally, Jack Kroll, in "Brilliant Nightmare," sees Stone's film as using advanced filmmaking for trailblazing social commentary. "A creature of the media himself [Stone is] assaulting the media for its crucial role in a process of dehumanization that seems to be an inescapable feature of mass society. . . . How does a filmmaker deal with the catch-22 of presenting extreme violence without luxuriating in it? Stone handles the problem in a brutally logical fashion, by subjecting the movie medium itself to violence. . . . [Stone speeds up] his stream of images (he says *Killers* has three thousand images) so that you have no rest, no place to collect your thoughts, to stabilize your senses, to get your bearings—physical, aesthetic, moral. Stone pulverizes the murderous acts of his youthful serial killers, Mickey and Mallory, into their behavioral particles: GLAM! goes the gun, and the 'realistic' image ripsaws into a grainy TV image, a black-and-white home movie, a cartoon demon, a newsreel flash, a fragment from some cesspool of dreams. . . .

"The sitcom ('I Love Mallory') . . . is part of the cultural mindlessness he's evoking. If his killers are 'brain dead,' then what of the consumers of this culture? . . . The movie is in fact a portrait of a New American Mind dislocated and stupefied by vicarious violence. Its extravagant surrealism reflects reality. . . .

"In *Natural Born Killers*, something revelatory happens. The movie is enlightening, not because it transmits new information, but in the way that movies enlighten, through a synergy of images and rhythms that make us sense the world in a new way. . . . Stone's flabbergasting movie cannot be dismissed, it must and will be fought over."[8]

There were also those that were less than enthusiastic. Perhaps the most incisive and unhappy was David Denby, a Stone enthusiast, who sees the ghost of Jim Morrison in the maker of *NBK*.

"*Natural Born Killers* is like bad sex and a bad drug trip combined. It's an ejaculatory farce, but without satisfaction or rest. Stone pushes well beyond plausibility, yet we are meant to take the movie seriously as the essential rabid truth of our times—we are meant to take it as satire. Stone can't successfully satirize anything, however, because he can't distance himself from his subjects. He's driven by the logic of his temperament to become what he hates, or what he claims to hate. His response to the media frenzy is to redouble it— the imitative fallacy with a vengeance. . . .

"It's Oliver Stone and no one else who encourages the audience to relish the young lean killers with their dark glasses and modish trash clothes as they kill some groveling fat person crawling on the floor. The jeering way in which many of the scenes are staged is a coarsening of Stone's spirit. And I'm not happy with the cockeyed moralism by which someone like (say) Geraldo Rivera is supposed to be worse than a serial killer like John Wayne Gacy. The murderer, you see, is pure, he merely kills your body, whereas the media hustler takes your soul. This is the kind of ersatz hip perception that normally (and with good reason) dies at first sign of daylight. The misfortune of *Natural Born Killers* is that Stone put his jangled disgust, his night thoughts, into a movie."[5]

The *New York Times* head reviewer Janet Maslin found much that was poorly thought out, equivocal, or otherwise inadequate, and discussed it in a review entitled: "Young Lovers with a Flaw That Proves Fatal."

"Mr. Stone assembles an arsenal of visual ideas and then fires away point-blank in his audience's direction. If viewers flinch during this tireless two-hour barrage, are they simply no match for the filmmaker's tough, unrelenting style? Or has he by now perfected his own form of exploitative fakery? While *NBK* affects occasional disgust at the lurid world of Mickey and Mallory, it more often seems enamored of their exhilarating freedom. If there is a juncture at which these caricatures start looking like nihilistic heroes, then the film passes that point many times. . . .

"Just before the credits roll, Mr. Stone shoots himself in the foot with a quick montage of tabloid television's greatest hits: the Bobbitt and Menendez trials, Tonya Harding, O. J. Simpson. For better or worse, those are spectacles that cast a long shadow. And for all its surface passions, *Natural Born Killers* never digs deep enough to touch the madness of such events, or even to send them up in any surprising way. Mr. Stone's vision is impassioned, alarming, visually inventive, characteristically overpowering. But it's no match for the awful truth."[10]

Peter Travers, in a *Rolling Stone* essay "Blood from a Stone," used the film as the basis of an attack on all Stone's filmmaking efforts:

"Stone's hypocrisy is galling. 'I'm only doing this one,' Stone told *Premiere*. 'I don't have a show that's doing this again and again.' Oh, really? Stone has been in the exploitation game as far back as *Seizure* (1974) and *The Hand* (1981). He traffics in war atrocities (*Salvador, Platoon*), glamour drugs (*The Doors*), rape (*Heaven and Earth*), and misanthropy (*Talk Radio*). And what about those assassination replays (slow, fast, still frame) in *JFK*? . . . A potent movie could be made about what draws us to warped behavior. And Stone could do it. He could expose his own demons and show us ourselves in them.

Instead he hides behind bulldozing style, denying his movie what it needs most: a heart.

"Stone calls this bile satire. But it's not satire to skewer idiots. Satire respects the insidious power of its targets. Satire takes careful aim. *Killers* is crushingly scattershot. By putting virtuoso technique at the service of lazy thinking, Stone turns his film into the demon he wants to mock: cruelty as entertainment."[14]

Geofrey Cheshire, in an essay, "The Cemetery of Good Taste," has his own amusing problems with the film's anachronistic style, befuddled morals, but redeeming mania.

"It is though unique in Stone's work for lacking any obvious, coherent moral viewpoint. . . . *NBK* is more a bong hit than a lecture. . . . The film's implicit attitude . . . basically *heh heh cool*— is seemingly meant as a dark mirror of the infotainment machinery that turns lethal thugs like Mickey and Mallory into tabloid fodder cum cult anti-heroes. The only real crime in murder, *NBK* chortles, is to kill without flair or notoriety. . . . We're supposed to react with thoughtful revulsion at the tabloid media's cartoonlike distortions and frenetic hyperbole? How can we, when the movie's not only rampantly indulging in the very same fraudulence, but clearly enjoying the hell out of it?

"Yet this, paradoxically, is where *NBK* begins to redeem itself. It is fun, and zanily revelatory—not despite being preposterously wrongheaded in so many ways, but because of that. When Stone loses all touch with reality and just goes goofy, it's hard not to be impressed by the maniacal energy and extraordinary skills. . . . The filmmaker's gifts aren't obscured by bombast but forever wedded to it. . . . Even a 'bad' Stone film like *NBK* will remind us that his reckless courting of the overblown and pretentious remains his saving grace, the talisman that inevitably wards off tasteful boredom."[3]

Stone's creative team made a number of insightful comments. Longtime lighting expert Ray Pesche: "When I saw an early screening, it became clear what he wanted to achieve was to make a piece of modern art, using the medium of filmmaking. It all comes back to colors, where you don't need a reason to use a certain color. It's totally avant-garde, and in that sense it's the first real movie of the nineties, it points to the future of techniques and ideas."[1]

Director of photography Richardson noted: "After doing eleven different films with him, I see that the devil comes in many different costumes. He can be extraordinarily peaceful, and he can be extraordinarily belligerent. . . . I think if one were to say *Killers* was about the evolution of demons, then Oliver was attempting to understand those demons, because he was part demon himself during the making of this film. But I don't mean that in a negative way. I mean that his whole creative spirit was definitely the devil, and he played with that. It was very difficult at times to want to stay in pace with that . . . a film about random killings on the road."[1]

Cowriter Veloz summed up: "I think the film asks the question whether or not our society creates innate evil people only so we can hunt them down in order to feel morally superior. Very few things, short of war, can bring a community together, so we almost secretly need or want an evil like that."[17]

Quentin Tarantino, source of the story, commented: "I never want my stuff to be able to be boiled down to one subject . . . where Oliver Stone . . . is very much about the big idea. . . . If I hadn't written it, it sounds like one of Stone's movies I'd get a big kick out of."[11]

Having worked on many of Stone's films, his recently divorced wife Elizabeth noted: "I think that technically it's brilliant. But as a movie I abhor it. I think it's awful and ugly and a complete waste of talent. Why is he wasting his talent? . . . All this sex and violence, sex and violence, he's like a dog chasing his tail."[12]

Warners executives, speaking on conditions of anonymity said the studio was uneasy about the violence, though they did not downplay it: billboards and coming attractions treat it as a social satire, rather than a drama about two killers:

"We knew this film would be incredibly controversial. We realized that from the beginning. There's obviously a level of concern that it will polarize the audience. It could do that. . . .

"It's a very difficult film to sell. How do you sell a film about two despicable people and the media turning them into heroes? How do you do that? It is a social satire. Implicit in the marketing of the film is its violence."[15]

One approach, part of the promotional materials such as Warners' program notes, was to give statistics showing that for better or worse society and the media do seem obsessed with such material, concluding: "Killers are the hottest media draw in town."

Stone tested the film with screenings in Seattle and Chicago. "We previewed it numerous times with younger audiences, and they laughed through the heavier parts. At that point, I knew we were in the ballpark."[4]

Charlotte Kandel, senior vice president of worldwide publicity and promotion for Warner Brothers: "It was going to be one of the most controversial and best films of the year. We didn't have to create it. . . . We don't have to whip anything up. We don't have to manufacture hype. We knew we could count on good reaction from both the public and the press."

In an interview near the end of shooting, Stone gave perhaps his clearest view of his project: "It's like Keystone Kops. Really, I'm not saying I'm doing slapstick, but I'm looking for the edge, where the physical becomes humorous. . . .We're satirizing the tabloids . . . but it's part of a larger canvas of modern America and crime and the media. We poke fun at the warden, at the system with a capital S. . . . We poke fun at the idea of justice, and the idea of righteousness, the concept that in America there's a right way and a wrong way. . . . "I knew it would be dangerous for somebody like me because there's no real up side. The subject matter is violent, and it doesn't have the broadest possible appeal . . . but fuck that."[11]

During its first weekend after release, *Natural Born Killers* was the number one U.S. box-office attraction, making an estimated $11.2 million on 1,510 screens. In subsequent weeks it continued to ride near the top in grosses.

12

PROBLEMS AND PROSPECTS

A RECENT COMMENT by Lawrence Wright, scriptwriter of Stone's ongoing project *Noriega,* confirms the writer-director continues to focus on the themes previously detailed: "When I was working with him, he had some suggestions that were very keen. There's a scene where Noriega is speaking at Harvard, and Oliver suggested that you would take the camera right into Noriega's eyes. And that single idea would trigger the whole flashback sequence, where you could tell Noriega's life story as he was being introduced. And the elegance of that was terrific."[5]

Stone himself has stated recently that his films come out of himself, not the seeking of social causes or fashionable ideas. In his own words: "I do my films to take me out of where I am. The questions the movies ask—those are the questions I'm asking myself at that point in time. In *JFK* I was saying, 'Yeah, if you do go for your truth, how far are you willing to push it? Are you willing to alienate everybody and everything? Lose your family?' I was asking that of myself. I use films as benchmarks, signposts. As therapy, also—I think I do. And I question that, too."[5] Stone's films are never conventional Hollywood "product."

Still, critical opinions gathered here suggest that as a filmmaker/artist Stone has several particular strengths and weaknesses. To sum up briefly, his strengths include:

Social and political engagement. Stone is almost alone as a Hollywood filmmaker confronting and exploring with some realism serious social and political issues. Yet recently he says of this: "I would rather not seek out a controversy; I really would not. This is something that people don't understand. Controversy just categorizes you; it's boring. I've had so many categories in my life . . . sometimes I don't recognize myself."[5]

In a sense, his two latest films represent alternatives to controversy: *Heaven and Earth*, a biography, and *Natural Born Killers*, a satirical comedy. In fact, a critic has defined comedy as "hostility enjoying itself" (e.g., Marx Brothers films, where "whatever it is, I'm against it.") Will Stone become our future hip Groucho Marx/ Lenny Bruce? It's possible. ("Controversy enjoying itself?")

Pure ambition and energy. Stone's films have enormous energy, they are involving, they create strong characters and dramatic situations. The larger social issues and historical problems and forces, it's been argued, may drift into the background, but the audience *is* held on to. Most important, he seeks new "film territory." As Stephen Schiff puts it, "Stone is genuinely a seeker, an adventurer of a kind that is no longer fashionable, with traits that may be undervalued in an effete, millennial age: physical courage, a yearning for transcendence, a hunger to taste all the fruits of the world."[5]

Showbiz sense. Stone is not a "kept" director, he is an active, powerful, knowledgeable force in the industry. He has friends and clout, and keeps going. Edward Pressman, a Hollywood producer/ friend: "He's got a very good business sense, and everyone considers him very practical and very responsible about budgets. And you have to remember that Oliver, up until *Heaven and Earth*, made a lot of good calls. He's very creative with his instincts. Oliver's gone with new writers and editors and cinematographers—he gave Robert Richardson his first job. He cast Michael Douglas before he was a big star. And Tom Berenger. He cast Tom Cruise against type. Those were not obvious choices at the time. So people respect his instincts."[5]

Stone has also produced or coproduced *Reversal of Fortune, Blue Steel, Iron Maze, South Central, Zebrahead, The Joy Luck Club, The New Age,* and *Wild Palms* (for television), suggesting he'll risk time and money to push notable projects through.

Self-promotion. Stone has promoted himself as a personality, a good thing careerwise. He's not a household name as Hitchcock may still be, but is well enough known to promote his films. (By comparison, current successful filmmakers like Reitman, Zemeckis and others keep a low profile.) In a sense, this reaches comic heights in *Natural Born Killers,* with BW bluish and color images of families on fifties TV shows, and a seated figure with its head chopped off, racing over to the TV to tune in Stone's latest excesses.

Several other aspects of Stone's work have been repeatedly criticized as flaws and weaknesses:

Excess. Excesses run from exaggerations, simplifications, and omissions of facts to dramatic and thematic extremes. Potentially, perhaps, any human behavior can be transformed into art. The challenge is conceptual treatment, point of view, and fine-tuning. (Andrew Sarris uses the example of Little Red Riding Hood; from the little girl's POV she's running for her life, from the wolf's she's an accidental subject of his tormenting, obsessive pathological weakness.)

For Stone enthusiast David Denby, the excesses of his latest film didn't work. *"Natural Born Killers* is all commentary and no text, an editing table folly. . . . Many of the scenes suggest a deep complicity with murder, which is Stone's upping the ante this time. He's letting us know how good it must feel to kill. Okay, I'm shocked. But what shocks me as well is that there's little regret or anguish in the scenes, but instead a mood of gleeful nuttiness and play as if in a degraded, Friday night horror movie made for kids."[2]

And Denby has yet to see Stone's director's cut where: "Essentially what we film is that great Jim Morrison line, 'the whole shithouse goes up in flames.' We had hundreds of real live prisoners throwing stuntmen off pedestals and hanging and impaling people. . . . We showed the whole world coming apart."[3]

And there are other limits. At least one source, using slow motion and freeze frame, claims to have found subliminal conditioning images (flashes of skulls, ghosts, religious figurines) running through *JFK.*[4] Though one can argue that *Natural Born Killers* is *only* subliminal conditioning images, stuck into a plot.

Treatment of women. Critics have repeatedly attacked Stone for being unable to create realistic women characters. Typically, Daryl Hannah's role in *Wall Street* was said to lack depth, being largely a plot function, and Meg Ryan's part as Jim Morrison's companion in

The Doors had Stone seemingly acknowledging the tendency, with her telling customs police her job was "ornament." Even in *Heaven and Earth*, critic Tye Burr argues: "The movie's signal fault is that Le Ly never really *does* anything. Rather, things are done unto her. . . . Events wash over passive Le Ly like water over a rock. . . . The real Le Ly appears to have been plenty active. . . . Stone can't show us this side of the woman, because then he'd have to give up his vision of the sainted martyr."[1]

Sentimentality/mawkishness/insincerity. Though critics characteristically attack Stone for excess, his films include notable sentimentalized and insincere scenes. In *Heaven and Earth*, Le Ly is introduced to prostitution with U.S. soldiers in a ridiculously sweet way, with a sympathetic charming sergeant pimping ("Do it for world peace!") for two shyer-than-Forrest Gump privates. (Her sister has a "balancing scene" with a crude father-insulting GI.) In *Wall Street*, Michael Douglas's Gordon Gekko is perhaps the most deethnicized New York City College graduate in its century-long history. Likewise, Stone's lifer sergeants in *Platoon* are Homeric noble fighters, displaying none of the sleazy, chiseling, crooked traits Stone found among real-life noncoms in Vietnam.[7]

In general, until *Natural Born Killers*, Stone tends to treat those with conventional status and authority with residual dignity, even if corrupt—money and power still talk in his films, and the lack of it whines and moans. But perhaps we'll someday see a *Salvador* with style and class swapped, as *Natural Born Killers* inverts *Seizure*.

Blind spots. Stone's films seem to have consistent blind spots, notably direct criticism of our business culture. *Wall Street* was in fact a curious view of the subject, with a lawbreaking youngster taking the rap for a big-time crooked trader who gets away free. In *JFK*, big-time arms makers and other businessmen are accused of the assassination, without details or dramatization (Stone has admitted *JFK* needed the "big conspiracy" element to be a commercial hit[6]). Again, evil arms makers are talked up in *Heaven and Earth*. (A scene at Dow Chemical's Third World Napalm Sales Division, however, admittedly might have been . . . impolitic?)

More generally, Stone's interviews reveal an exhaustive knowledge of "functional" film history, how films "work" and which ones made money and why. Despite such stunning counterexamples as *Natural*

Born Killers, one hopes this encyclopedic knowledge will not unconsciously creep out to inhibit the writer-director.

In my own view, Stone remains a youthful, relatively idealistic filmmaker obsessed with the special American experience. His situation recalls two pieces of advice the older journalist gives the protagonist in Graham Greene's *The Quiet American.* First the character speaks unfavorably of books by a man who "always had a return ticket." Similarly, Stone's least-successful films—*Talk Radio, The Doors, Heaven and Earth*—were those with "easy dramaturgical return tickets"—foreign religions, suicide, "show-business mysticism," for their characters' confrontations with America. Graham Greene's character then reads a poem, without comment, which speaks to the special situation, ambitions, and temptations, of being an American—which could in fact have been the epigraph to any of Stone's films:

> I drive through the streets and I care not a damn.
> The people they stare, and they ask who I am;
> And if I should chance to run over a cad
> I can pay for the damage if ever so bad.
> > So pleasant it is to have money, heigh ho!
> > So pleasant it is to have money!

NOTES

CHAPTER 1: Beginnings

1. Bennett, Leslie. "Oliver Stone—Easing Out of Violence." *New York Times Arts & Entertainment*, April 13, 1987.
2. Blauer, Peter. "Coming Home." *New York*, December 1986.
3. Canby, Vincent. "Films." *New York Times*, March 23, 1975.
4. Corliss, Richard. "Platoon." *Time*, January 26, 1987.
5. Pfeifer, Chuck. "Oliver Stone." *Interview*, February 1987.
6. Herridge, Francis. "Movie Scene." *New York Post*, March 31, 1975.
7. Martin, Rob. "Oliver Stone and *The Hand*." *Fangoria*, 12, December 19, 1977.
8. *Oliver Stone: Inside Out* (1989), from Pacific Street Films, Hastings on the Hudson, NY.
9. Orth, Maureen. "Talking to . . . " *Vogue*, December 1987.
10. Oster, Jerry. *New York Daily News*, March 13, 1975.
11. "Playboy Interview: Oliver Stone." *Playboy*, February 1980.
12. *Seizure*, rent from Kim's Video, New York City.
13. Stone, Oliver. "The Next Vietnam?" *U.S.*, June 15, 1987, p. 37.

CHAPTER 2: False Starts

1. Aufderheide, Paula. "Ken and Barbie in Fantasyland." *Chicago Reader*, December 1980.
2. "Berg." "Conan the Barbarian." *Variety*, March 17, 1982.
3. Biskind, Peter. "Cutter's Way." *Premiere*, February 1989.
4. Blauner, Peter. "Coming Home." *New York*, December 8, 1986, p. 60.
5. Brandel, Mark. *The Lizard's Tail*.
6. Canby, Vincent. "Film: *The Hand* Clever Horror Tale." *New York Times*, April 24, 1981.

7. ———. "Film: Fighting, Fantasy in *Conan the Barbarian*." *New York Times*, May 15, 1982.
8. ———. "Screen: Al Pacino Stars in *Scarface*." *New York Times*, December 9, 1983.
9. Denby, David. "Movies: *Eight Million Ways to Die*." *New York*, May 12, 1986.
10. ———. "Movies: Sweat and Strain." *New York*, May 24, 1982.
11. ———. "Movies: Snowed Under." *New York*, December 19, 1983.
12. Farber, Steven. "Films." *New West*, November 20, 1973, p. 174.
13. Fernandez, Enrique. "*Scarface* Died for My Sins." *Village Voice*, December 20, 1983.
14. Goodman, Walter. "Stone Cold." *New York Times*, December 20, 1983.
15. Hayes, Billy, with William Hoffer. *Midnight Express*. New York: E. P. Dutton, 1977.
16. Kael, Pauline. *State of the Art*. New York: E. P. Dutton, 1985.
17. ———. "The Last White Hope." *New Yorker*, September, 1985.
18. ———. "Movie Yellow Journalism." *New Yorker*, November 27, 1978.
19. ———. "Eight Million Ways." *New Yorker*, May 19, 1986.
20. Lehmann-Haupt, Christopher. "Midnight Express." *New York Times*, October 26, 1978.
21. Kraft, David. "Behind the Scenes with Edward Pressman." *Conan the Barbarian Comic Book*, August 1982.
22. Martin, Bob. "Oliver Stone and *The Hand*." *Fangoria*, December 12, 1981.
23. Maslin, Janet. "Two Hit Films without Gimmicks." *New York Times*, December 14, 1978.
24. ———. "Film: *The Year of the Dragon*: Cimino in Chinatown." *New York Times*, August 16, 1985.
25. Perry, Gerald. "The Hand," *Real Paper*, May 28, 1981.
26. "Playboy Interview: Oliver Stone." *Playboy*, February 1980.
27. Plutzik, Roberta. "Billy Hayes, It's Only Love." *Soho Weekly News*, October 12, 1978, p. 30.
28. Sarris, Andrew. "Pacino's Cuban Capone Comes a Cropper." *Village Voice*, December 20, 1978, p. 78.
29. Sarris, Andrew. "Little Night Kvetch." *Village Voice*, October 16, 1978.
30. ———. "The Matrix of Movie Reviewing." *Village Voice*, May 13, 1981.
31. ———. "Year of the Dragon." *Village Voice*, August 20, 1985.
32. Vineberg, Steve. "To Snort and Die in L.A." *Phoenix Post*, September 27, 1986.
33. Wolcott, James. "The Godfather Goes Slumming." *Texas Monthly*, January 1984.

CHAPTER 3: Salvador

1. Blauner, Peter. "Coming Home." *New York*, December 8, 1986, p. 60.
2. Bonner, Raymond. *Weakness and Deceit: U.S. Policy and El Salvador.* New York: *New York Times Books*, 1984.
3. Brooks, David. "*Salvador:* Where the War Isn't Won." *Insight*, April 28, 1986.
4. "Cart." "*Salvador.*" *Variety*, March 3, 1986.
5. Chomsky, Noam. *What Uncle Sam Really Wants.* Berkeley, CA: Odonian Press, 1992.
6. Corliss, Richard. "Platoon." *Time*, January 27, 1987.
7. Crowdus, Gary. "Personal Struggles and Political Issues: An Interview with Oliver Stone," *Cineaste*, no. 3, 1986, p. 18.
8. Denby, David. "Movies." *New York*, March 24, 1986.
9. Gleiberman, Owen. "*Salvador:* Oliver's Army Crosses through the Horror." *Boston Phoenix*, April 1, 1986.
10. Goodman, Walter. "Screen: *Salvador* by Stone." *New York Times*, March 24, 1986.
11. Hibbin, Sally. "Blood from a Stone." *Films and Filming*, January 1987, p. 18–19.
12. Jensen, Lisa. "Human Truth, Tragedy, Tangle in *Salvador.*" *Good Times* (Santa Cruz, CA) September 11, 1986.
13. Kael, Pauline. "Pig Heaven." *New Yorker*, July 23, 1986.
14. Kehr, Dave. "The Left Stuff." *Reader*, April 25, 1988.
15. "Playboy Interview: Oliver Stone." *Playboy*, February 1980.
16. Production Notes. *Salvador,* Hemdale Films.
17. Stone, Oliver. *Platoon and Salvador Scripts.* New York: Vintage Books, 1985.
18. Stone, Robert. "Oliver Stone U.S.A." *New York Review of Books*, February 17, 1994.
19. Thompson, Anne. "The Direct Approach—Oliver Stone in Havana." *Movieline,* January 8, 1991.
20. Wood, Robin. "Oliver Stone." *International Dictionary of Films and Filmmakers.* Chicago and London: St. James Press, 1988.

CHAPTER 4: Platoon

1. Blauner, Peter. "Coming Home." *New York*, December 8, 1986.
2. Canby, Vincent. "Film: The Vietnam War in Stone's Platoon." December 19, 1986.
3. "Cart." "Platoon." *Variety*, December 3, 1986.
4. Cawley, Leo. "An Ex Marine See Platoon." *Monthly Review,* June 1987.

5. Corliss, Richard. "Platoon." *Time*, January 26, 1987.
6. Crowdus, Gary. "Personal Struggles and Political Issues." *Cineaste*, vol. 16, no. 3, 1986.
7. Denby, David. "Bringing the War Back Home." *New York*, December 15, 1986.
8. Gleiberman, Owen. "Ground Zero: *Platoon* Gets Down to Too Little." *Boston Phoenix*, January 13, 1987.
9. Harmetz, Aljean. "Unwanted Platoon Finds Success as U.S. Examines the Vietnam War." *New York Times*, 1987.
10. Hoberman, J. "At War with Ourselves." *Village Voice*, December 15, 1986.
11. Kael, Pauline. "Platoon." *New Yorker*, January 12, 1987.
12. Kramer, Sydelle. "Platoon." *Cineaste*, vol. 15, no. 3, 1987.
13. Lewis, Anthony. "The Lying Machine." *New York Times*, June 6, 1994.
14. "Playboy Interview: Oliver Stone." *Playboy*, February 1980.
15. Sklar, Robert, et al. "Platoon on Inspect." *Cineaste*, vol. 15, no. 4, 1987.
16. Stone, Oliver. "The Next Vietnam." *U.S.*, June 15, 1987.
17. ———. *Platoon: Screenplay*, New York: Vintage Books, 1986.

CHAPTER 5: Wall Street

1. Biskind, Peter. "Stone Raids Wall Street." *Premiere*, December 1987.
2. Boozer, Jack, Jr "Wall Street." *Journal of Popular Film and Television*, 17, Fall 1989.
3. "Bast." "Wall Street," in *Variety*, December 9, 1987, p. 13.
4. Canby, Vincent. "Stone's Wall Street." *New York Times*, December 1, 1987.
5. Chomsky, Noam. *The Prosperous Few and the Restless Many*. Berkeley, CA: Oponian Press, 1993.
6. Crowdus, Gary. "Personal Struggles and Political Issues." *Cineaste* 16, no. 3, 1988.
7. Denby, David. "Wall Street." *New York*, December 14, 1988.
8. Edelstein, David. "Raiders of the Lost Market," *Village Voice*, December 15, 1987.
9. Fabrikant, Geraldine. "Wall Street Reviews 'Wall Street'." *New York Times*, December 10, 1987.
10. French, Sean. "Breaking News." *Sight and Sound*, Spring 1988, p. 136.
11. Gardner, James. "Films: Wall Street." *Nation*, January 23, 1988.
12. Madrick, Jeffrey. "Wall Street: The Banality of Greed." *New York Times*, January 17, 1988.
13. "Playboy Interview: Oliver Stone." *Playboy*, February 1980.
14. Powers, John. "For Love or Money." *Los Angeles Weekly*, December 25, 1987.

15. Rickey Carrie. "A World of Lowlifes in High Finance." *Philadelphia Inquirer,* December 11, 1987.
16. Ritzer, George. *The McDonaldization of Society.* Thousand Oaks, CA: Nine Force Press, 1993.

CHAPTER 6: Talk Radio

1. Bogosian, Eric. "Barry Champlain, Sculptured by Stone." *New York Times,* December 18, 1988, Section 2, 1.
2. Canby, Vincent. "The Nights of a Big Radio Mouth." *New York Times,* December 21, 1988, Section 3, 28.
3. "Cart." "Talk Radio." *Variety,* December 25, 1988, p. 25.
4. Corliss, Richard. "Talk Radio." *Time,* December 19, 1988, p. 79.
5. Denby, David. "Raging Bull." *New York,* December 12, 1988.
6. Gleiberman, Owen. "Making Waves."
7. Hoberman, J. "Freedom Now." *Village Voice,* December 20, 1988, p. 83.
8. Kauffmann, Stanley. "Justice Collectors." *New Republic,* December 13, 1989, p. 26.
9. Portan, Richard. "Talk Radio." *Cineaste,* no. 2, 1989, p. 53.
10. Rosenberg, Jonathan. "Performance Art." *Chicago Reader,* summer, 1988.
11. Tomasulo, Frank. "The Spectator in the Tube: The Rhetoric of Donahue." *Journal of Film and Video,* Spring 1984.
12. Wood, Robin. "Oliver Stone." *International Dictionary of Films and Filmmakers: Directors.* Chicago and London: St. James Press.

CHAPTER 7: Born on the Fourth of July

1. Appy, Christian. "Vietnam According to Oliver Stone," *Commonweal,* March 13, 1990, p. 188.
2. Biksin, Peter. "Cutter's Way." *Premiere,* February 19, 1990, p. 68.
3. Canby, Vincent. "How an All American Boy Went to War and Lost His Faith." *New York Times,* December 20, 1989.
4. Collins, Glenn. "Oliver Stone Is Ready to Move on from Vietnam." *New York Times,* December 2, 1990, p. 13.
5. Corliss, Richard. "Tom Terrific." *Time,* December 25, 1989.
6. Covino, Michael. "Return of the Native," essay, Museum of Modern Art, Film Division.
7. "Daws." "Born on the Fourth of July," *Variety,* December 20, 1989.
8. Denby, David. "Days of Rage." New York, December 18, 1989, p. 101.

9. Hinson, Hal. "Born on the Fourth of July." *Washington Post*, December 20, 1989.
10. Hoberman, J. "The Worst Years of Our Lives." *Village Voice*, December 9, 1989.
11. Jacobson, Kurt. "Unfinished Business," essay, Museum of Modern Art, Film Division.
12. Kael, Pauline. "Potency." *New Yorker*, January 22, 1990.
13. Mirabella, Alan. "The War Within." *New York Daily News*, January 20, 1990.
14. Seidenbert, Robert. "To Hell and Back." *American Film*, January 1990, p. 28.
15. Sharett, Christopher. "Born on the Fourth of July," *Cineaste*, no. 4, 1990, p. 48.
16. Sheer, Robert. "Born on the Third of July." *Premiere*, February 1990, p. 51.
17. Stone, Robert. "Oliver Stone's USA." *New York Review of Books*, February 17, 1994.
18. Zinn, Howard. *A People's History of the United States*. New York: Harper Colophon, 1980.

CHAPTER 8: The Doors

1. Carr, Ray. "The Man behind *The Doors*." *Boston Globe*, March 1, 1991, p. 25.
2. Chutcow, Paul. "Oliver Stone and 'The Doors.'" *New York Times*, February 24, 1991.
3. Cohen, Jessica. "Neo Macho." *American Film*, June 1991.
4. Collins, Glenn. "Oliver Stone Is Moving on from Vietnam." *New York Times*, January 2, 1990.
5. Corliss, Richard. "Come On Baby Light My Fizzle." *Time*, March 11, 1991.
6. Denby, David. "The Doors." *New York*, March 25, 1991.
7. Dieckmann, Katherine. "Rider on the Storm: On *The Doors* Set with Oliver Stone." *Village Voice*, February 26, 1991.
8. Gleiberman, Owen. "Wild Child." *Entertainment Weekly*, March 8, 1991.
9. Goldstein, Richard. "The Lizard King Plays Himself." *Village Voice*, February 26, 1991.
10. Hoberman, J. "The Lizard King's New Clothes," *Village Voice*, March 8, 1991.
11. Hopkins, Jerry. *The Lizard King*. New York: Collier Books, 1993.
12. Horton, Robert. "Riders on the Storm." *Film Comment*, 27, May–June 1991, p. 57.

13. Kilday, Gregg. "Love Me Too." *Entertainment Weekly*, March 1, 1991.
14. Maslin, Janet. "Flying, Falling: Days of the Doors." *New York Times*, March 1, 1991, p. C.1.
15. Rafferty, Terrence. "Stone Again." *New Yorker*, March 11, 1991.
16. Richardson, J. H., and Judson Klinger. "People Are Strange." *Premiere*, March 1991.
17. Rowland, March. "Stone Unturned." *American Film*, March 1991.
18. Sarris, Andrew. "The Doors." *Village Voice*, March 11, 1991, p. 51.

CHAPTER 9: JFK

1. Albert, Michael. "*JFK* and Us." *Z*, February 1992.
2. Ansen, David. "A Troublemaker for Our Time." *Newsweek*, December 23, 1991.
3. Anson, Robert Sam. "The Shooting of JFK." *Esquire*, November 1991.
4. Canby, Vincent. "When Everything Amounts to Nothing." *New York Times*, December 30, 1991, p. C.1.
5. Cockburn, Alex. *The Nation*. Letter, March 9, 1992.
6. Crowdus, Gary. "Clarifying the Cost: An Interview with Oliver Stone." *Cineaste*, vol. 19, no. 1, 1992.
7. ———. "Getting the Facts Straight: An Interview with Zachary Sklar." *Cineaste*, vol. 19, no. 1, 1992.
8. ———. "Striving for Authenticity: An Interview with Jane Rusconi." *Cineaste*, vol. 19, no. 1, 1992.
9. Denby, David. "Thrill of Fear." *New York*, January 6, 1992, p. 50.
10. Ebert, Roger. "Interview with Oliver Stone." *Universal Press Syndicate*. December 1991.
11. Mailer, Norman. "Footfalls in the Crypt." *Vanity Fair*, February 1992.
12. Maslin, Janet. "Oliver Stone Manipulates His Puppet." *New York Times*, January 5, 1992, Section 2, p. 15.
13. Production Notes. Interview, *JFK*, United Artists, November 25, 1991.
14. Simon, Art. "The Making of Alert Viewers." *Cineaste*, vol. 19, no. 1, 1992.
15. Stone, Oliver. "Oliver Stone Talks Back." *Premiere*, January 1992.
16. ———. Speech to National Press Club, January 1992.
17. ———. *JFK: The Book of the Film*, New York: Applause Books, 1992.
18. Weinraub, Bernard. "Hollywood Wonders If Warner Brothers Let *JFK* Go Too Far." *New York Times*, December 23, 1991.
19. ———. "Valenti Calls *JFK* Hoax and Smear." *New York Times*, April 2, 1992.

CHAPTER 10: Heaven and Earth

1. Carr, Jay. "Stone's Heaven Hits Relentlessly Hard." *Boston Herald*, December 24, 1993.

2. Dowell, Pat. "Heaven and Earth." *Cineaste,* vol. 20, no. 3, p. 56.
3. Frumkeyes, Roy. "Twenty Minutes with Oliver Stone." *Film Journal,* July 1994.
4. *Heaven and Earth.* Production Information. Warner Brothers.
5. McCarthy, Todd. "Heaven and Earth." *Rolling Stone,* December 27, 1993.
6. Schiff, Stephen. "The Last Wild Man." *New Yorker,* August 8, 1994.
7. Singer, Michael. "The Story behind the Story in *The Making of Oliver's Stone's "Heaven and Earth."* Boston: Charles E. Tuttle Co., 1993.
8. ———. *The Making of Oliver Stone's "Heaven and Earth."* Boston: Charles E. Tuttle Co., 1993.
9. Smith, Gavin. "The Camera for Me Is an Actor: Interview with Oliver Stone." Film Comment, January–February 1994.
10. Stone, Oliver. "Vietnam: The Reverse Angle." *The Making of Oliver Stone's "Heaven and Earth."* Boston: Charles E. Tuttle Co., 1993.
11. ———. *Heaven and Earth* script, 5th draft, May 15, 1992, Ixtlan, Inc. Santa Monica, CA.
12. Stone, Robert. "Oliver Stone's USA." *New York Review of Books,* February 17, 1994.
13. Vermiere, James. "Film View: *Heaven and Earth.*" *Boston Herald,* December 24, 1993.

CHAPTER 11: Natural Born Killers

1. Blair, Ian. "Natural Born Killers." *Film and Video,* August 1994.
2. Brown, Corrie. "American Maniacs." *Premiere,* August 1994.
3. Cheshire, Godfrey. "The Cemetery of Good Taste." *New York Press,* August 24, 1994.
4. Corliss, Richard. "Cinema: Stone Crazy." *Time,* August 23, 1994.
5. Denby, David. "Dead Heads." *New York,* September 5, 1994.
6. Hoberman, J. "True Romance." *Village Voice,* August 30, 1993.
7. Kagan, Norman. *The Cinema of Stanley Kubrick.* New York: Continuum, 1989.
8. Kroll, Jack. "Brilliant Nightmare." *Newsweek,* August 29, 1994.
9. McCarthy, Todd. "Stone's Killer: A Bloody Good Show." *Variety,* August 29, 1994.
10. Maslin, Janet. "Young Lovers with a Plan that Proves Fatal," *New York Times,* August 26, 1994.
11. Russo, Francine. "Welcome to the Jungle." *Entertainment Week,* September 9, 1994.
12. Schiff, Stephen. "The Last Wild Man." *New Yorker,* August 8, 1994.
13. Tarantino, Quentin. *Natural Born Killers,* draft 3 (rev.), March 12, 1991.

14. Travers, Peter. "Blood from a Stone." *Rolling Stone*, September 8, 1994.
15. Weinraub, Bernard. "How a Movie Satire Turned into Reality." *New York Times,* August 16, 1994.
16. Williams, Dave E. "Oliver Stone Interview." *Film Threat*, October 1994.
17. ———. "Overkill." *Film Threat*, October 1994.

CHAPTER 12: Problems and Prospects

1. Burr, Tye. "Stone Unturned." *Entertainment Weekly*, July 8, 1994.
2. Denby, David. "Dead Heads." *New York*, September 5, 1994.
3. Fuller, Graham. "Interview with Oliver Stone." Interview, September 1994.
4. Grace, Dean. "Subliminal Images in Oliver Stone's *JFK*." *Secret and Suppressed*, Jim Keith, editor. Portland, Oregon: Feral House, 1993.
5. Schiff, Stephen. "The Last Wild Man". *New Yorker*, August 8, 1994.
6. Smith, Gavin. "Interview with Oliver Stone." *Film Comment*, January–February 1994.
7. Stone, Oliver. "The Next Vietnam." *U.S.*, June 15, 1987.

FILMOGRAPHY

Seizure (Cinerama via American International Pictures, 1974)
Director: Oliver Stone.
Producers: Garrard Glenn and Jeffrey Kapelmann.
Screenplay: Edward Mann and Oliver Stone, based on a story by Stone.
Photography: Roger Racine.
Art direction: Najwa Stone.
Music: Lee Gagnon.
Cast: Jonathan Frid, Martine Beswick, Joe Sirola, Christina Pickles,
    Roger de Koven, Mary Woronov, Herve Villechaize, Richard Cox,
    Henry Baker, Timothy Ousey, Lucy Bingham, Alexis Kirk, Emil
    Meola.

Midnight Express (Columbia Pictures, 1978)
Director: Alan Parker.
Producers: Alan Marshall and David Puttman.
Screenplay: Oliver Stone, based on the book by William Hayes with
    William Hoffer.
Photography: Michael Seresin.
Music: Giorgio Moroder.
Cast: Brad Davis, Irene Miracle, Bo Hopkins, Paolo Bonacelli, Paul
    Smith, Randy Quaid, Norbert Wiesser, John Hurt, Mike Kellin,
    Franco Diogene, Michael Ensign, Peter Jeffrey.

The Hand (Orion Pictures released through Warner Brothers, 1981)
Director: Oliver Stone.
Producer: Edward R. Pressman.
Screenplay: Oliver Stone, from the novel *The Lizard's Tail* by Marc
    Brandel.

Photography: King Baggot.
Music: James Horner.
Cast: Michael Caine, Andrea Marcovicci, Annie McEnroe, Bruce McGill,
Viveca Lindfors, Rosemary Murphy, Mara Hobel, Pat Corley, Bill
Marshall, Charles Fletcher.

Conan the Barbarian (A Dino De Laurentis presentation of an
Edward R. Pressman Production, 1982)
Director: John Milius.
Producer: Edward R. Pressman.
Screenplay: John Milius, Oliver Stone.
Photography: Duke Callaghan.
Production design: Ron Cobb.
Art design: Pierliugi Basile, Benjamin Fernandez.
Music: Basil Poledouris.
Cast: Arnold Schwarzenegger, James Earl Jones, Max von Sydow,
Sandahl Bergman, Ben Davidson, Cassandra Gaviola, Gerry Lopez.

Scarface (Universal Pictures, 1983)
Director: Brian De Palma.
Producer: Martin Bregman.
Screenplay: Oliver Stone.
Photography: John A. Alonzo.
Art direction: Ed Richardson.
Music: Giorgio Moroder.
Cast: Al Pacino, Steven Bauer, Michelle Pfeiffer, Mary Elizabeth
Mastrantonio, Robert Loggia, Miriam Colon, F. Murray Abraham,
Paul Shenar, Harris Yulin, Angel Salazar, Pepe Serma.

Year of the Dragon (MGM-United Artists, 1985)
Director: Michael Cimino.
Producer: Dino De Laurentis.
Screenplay: Oliver Stone and Michael Cimino, based on the book by
Robert Daley.
Photography: Alex Thomson.
Music: David Mansfield.
Cast: Mickey Rourke, John Lone, Ariane, Leonard Termo, Ray Barry,
Caroline Kava, Eddie Jones, Joey Chin, Victor Wong.

Eight Million Ways to Die (Tri-Star Pictures, 1986)
Director: Hal Ashby.
Producer: Steve Roth.

Screenplay: Oliver Stone and David Lee Henry, based on the novel by
Lawrence Block.
Photography: Stephen H. Burum.
Music: James Newton Howard.
Cast: Jeff Bridges, Rosanna Arquette, Alexandra Paul, Randy Brooks,
Andy Garcia, Lisa Stone, Christa Denton.

Salvador (**Virgin Films, 1986**)
Director: Oliver Stone.
Screenplay: Oliver Stone and Richard Boyle.
Photography: Robert Richardson.
Music: Georges Delerue.
Production: Pasta Productions, Hemdale.
Cast: James Woods, James Belushi, Elepedia Carrillo, Michael Murphy,
John Savage, Tony Plana, Cynthia Gibb, Colby Chester, Will
MacMillan, Jorge Luke, Valerie Wilman, Jose Carlos Ruiz, Juan
Gernandez.

Platoon (**Hemdale, 1986**)
Director: Oliver Stone.
Producer: Arnold Kopelson.
Screenplay: Oliver Stone.
Photography: Robert Richardson.
Music: Georges Delerue.
Art direction: Rodel Cruz, Doris Sher Williams.
Cast: Tom Berenger, Willem Dafoe, Charlie Sheen, Forest Whitaker,
Francesco Quinn, John C. McGinley, Richard Edson, Kevin Dillon,
Reggie Johnson, Keith David, Johnny Depp, David Neidorf, Mark
Moses, Chris Pedersen, Corkey Ford, Corey Glover, Bob Orwig.

Wall Street (**Twentieth Century-Fox, 1987**)
Director: Oliver Stone.
Producer: Edward R. Pressman.
Screenplay: Stanley Weiser and Oliver Stone.
Photography: Robert Richardson.
Art direction: John Jay Moore, Hilda Stark.
Music: Stewart Copeland.
Cast: Michael Douglas, Charlie Sheen, Daryl Hannah, Martin Sheen,
Terence Stamp, James Spader, Sean Young, Millie Perkins, John C.

McGinley, Hal Holbrook, Tamara Tunie, Franklin Cover, Sylvia Miles, Sean Stone.

Talk Radio (Universal Pictures, 1988)
Director: Oliver Stone.
Producer: Edward R. Pressman.
Screenplay: Eric Bogosian and Oliver Stone, based on the play *Talk Radio* by Eric Bogosian and the book *Talked to Death: The Life and Murder of Alan Berg* by Stephen Singular.
Photography: Robert Richardson.
Music: Stewart Copeland.
Production design: Bruno Rubeo.
Cast: Eric Bogosian, Ellen Greene, Leslie Hope, Alec Baldwin, John C. McGinley, John Pankow, Michael Wincott, Linda Atkinson, Robert Trebar, Zach Grenier, Anna Levine, Rockets Redglare. Tony Frank, Harlan Jordan.

Born on the Fourth of July (Universal Pictures, 1989)
Director: Oliver Stone.
Producer: A. Kitman Ho.
Screenplay: Oliver Stone and Ron Kovic, based on the book by Ron Kovic.
Photography: Robert Richardson.
Production design: Bruno Rubeo.
Music: John Williams.
Cast: Tom Cruise, Kyra Sedgwick, Caroline Kava, Raymond J. Barry, Jerry Levine, Frank Whaley, Willem Dafoe, Tom Berenger, Bryan Larkin, Josh Evans, Tony Frank, Jayne Hayes.

The Doors (Tri-Star Pictures, 1990)
Director: Oliver Stone.
Producers: Graham Harari, A. Kitman Ho.
Screenplay: J. Randal Johnson, Oliver Stone.
Photography: Robert Richardson.
Executive music producer: Budd Car.
Production design: Barbara Ling.
Art direction: Larry Fulton.
Cast: Val Kilmer, Meg Ryan, Kevin Dillon, Kyle MacLachlan, Frank Whaley, Michael Madsen, Kathleen Quinlan, Michael Wincott,

Dennis Burkley, Josh Evans, Paul Williams, Kristina Fulton, Crispin Glover.

JFK (Warner Brothers, 1991)
Director: Oliver Stone.
Producers: A. Kitman Ho, Oliver Stone.
Screenplay: Oliver Stone and Zachary Sklar, based on the books *On the Trail of the Assassins* by Jim Garrison and *Crossfire: The Plot That Killed Kennedy* by Jim Marrs.
Photography: Robert Richardson.
Production design: Victor Kempster.
Music: John Williams.
Cast: Kevin Costner, Sissy Spacek, Joe Pesci, Tommy Lee Jones, Gary Oldman, Joe O. Sanders, Laurie Metcalf, Michael Rooker, Jack Lemmon, Walter Matthau, Donald Sutherland, Kevin Bacon, Edward Asner, Brian Doyle-Murray, Jim Garrison.

Heaven and Earth (Warner Brothers, 1994)
Director: Oliver Stone.
Producers: Oliver Stone, Arnon Milchau, Robert Kline, A. Kitman Ho.
Screenplay: Oliver Stone.
Photography: Robert Richardson, A.S.C.
Production design: Victor Kempster.
Music: Kitaro.
Cast: Tommy Lee Jones, Joan Chen, Haing S. Ngor, Hiep Thi Le.

Natural Born Killers (Warner Brothers, 1994)
Director: Oliver Stone.
Producers: Jane Hamsher, Don Murphy, Clayton Townsend, Aron Milchan, Thom Mount, Rand Vossler.
Screenplay: David Veloz, Richard Rutowski, Oliver Stone.
Photography: Robert Richardson.
Production design: Richard Kempster.
Editing: Hank Corwin, Brian Berdan.
Cast: Woody Harrelson, Juliette Lewis, Robert Downey, Jr., Tommy Lee Jones, Rodney Dangerfield.

INDEX

INDEX